RAILROADING
COAST TO COAST

Front end of Southern Pacific
4-8-4 type GS-4 Class.
No. 4449 Used on Freedom Train

Tractive Effort	64,800 lbs.
Drivers Diameter	80 in.
Weight on Drivers	275,700 lbs.
Total Weight	475,000 lbs.
Steam Pressure	300 lbs.
Tender Capacity	23,300 Gals. Water.
	5,880 Gals. Oil.

Other Books by S. Kip Farrington, Jr.

Labrador Retriever: Friend and Worker
The Trail of the Sharp Cup
Fishing with Hemingway and Glassell
Skates, Sticks and Men
The Santa Fe's Big Three
Atlantic Game Fishing
Pacific Game Fishing
Fishing the Atlantic Offshore and On
Fishing the Pacific Offshore and On
A Book of Fishes
Sport Fishing Boats
Cabo Blanco World's Fishing Capital
The Ducks Came Back
Interesting Birds of our Country
Ships of the U.S. Merchant Marine
Railroading from the Head End
Railroading from the Rear End
Railroading the Modern Way
Railroads at War
Railroads of Today
Railroading Around the World
Railroads of the Hour
Giants of the Rails

JUVENILE
Bill the Broadbill Swordfish
Tony the Tuna

RAILROADING COAST TO COAST

Riding the Locomotive Cabs
Steam, Electric and Diesel
1923-1950

By S. Kip Farrington, Jr.

BONANZA BOOKS
New York

This edition is published by Bonanza Books,
distributed by Crown Publishers, Inc.,
by arrangement with Hastings House, Publishers, Inc.
h g f e d c b a
1981 EDITION

Manufactured in the United States of America

Library of Congress Cataloging in Publication Data

Farrington, S. Kip (Selwyn Kip), 1904-
Railroading coast to coast.

Includes index.
1. Railroads—United States—History.
2. Locomotives—United States—History.
I. Title.
TF23.F298 1981 385'.0973 81-12296
ISBN 0-517-35772-0 AACR2

Dedicated

To the following railroads of the United States and Canada who did so much to improve and modernize their passenger trains, service, and speed. They spent millions of dollars on building new lightweight, streamlined cars including coaches, parlor, all room sleepers, dining, dormitory, lunch counter, club and lounge.

In the same period they introduced the expensive vista domes and dome diners. In addition to the above equipment, the most modern postal and express cars were also acquired and these railroads made a tremendous and very costly effort to keep their passenger trains operating in service, even after losing the U.S. mail.

Their usual on time standards were still rigidly adhered to as always.

Atchison, Topeka & Santa Fe
Atlantic Coast Line
Baltimore & Ohio
Bangor & Aroostock
Boston & Maine
Canadian Pacific
Canadian National
Central of Georgia
Chesapeake & Ohio
Chicago, Burlington & Quincy
Chicago & Eastern Illinois
Chicago & Great Western
Chicago, Milwaukee, St. Paul & Pacific
Chicago & North Western
Chicago, Rock Island & Pacific
Colorado & Southern

Delaware, Lackawanna & Western
Denver & Rio Grande Western
Erie
Florida East Coast
Ft. Worth & Denver
Great Northern
Gulf, Mobile & Ohio
Illinois Central
Kansas City Southern
Lehigh Valley
Louisville & Nashville
Missouri, Kansas & Texas
Missouri Pacific
Nashville, Chattanooga & St. Louis
New York Central
New York, New Haven & Hartford
Norfolk & Western
Northern Pacific
Pennsylvania
Richmond, Fredericksburg & Potomac
St. Louis—San Francisco
Seaboard
Southern Pacific
Southern
Texas & Pacific
Union Pacific
Wabash
Western Pacific

Contents

SECTION THREE

SECTION FOUR

The Author

S. Kip Farrington, Jr. has spent a lifetime riding locomotives. He had his first ride at the age of four and from the time he was fourteen on he was on railroads all over North America. Inspecting fifty-two properties in thirty-seven foreign countries he rode many many more miles on the locomotives.

In all his railroad trips he kept comparatively few transcripts of locomotive runs, over two hundred. Although he kept two personal notebooks from 1930 to 1940, his usual procedure was to write down any run in which he was interested on the operating timetable of the division he was riding. The few that he saved have been gathered for this book, his tenth on railroading. Nine of his previous books are on the United States and one on Railroading Around the World.

Many of America's leading railroad photographers have contributed great photographs to embellish the text. The excellent builders' photographs opposite the runs with the statistics and comments on the locomotives are of great interest to all students of locomotive practices. Thirty-three types of locomotives are portrayed. There are many action pictures with explanations, locations, divisions and engine statistics. The transcripts of these runs cover thirty-three North American Railroads and many of this country's foremost grades. These include the Santa Fe's Raton Pass, Glorieta, the Arizona Divide and Cajon Pass; the Southern Pacific's Santa Margarita Grade, Beaumont Hill, Tehachapi, Cascade Summit and the Sierra Nevadas. On the Great Northern the reader can picture crossing the Continental Divide over Maria's Pass and in the Cascades; the Milwaukee's Pipestone Pass; the Northern Pacific's Butte Mountain, and the Rio Grande's Tennessee Pass, Soldier Summit and the Moffat Tunnel Route; the Union Pacific's Sherman Hill and Wasatch Grades.

The Allegheny's Blue Ridge and lesser foothills are crossed and recrossed on the Chesapeake and Ohio, Norfolk and Western, Baltimore and Ohio, Western Maryland, Pennsylvania Railroad and Virginian. The Poconos on the Lackwanna and Lehigh Valley are included with the pictures of all the engines used on these grades.

Mr. Farrington gives extensive coverage of the train makeup, weather conditions, and on some runs even names the crew members. All detentions and other descriptive data are included in his transcripts. He has ridden every division of the Canadian Pacific by day from St. Johns, New Brunswick to Niamano, British Columbia including the south and north lines, and also most of the Canadian National Railroad. He has inspected extensively by rail in Europe, South America, Australia, New Zealand, the Far East and other countries.

S. Kip Farrington is an honorary member of five foreign railroad clubs and belongs to the Pacific Railway Club, the Northwest Maintenance of Way Club, the Western Railroad Club of Chicago, the New York Railroad Club and the Railway and Locomotive Historical Society. For his writings about their railroads, he has received decorations from Chile in 1943 and Peru in 1956. He was the only author ever listed in Who's Who in Railroading. He has ridden business cars on eighty-five Class I railroads.

The author's last book, the Santa Fe's Big Three is a biography of three great steam locomotives. His previous writings were all on modern railroad practices. He wrote the only book on the great job the United States railroads did to help win World War II.

You may be assured that Kip Farrington is the only person who had the experience of riding all the steam locomotives on so many railroads to be able to produce this book, with thirty-nine railroads covered and more than two hundred pictures of locomotives included—steam, diesel and electric.

Valuable information is also included on the mountain operation of the Southern Pacific's Sierra Nevada Grade, the Great Northern Railroad's ore move, Scooping Water on the Run and there are complete sections on Western Maryland Dynamometer Car tests with Resulting Tonnage Ratings, Bridge Ratings and Clearances, including Graphs, Charts and Nine Photographs. There is also a complete section on Passenger Train On Time Movements over thirty railroads, 1962 to 1965 with twelve photographs.

Introduction

RIDING THE HEAD END

Back in 1944 I once saw the air speed indicator in my P-51 Mustang hit 550 miles per hour in a high altitude dive over Europe. A few years later on a cold, clear, predawn morning in Fort Wayne, Indiana I climbed into the cab of Pennsylvania Railroad's huge, sleek, passenger hauling steam locomotive, #5510 T-1 class, with 80 inch driving wheels. Between Warsaw and Plymouth our speed reached 93 miles an hour. For a sense of real speed, for sheer emotional impact, and incredibly noisy, consuming excitement there simply was no contest—the 5510 erased the memory of the Mustang with a roaring stack, white hot fire, wind whipped coal dust in our faces, and the piercing wail of the melodious chime whistle challenging countless rural grade crossings as we raced toward Chicago. Four hundred and seventy tons of steel, coal, and water providing the ultimate thrills of speed and motion, unchallenged and unforgettable to this day!

Kip Farrington understands! He has ridden more miles in more classes of locomotives on more railroads than any man in history. He was already a veteran "head-ender" when he rode his first Santa Fe engine, age twelve, and he still rides the head end on many occasions. In the single year of 1943 Kip rode over 25,000 miles in locomotive cabs, including more than one ride of 1,234 miles between La Junta, Colorado and Los Angeles in the cabs of Santa Fe's great 3776 class 4-8-4 type heading the fabled "Chief." He wrote of these incredible, long distance rides in "Railroads at War," and this is the most factual, thorough, yet emotionally moving account of a locomotive cab ride I have ever read, a moving tribute to what was probably the greatest steam locomotive ever built in this country. A book could be written about Kip and his locomotive rides, and it has been written, and this is it—his tenth railroad book!

If you were to ask Kip why he rode so many locomotive cabs, his rather laconic reply would be, "... mainly to observe the locomotive's performance and the railroad operation." This is only half an answer, for the true sportsman's blood is in his veins, whether it be landing a record breaking black marlin off the Peruvian coast, or catching a hard driven hockey puck as a veteran amateur hockey goaltender—or riding a fast moving locomotive! He knows, and I know, and every man who was ever a "guest" aboard a working steam locomotive knows that it was a sporting event with the inherent elements of fast action, noise, weather, and raw excitement plus the opportunity to watch an extremely skilled team at work—the engineer and fireman. It should, by the way, be stated for the record that, taken as a group, this country's steam locomotive enginemen were just about the finest bunch of men who ever earned wages—and I do mean earned them!

Between 1923 and the mid-fifties, Kip documented many of his cab rides with meticulously kept logbooks, and these logs are the heart of *Riding the Head End, Railroading Coast to Coast.* When you ride with him, you will know the engine number and class, crew names, dates, weather conditions, and schedule. You will learn the consist and tonnage of the train, what speeds were attained, what delays were encountered—in short you will know the total performance of that engine on that train on that date. You will also find a builder's photo, with specifications, and in most cases an action photo of the particular locomotive ridden. You will ride over thirty-nine of the Class I railroads in the country by day and by night, on freight and passenger trains, in steam, diesel, and electric locomotive cabs. You will cover the United States from coast to coast—around Horseshoe Curve, over Donner Pass, up Saluda Hill in North Carolina, over Sand Patch grade in Pennsylvania, Pipestone Pass, Sherman Hill, Moffatt Tunnel, Raton Pass! Where helper engines were used you will ride them.

Eighteen pages of dynamometer car tests on the Western Maryland provide a fascinating and unique record of locomotive performance and comparison. On the Bessemer & Lake Erie, it is steam vs. diesel in another factual, personally recorded log of performance. To sum up, *Riding the Head End* is a totally unique and authentic record, amply illustrated, of U.S. locomotive performance during the finest years of steam and electric operation, and on into the diesel era of increased economy and efficiency. Nothing like this volume has ever been published before, for only Kip Farrington could do it!

Something more needs to be said here, and the careful reader of this book will find ample, supporting testimony. Despite growing public apathy, ridiculous governmental over-regulation and taxation, curtailment of passenger service, and an increasingly complex management-union relationship America's railroads have done a fantastic job of providing the nation with an indispensable and irreplaceable life-line. Without our railroads, we might have lost World War II, yet the average citizen today is totally unaware of the fact that in 1972 the much maligned railroads hauled more tonnage than during any year of that all-consuming war. As for passenger trains, the railroads spent millions upon millions of dollars, without one penny of government subsidy, on passenger equipment, providing frequent, dependable, service between all the key cities and towns in the country. Today, all I seem to hear is how great the European and Japanese rail service is, and why not? They are all government owned and operated, and their passenger service losses are staggering. Guess who pays for these deficits—the taxpayers! Contrast this with America's privately run and financed railroads who, starting with the depression years of the early thirties, and continuing into the mid-fifties or later, provided the finest, most luxurious, safest, best operated passenger trains the world has ever seen, and with few exceptions lost money all the while they were running these great trains. To state that the railroads of this country deserted their passengers is utter nonsense! Exactly the reverse is the truth—America deserted the passenger train! They were destroyed by 80 mile an hour automobiles traveling a vast network of superhighways, high flying jet aircraft, and near maniacal increases in costs, and the real wonder is that they provided service of any sort until the beginning of Amtrak in May of 1971. Certainly there are many people today who like to ride trains, but when nearly ninety percent of the people in this nation travel between cities in private autos, even Amtrak can have no realistic hope for profits.

I salute the railroads of the United States! For all their struggles, over-regulation, sometime lack of good competitive thinking and cooperation, most have survived squarely on their own feet against all odds. Bankrupt or prosperous, deferred maintenance or ninety mile an hour welded rail, mismanaged or brilliantly operated, they are still here. The author of this book believes in them, I believe in them, and the American public had better start believing in them (and let Washington, D.C. know it!), for the railroads are *still* absolutely indispensable to the nation's well-being, and their future is as bright as the thinking people of this country will permit.

Now a toast to S. Kip Farrington, Jr., a skilled author, a man of rare physical courage, internationally known sportsman, a prolific and accurate chronicler of railroad operations—and my friend. This is a man qualified to ride the head end!

HOWARD FOGG

Boulder, Colorado

Foreword

Never having been a saver of anything except Track Charts, Mechanical Data, Locomotive Rosters, Rule Books, Locomotive Diagram Books and Operating Timetables of the railroads I am closest to or working on, I was fortunate to find more than two hundred transcripts that I had made on the locomotives of the American Railroads. This is a small part of over two thousand rides on the head end between 1920 and 1950. And I made many, many more on diesels since then.

In this volume I have included 196 train movements of on time performances of passenger trains on United States railroads from 1961 to 1963 with only ten late arrivals. I have given all facts and figures accurately and held back nothing regarding the detentions, failures or other problems that I observed. My only regret is that there are no Delaware and Hudson, Clinchfield and Nashville, Chattanooga and St. Louis transcripts of runs recorded. I spent many days on these fine properties but could not find any of their operating timetables with records of my locomotive runs. As there are so many Pennsylvania and New York Central runs, I have tried to avoid an inundation of them. Instead I have added outstanding photographs of the Chesapeake & Ohio, Baltimore & Ohio and Norfolk & Western.

I hope that the many devotees of the steam locomotive, students of all types of motive power and railroad enthusiasts will approve of this volume. Once again, I am indebted to Richard H. Kindig, Preston George, Bruce D. Fales, H. Reid, W.H. Thrall, H.W. Pontin, Glen Gabriel and other photographers and the late Otto C. Perry. Bert Pennypacker, G.M. Best, T.W. Taber, Al Staufer and H.L. Broadbelt, all master photographers, and like Kindig and Reid, excellent writers with the finest railroad books to their credit have also contributed to this book.

I cannot express my appreciation and thanks strongly enough and I like to feel that this book is a tribute to them.

My sincere gratitude and acknowledgement is due Marie Rieman of Watermill, Long Island, and to Guendolyn P. Kelley of Amagansett, Long Island for their work on this manuscript.

S. Kip Farrington, Jr.
"Finning Out"
East Hampton, Long Island, New York

Section One

THE AUTHOR'S FAVORITE LOCOMOTIVES

Howard Fogg, in his very flattering introduction for this volume, says that in reply to the question why I had ridden so many locomotives I had answered it was mainly to observe the locomotives' performances, and of course, the railroad operation. But it was more than that. I like the elements, particularly cold weather and snow, which are, naturally, a railroad's enemy. It always gives me a thrill to be isolated from people with the wild game and many birds to be seen. There are ducks, geese, doves, quail and pheasants in particular, and the other animals including livestock.

I enjoyed meeting the people, of course: the engine crews, travelling engineers, road foremen of engines and the head brakemen in freight service, and made it a point to stay on locomotives and cabooses when out with the men. By this policy, I passed up many a good ride and meal in a business car. But when invited by officials, I always accepted their kind invitation to ride with them, unless there was some particular reason for riding a new locomotive or watching its latest innovation.

All of this isn't as glamorous as it may seem. Some of the roads never had second seats in the cab. The reasoning behind this was that it would keep the head brakeman constantly alert looking the train over. I have ridden many miles sitting on sand boxes fortunately provided for the oil burners. All of the later modern steam engines, however, were equipped with a fine extra seat behind the fireman and perhaps another behind the engineer.

Riding the Dog House on top of the tender is a great place to view the countryside and look the train over but it is not by any means the same as riding in the locomotive's cab. The longest trip taken standing, I can remember, was from Buffalo to Newark on the Lehigh Valley with the exception of helpers out of Ithaca and Wilkes Barre, and on the Union Pacific from Los Angeles to Caliente. The longest runs without getting off were three or four round trips from Los Angeles to La Junta—on the Santa Fe, but not all at the same time!

My longest rides on the Southern Pacific, Union Pacific, and the Great Northern were Oakland Pier to Ogden, Ogden to Omaha, and Spokane to Harve respectively. People ask me why I gave myself such a licking but remember, I was always on short time away from business or going to or from some very good duck shooting.

While I fired a few locomotives with the scoop, I have no desire to ever try it again and had no particular interest in firing them with the stoker or an oil burner. I have run them all, steam, diesel and electric, but I had no desire to do that either on those engines. It takes too much concentration plus calling the signals. I was there strictly to observe and was interested in learning the road.

About airplanes, I feel the same: it's interesting to be in the cockpit, particularly during approaches, landings and takeoffs but learning to fly has never been one of my goals. I have no desire to steer a fishing boat, or to give orders in the wheel house, or on the bridge of a large ship, even though I have never made an ocean voyage where I did not stand the regular watches with particular attention to navigation. The sixteen hour law did not apply to me aboard ship as well as as railroad locomotives or cabooses where I spent so many, many days.

People ask why I rode cabooses. It was so that I could watch the operation from the rear end of a long freight train, to be with the crew and to observe the conductor making out his work reports. On no occasion did I ever ride a head or rear end without the operating timetable and track charts of the division on which I was riding. The most helpful way to learn the road was during daylight hours, because charts were not readable in the dark. Without the track charts, I would never have known the U.S. railroads as I do.

The best place from which to learn the railroad, however, is the rear end of a business car, particularly with its side mirrors and track lights. With the diesels it was a great deal easier to see the railroad and countryside from the head end. Their cleanliness, ease of operation and fine seats should have added a lot of years to many engine crews. I am sure they did so for me. I saw one, and only one, locomotive outfitted with a desk: the diesel unit of the Talgo Train in Spain, which had an excellent table before the fireman's seat.

People ask me why I did all that. Maybe it's the urge to try to improve one's knowledge by looking into and doing many different things. In golf, I tried to play many courses, sometimes a new one every evening after Wall Street hours. I made it my business to fish in all the great salt water hot spots of the world and was fortunate to catch some of all the species of game fish, large and small. I've shot ducks in thirty-two states, all the Canadian provinces, Mexico, Cuba, Chile and Argentina. I was attracted to the various species of water fowl and upland birds, just as I was drawn to all other species of bird life. It was always a great challenge and big interest for me to be able to play hockey in various rinks so it was only natural I guess, that a variety of locomotives and railroads were my game too.

The Author's Favorite Locomotives

If you want to know my favorite steam locomotives of all that I rode, I'll pick no more than four of each going back as far as the American and Mogul types:

The best of the eight wheelers or 4-4-0 type would be the Pennsylvania's D-16sb. They could do more with their 68-inch driving wheels than any other I ever rode and were excellent in suburban service with light trains and easy grades.

By all odds the finest Mogul or 2-6-0 type, which I will never forget, was the Southern Pacific's M-11, their class designation M-63 21/28 153-S. With their 200 lb. boiler pressure and a tractive force of 36,570 lbs., they really were amazing.

My number one Prairie 2-6-2 type would be the Santa Fe's 1800 class of which 86 were built. With 69-inch driving wheels, 200 lb. boiler pressure and a tractive force of 43,200 lbs., they did an outstanding job.

I will never forget them in World War II when they were pinch hitting in all classes of service and did a fine job in "Main" train service. I once rode one with third No.3, the California Limited and we made running time on that train's schedule from Needles to Barstow with no helper from Cadiz to Ash Hill. Of course, we had a helper from Needles to Goffs.

My Atlantic type favorites would be the Pennsylvania E-6 and the Milwaukee oil burning Class A for Hiawatha Service.

My number one 4-6-0 ten-wheel type is a difficult choice but there is no question that the Pennsylvania G-5 was the most powerful, if kept strictly to the service for which it was designed and built, hauling suburban trains out of Pittsburgh on the Eastern,Pan Handle and Pittsburgh Divisions. The 68 inch wheels were high enough for this service. But when brought to the Long Island Railroad to make 100 mile runs with fairly sustained speeds in passenger service, these engines were very rough riders, hard to fire and bad on water. On the Long Island commuting trains, though, running 45 to 50 miles, they did well enough but were bad in heavy snow as it clogged their low air pump.

My choice of the Pacific type would be the Baltimore & Ohio's F-7 as the very finest, followed by the Chesapeake & Ohio's F-19, the Santa Fe's modernized 3400 and the Pennsylvania's K-4.

For the Mountain, or 4-8-2 type, I would take the Boston and Maine R-1 which were later sold to the Baltimore & Ohio. The Lehigh & Hudson also had three of them. The Pennsylvania's M-1a would be my second choice.

There were only two 4-10-2 types and both were owned and operated by the Southern Pacific and the Union Pacific. I preferred the Southern Pacific's but really did not care for a 3-cylinder locomotive and the Union Pacific did not waste much time in removing their 3rd cylinder.

The 4-12-2 type was, of course, only built for Union Pacific and did a very fair job without being too tough on the rail but once again was a 3-cylinder locomotive. This type proved to be very fine in heavy snow.

My choice for the Consolidation or 2-8-0 type would be the Western Maryland H-9 with no others even close although the Philadelphia and Reading had a very able one.

For the Mikado 2-8-2 type, my favorites would be the Chesapeake & Ohio's K-3 and the Baltimore & Ohio's Q-4. While the Great Northern had the largest and heaviest with the highest drivers, I was not so impressed with their 0-5, and would put it in third place.

For the 2-10-0 Decapod type, I'll take the Western Maryland I-2 with the Pennsylvania Railroad's I-1 following a long way behind.

My favorites of the Santa Fe type 2-10-2 were the Baltimore & Ohio's S-1-2, the Santa Fe's 3800 and 3900 classes and the Missouri Pacific's 1720 class.

Of the many fine 2-8-4 types with various names given by the roads that owned them, I would choose the Chesapeake & Ohio's K-4, the Louisville & Nashville's M-1, the Nickel Plate S-1 and the Erie S-4 as all being outstanding.

For the magnificent Texas or 2-10-4 type, my big four most emphatically, would be the Santa Fe's 5001, 5011 classes, the Kansas City Southern 900 class, the Chesapeake & Ohio's T-1 and Pennsylvania's J-1 which was copied after the Chesapeake & Ohio's T-1.

My choice of 4-6-4 type would be the three designed with the 84 inch driving wheels, the Santa Fe's 3460 class, the Milwaukee's F-7 and the North Western's E-4. The Lackawanna's 1151 class was another good one with 80 inch drivers.

Readers might be surprised to know that I put the very popular and the pioneer Hudson type, New York Central's J classes at the bottom of the list. They had many more troubles with them than were ever made public although they did lead the parade.

The booster never made much impression on me. It was just one more extravagance to get out of order and was so many times never "cut in." One would in fact, be amazed at what little usage boosters received, and the roads that never had them seemed to get alone fine with no regrets.

For the magnificant Four-eight-four, there is no question in my mind that it was the greatest all-around steam locomotive ever built. Originally it was called the Northern Type because it was first used on the Northern Pacific but was known as the Niagara on the New York Central; Greenbrier on the Chesapeake & Ohio; Pocono on the Delaware, Lackawanna & Western; Wyoming on the Lehigh Valley; General Service on the Southern Pacific, as I recall but a few. Having ridden them all, my choices would be the Santa Fe's 3776 and 2900 classes, the Union Pacific's 820's, Southern Pacific's GS3-4 and the Atlantic Coast Line's 1800.

The first with 80 inch driving wheels, the Great Northern's S-2 should be mentioned here as well as the New York Central's S-1 with 79 inch driving wheels.

Needless to say, I preferred any oil burner over a coal burning locomotive.

Of the 2-6-6-2 type, I would prefer the Chesapeake & Ohio's H Engines even though they were the only locomotives to ever affect me by smoke, heat and fumes. This occurred while passing through the Millboro Tunnel on one of the H-3's which was working water with a very light train. The fireman lost his lunch and I must say, it was very difficult to breathe. This was on the Mountain Sub-Division of the Clifton Forge Division.

Of the 2-8-8-2 type, my preference would be the Rio Grande's L-131, the Great Northern's R-2 and the Norfolk & Western's Y-6.

Of the 2-8-8-4's, I could never see much difference between the Missabe's M-4 and the Northern Pacific's Z 7-8. Both of these engines performed excellently in the service for which they were built.

Of the 2-6-6-4's, I would take the Norfolk & Western's class A ahead of the others that were built and would choose it over the Chesapeake & Ohio's H-8 and Virginian's 2-6-6-6 type, their class AG, even though the Norfolk & Western's class A was not used in a comparative service.

The Union Pacific's 4-8-8-4 type was, of course, the only one built, performed a great job and really produced the horsepower and speed. I was present at all the tests when these locomotives were first brought out and always thought that they would have been better with a feed water heater rather than an exhaust steam injector and that they were also a trifle hard to fire.

The Southern Pacific's 4-8-8-2 cab ahead AC Engines were, of course, my great favorites, particularly as they were used on mountain grades with many snow sheds and tunnels. However, they did remarkably well in hauling heavy passenger trains and I have ridden one 65 mph between Palmdale and Lancaster with Train No. 59. To me, they were outstanding and I never saw any failure while riding them.

Of all the many magnificient 4-6-6-4 types, my number one favorite would be the Rio Grande's L-105 with the Northern Pacific's Z-6 and Union Pacific's 3800 and 3900 class following.

Of all the electric engines I have ridden in the United States, I would pick the Pennsylvania Railroad's G-G1, the Great Northern's Y1 and the Virginian's EL2b. I have, of course, ridden all of the electric power in Switzerland, France, Sweden, Norway, Italy, Holland, New Zealand and other countries.

For the diesels, one always was as good as the other, if they were built by the Electro Motive Division of General Motors.

Well to close this chapter, I wish to say that I have never flown in the United States west of Minneapolis, St. Paul, Omaha, Kansas City and Houston even after all the flying I have done outside the United States. I once flew in 16 different type aircraft on 16 consecutive flights. This variation happened to break that way over a four-month period in North and South America.

Wait, I will take that "never" back. I once flew from Sacramento to Los Angeles to catch the Super Chief east.

I have neglected the airlines because of my desire to see my many friends on the various railroads in all classes of service as well as the physical property, country and cities though which they pass.

Many of my railroad friends like to call me the North American 'Boomer." I do not regard it as a compliment but then they tell me, "look at all the home terminals you have had," meaning the division points that I almost lived and worked in and out of both ways.

Winslow on the Santa Fe, Sparks on the Southern Pacific, Whitefish on the Great

Northern, Portola on the Western Pacific and Ogden on the Union Pacific saw the most of me on the Western roads. On the Pocahantas roads, Charlottesville and Huntington saw the most of me on the Chesapeake & Ohio, Roanoke on the Norfolk & Western, Scranton on the Lackawanna, Port Jervis of the Erie and on the Pennsylvania, I was everywhere.

Born on the Lackawanna, I summered on the Central Railroad of New Jersey and was taken on one of their steam engines for my first ride at the age of four on the Daily, Except Sunday, Evening Fish Train from Galilee (Seabright) to Atlantic Highlands. I attended boarding schools on the Lackawanna, New Haven, Erie and Pennsylvania and lived the last 52 years in East Hampton, Long Island on the railroad of that name where from 1926 to 1941 I commuted every day, sometimes even Saturdays, a 206-mile round trip to my office in New York City. I *must* have liked the railroads!

I wanted to go to the Pennsylvania Railroad's Mechanical school at Altoona, a very fine one at the time, and was accepted, but my old man hauled me into Wall Street. It was probably just as well, since a working railroader has to be on call 24 hours a day. So for me, there would have been no shooting, fishing or hockey. I am lucky to have seen and known the railroads just by buying a ticket.

Long Island No. 138, 4-6-0 type, class G-53sd

Tractive Force	33,771 lbs.
Drivers Diameter	60½ in.
Weight on Drivers	150,500 lbs.
Total Weight	188,800 lbs.
Steam Pressure	200 lbs.
Tender Capacity	6,000 gals.
	14½ tons

This was the premier freight engine on the Long Island until the arrival of the H-6sb from the P.R.R.

1923
December 27th
L. I. R. R.

Holben Yard (Jamaica)—Amagansett via Montauk Branch, Valley Tower Train Big Bertha Extra 139 East, 29 cars to Speonk. 1435 tons where work began.

Engine 139 4-6-0 type class G-53c
LV Holben Yard 5:40 a.m.
LV Y Cabin 8:25-end of double track
ARR Patchogue 9:18-coal and water, also took water at Babylon met #27
LV Patchogue 10:38-after #8 went.
ARR Speonk 11:30-water
LV Speonk 12:15-left 4 cars
Westhampton 12:29-left 5 cars
Quogue 1:25
Hampton Bays 2:15-left 7 cars met #19
ARR Southampton 4:25-left 7 cars
ARR Bridgehampton 5:35-left 3 cars, picked up 2 empties, met #21
LV Bridgehampton 6:32
ARR East Hampton 6:51-left 3 cars, picked up 4 empties
Headed in for #20
ARR Amagansett 7:25 ahead of #26
Tied up 7:32
Snowing Temp 22

Long Island No. 18, 4-6-0 type, class G-54sa

Built by Baldwin in 1902: 72 inch driving wheel. With James C. Eichhorn, Sr. in cab. Fireman George Cogne of Greenport.

Engine named for Eichhorn who started with L. I. R. R. 6/28/1887 and retired 12/28/1937

1923
May 7th
L. I. R. R.

New York—Montauk
Train#20—The Cannonball
Motor 347 to Jamaica DD1
Engine #18 4-6-0 type G54sa
LV Jamaica 4:18
LV Speonk 5:46
LV Southampton 6:24
LV East Hampton 6:51
ARR Montauk 7:18
7 cars, 2 PL, 1 combine, 4 coaches, 10 cars to MR.
Took water at Speonk
OT at Montauk
via Main Line-MR

Long Island No. 4, 4-4-2 type
Built by Baldwin 1901 seventy-six inch driving wheels.

1923
June 6th
L. I. R. R.

Montauk—Jamaica
Train #3, Cannonball—5 coaches, 3 Parlors, 1 combine from MR 7 from MY.
Engine #1 4-4-2 type E51
LV Montauk 6:20
LV East Hampton 6:52
LV Southampton 7:15
LV Speonk 7:48
ARR Jamaica 9:14—9 minutes late
LV Jamaica 9:18
ARR Penn Station 9:35—12 minutes late—motor 346 DDI
Engine #1 had trouble handling train, the usual rough ride on a camelback.
via MR Mainline

Long Island NO. 7, 4-6-0 type before Superheater

1923
August 14th
L. I. R. R.

Penn Station—Montauk
Train #18, Sunrise Special
Engine #7 4-6-0 G54sa
Helper Engine #4 4-4-2 type E51
LV N.Y. 3:25 Motor 349 DDI
LV Jamaica 3:55
Water for both engines at Speonk
ARR Southampton 5:40, 9 minutes late
ARR East Hampton 6:24, 14 minutes late
ARR Amagansett 6:30
ARR Montauk 7:02, 21 minutes late due to second stops at each station
Friday only, 7 PL, 2 lounge
via Montauk Branch

Long Island Railroad 4-4-0, type D-16sb
Built at P.R.R. Juanita Shops, Altoona, 1906

Tractive Force	22,750 lbs.
Drivers Diameter	68 in.
Weight on Drivers	98,150 lbs.
Total Weight	142,100 lbs.
Steam Pressure	175 lbs.
Tender Capacity	5,600 gals.
	13 tons

1924
May 20th
L. I. R. R.

Amagansett—Greenport Train 187
The Scoot—Engine 220 4-4-0 type D16sb
LV Amagansett 10:25
ARR Eastport 11:35 Met No. 8
ARR Manorville 11:59
Train 282
LV Manorville 12:01
LV Riverhead 12:23
ARR Greenport 1:10

1924
May 20th
L. I. R. R.

Train 283, The Scoot
Engine 84 4-4-0 type D56
LV Greenport 2:10
ARR Riverhead 2:55
LV M.R. 3:25
Train 186
LV Speonk 3:45 Met No. 19
ARR Amagansett 5:20
2 cars all the way, 1 combine, 1 coach
Took water Speonk, Riverhead both ways. OT all the way
Engineman—James Eichhorn, Sr.
Fireman—Wilber Bennett

Long Island R.R. No. 84, 4-4-0 type, class D-56

This engine was named the James Eichhorn, Sr. East End Engineer, standing at the front end.

1926
March 25th
L. I. R. R.

Jamaica—Montauk
Train #20, The Cannonball
Engine 23 4-6-0 type G5s
LV Jamaica 4:20
LV Speonk 5:46
LV Southampton 6:26
LV Easthampton 6:51
ARR Montauk 7:14
5 cars, 1 PL, 1 combine, 3 coaches, 8 cars to Manorville
Water at Speonk, OT all the way
Engineman—Frank Brewster
Fireman—Tanky Bell
Conductor—Leo Hantz
Flagman—Walter Hudson
via Mainline and MR

Long Island No. 23, 4-6-0 type, class G-5s

Tractive Force	41,330 lbs.
Drivers Diameter	68 in.
Weight on Drivers	178,000 lbs.
Total Weight	237,000 lbs.
Steam Pressure	205 lbs.
Tender Capacity	7,800 gals.
	15 tons

L-R John "Tanky" Bell Fireman, Leo Hantz, conductor, Walter Hudson, brakeman, Frank Brewster, engineman
While taking water at Speonk.

1927
July 25th
L. I. R. R.

Montauk—New York
Train #4015—Sundays only
Engine #36 4-6-0 type G5s
Helper Engine #13 4-6-0 type G54sb
LV Montauk 7:10 p.m. NY
LV East Hampton 7:44 HA
LV Southampton 8:05 SH
LV Speonk 8:43
LV MR 9:01
ARR J 10:15 p.m.
Lost 6 minutes both engines taking water at Speonk
ARR New York 10:43, Motor 360, 14 cars, 1 PLC, 12 PL, 1 OBS lounge via Manorville and Main Line

Long Island No. 36, 4-6-0 type, class G-5s at Greenport, L.I., N.Y. with James Eichhorn, Sr. standing on pilot's step. Note the similarity of this front end with the P.R.R. K-4 in the next photograph.

Long Island No. 18, 4-6-0 type, class G-54sb
Built by Baldwin in 1902 with 68 inch driving wheels.

At Morris Park Engine Terminal NY

1927
July 25th
L. I. R. R.

New York—Montauk
Dead head equipment cast
LV Penn Station 11:40 p.m. Motor 366
LV J 12:10—Engine #23 4-6-0 G-5s (Extra 23 East
LV B 12:42
LV Babylon 12:50
LV Speonk 1:47—water
ARR Montauk 2:58 a.m.
13 PL, 2 lounge, 1PLB, 10BS lounge, 17 cars
via B Tower Central Branch Montauk branch
Engineman James Eichhorn, Jr.
Fireman Gardiner See
Conductor Leo Hantz
Flagman George Bookstaver

5495

1931
February 5th
P. R. R.

North Philadelphia—Washington
Train 2-139
Engine 3885 K4s
14 cars, 12 SL 2 D-70
Temperature 20° very bad coal. Started train 9 times taking slack only once. Pulled out of W. Phila. hole at K tower without taking slack. Flag with Fussee at Newport freight cooling hot journal, left there 20 minutes late, arrived Washington 23 minutes late. Brakes in emergency at Perryville. Left North Phila. 16 minutes late. Coal shoveled down at Baltimore. L 1s helper through B. & P. tunnel.
Engineman Schaller
Fireman C. C. Taylor
Conductor C. Martin

Pennsylvania No. 5495, 4-6-2 type, class K-4s

Tractive Force	44,460 lbs.
Drivers Diameter	80 in.
Weight on Drivers	201,830 lbs.
Total Weight	308,890 lbs.
Steam Pressure	205 lbs.
Tender Capacity	11,980 gals.
	18½ tons

1931
February 13th
S. A. L.

Raleigh—Weldon, N. C.
Train 192 NY—Florida Lim., 14 cars
Engine 264 4-8-2
Detoured from Norlina account freight wreck at McKinney. Had ½ of #8, ran as second-192.
Met #5 at Littleton. Had engineman pilot out of Norlina. Two trains annulled.
Clear and cold

Seaboard Air Line No. 264, 4-8-2 type

Tractive Force	48,200 lbs.
Drivers Diameter	72 in.
Weight on Drivers	213,450 lbs.
Total Weight	320,900 lbs.
Steam Pressure	200 lbs.
Tender Capacity	9,000 gals.
	17 tons

Pennsylvania 4-6-2 type, class K-5

Tractive Force	54,675 lbs.
Drivers Diameter	80 in.
Weight on Drivers	208,250 lbs.
Total Weight	327,560 lbs.
Steam Pressure	250 lbs.
Tender Capacity	13,475 gals.
	22 tons

1931
February 20th
P. R. R.

Baltimore—Harrisburg
Liberty Limited #59 11 cars
Engine 5698 4-6-2 type, class K5 with Walschaert Valvegear Tractive effort 54675 lbs. most amazing no stoker.
LV Baltimore 4:23
ARR York 5:57 water
LV York 6:00
ARR Harrisburg 6:37
No track pans on Old Northern Central now Baltimore Division. Plenty of exhaust in cab—very dirty. Did all right on New Freedom hill.

Pennsylvania R.R. 4-6-2 type, class K-5 Poppet Valves and Caprotti Valve Gear

Tractive Force	58,092 lbs.
Drivers Diameter	80 in.
Weight on Drivers	208,370 lbs.
Total Weight	321,560 lbs.
Steam Pressure	250 lbs.
Tender Capacity	13,475 gals.
	22 tons

1931
February 21st
P. R. R.

Harrisburg—Baltimore

Golden Arrow #978 13 cars

Engine 5699 4-6-2 type, class K-5, Poppet valves, Caprotti valve gear removed in 1937. Tractive effort 58,092 lbs. Hand-fired. This valve gear and Poppet valve were replaced by Piston valves and Walschaert valve gear which made it identical with 5698.

LV Harrisburg 7:05 a.m. 20 minutes late

LV Cly 7:23

York 7:50 water

New Freedom 8:28

ARR Baltimore 9:25 20 minutes late

Made running time—lagged on New Freedom hill. Amazing no stoker, P.R.R. thinking, the first M-1s were hand-fired also. Stokers afterwards added. Wanted to ride one making some stops.

They were put on this 83 mile Baltimore Division after exhaust blowing back in cab particularly when drifting. Quickly took them off Philadelphia-Pittsburgh trains #35 and #36. Only two were built.

P.R.R. K-4s class, 4-6-2 type with 25,000 gallon tender. This innovation did not last long as the extra weight totaled more than a car.

Photo from H. L. Broadbelt collection.

1931
March 1st
P. R. R.

Manhattan Transfer—Washington
2-139
Engine 5339 K4s
Steaming badly. 12 cars out of New York, 13 out of Wilmington getting Roskalbs business car.
68 miles in 65 minutes Wilmington to Baltimore.
Plugged Severen proceeded as unequipped train to Bowie, lost 8 minutes.
L1s helper through B. & P. hole.
Clear with light fog 1/2 moon
Engineman Schaller
Fireman Taylor

Pennsylvania R.R. 4-8-2 type, class M-1

Tractive Force	64,550 lbs.
Drivers Diameter	72 in
Weight on Drivers	266,500 lbs.
Total Weight	382,400 lbs.
Steam Pressure	250 lbs.
Tender Capacity	11,000 gals.
	17½ tons

Photo from H. L. Broadbelt collection

1931
March 23rd
P. R. R.

NK (N. Elizabeth) to Enola via Trenton cutoff, Conestoga and Columbia.

Train P5, 121 cars, 6180 tons, 16th and 17th cars of explosives

Engines 6752 M1, 6952 M1a

Howelville for water, also Columbia on the low grade. Left NK at 8:20 p.m. arrived Enola 1:35 a.m.

Approx. 28 tons of coal used on M1a, fine run, clear, cold.

Enginemen—Miller and Houseal

Firemen—Watson and Lotz

P.R.R. 4-6-2 type, class K-4s

The 5400's were the last of this famous class to be built coming out of Baldwin in 1927.

Photo from H. L. Broadbelt collection

1931
April 21st
P. R. R.

West Phila.—Washington
Train 131
Engine 5401 K4s, 7 cars
Ran the freight track Aberdeen—North Point
Very heavy rain O.T. all the way
Engineman—Terhune
Fireman—Harmon

B&O No. 5304, 4-6-2 type, P-7d class hauling No. 21, the Washingtonian in a snowstorm two miles west of Silver Spring, Md. running 50 mph with nine cars. Photo taken in December 1948 by Bruce D. Fales. Baltimore Div.

Tractive Force	50,000 lbs.
Drivers Diameter	80 in.
Weight on Drivers	211,000 lbs.
Total Weight	347,500 lbs.
Steam Pressure	250 lbs.
Tender Capacity	20,000 gals.
	25 tons

1931
April 22nd
B & O

Washington—Jersey City
9 cars out of Washington, 10 out of Baltimore
Engine 5320 P-9 President Cleveland 4-6-2
Lots of dead time, slow schedule, O.T. all the way
Engineman—Allen
Fireman—Ecker

B&O No. 5304 streamlined 4-6-2 type, class P-7D

Especially remodelled for the Cincinatian in 1946. Climbs Cranberry Grade with No. 76 East of Rodemer, W. Va. Cumberland Div.-West End 5 cars
Speed 20 mph
Grade 2.02%

Photo taken in November 1948 by Bruce D. Fales

1931
April 29th
P. R. R.

N. Phila.—Washington
Train 177—The Senator, 8 cars
Engine 3853 K4s
Overtook #133 at Gwens Run, Doubleheader with 15 cars. Helper cut off at Loudon Park, broken spring hanger
We picked up Fussee and had order to run around which was annulled as signals cleared. Followed 133 into Washington 10 minutes late
Engineman—Frank Springstead

Lehigh Valley No. 2143, 4-6-2 type, K5a class

Tractive Force	48,273 lbs.
Drivers Diameter	73 in.
Weight on Drivers	203,300 lbs.
Total Weight	316,480 lbs.
Steam Pressure	200 lbs.
Tender Capacity	10,500 gals.
	22 tons

Photo from collection of H. L. Broadbelt

1931
May 3rd
L. V.

Manhattan Transfer N. J.—Wilkes Barre, Pa.
Train No. 3—Lehigh Limited
Engine 2138 K6b to Mauch Chunk OT

1931
May 3rd
L. V.

Mauch Chunk (now Jim Thorpe)—Wilkes Barre, Pa.
Engine 5001, Class S2, 3 Cylinder, 4-8-2
Train No. 3, Lehigh Limited
Clear, full moon, O.T. all the way, good run.
Always a beautiful ride up the Lehigh Gorge in any conditions.
Met No. 1111, the Timken Demonstrator with an eastward extra at Gracedale. The author afterwards rode this engine on both the Lehigh Valley, Lackawanna and Pennsylvania but has lost all his records of these tests. I well remember what a great impression the roller bearings made on all the operating and mechanical force heads just as it did on me. I, many years later, rode this engine again after it was sold to the Northern Pacific.

Lehigh Valley No. 5001, 4-8-2 type, S class 3 cylinder

Tractive Force	61,801 lbs.
Drivers Diameter	69 in.
Weight on Drivers	252,400
Total Weight	370,000 lbs.
Steam Pressure	200 lbs.
Tender Capacity	12,000 gals.
	22 tons

Photo taken at Mauch Chunk, Pa., Sept. 1936 showing the 5001 helping Engine 2058, 4-6-2 type, K4 class with No. 9, the Black Diamond. Photo by Bert Pennypacker. Rebuilt at Sayre, Pa. 1939 when 3rd cylinder was removed

B&O 2-8-2 type, class Q-4

Helper for No. 2 National Limited just before midnight ready to leave M & K Jtc. to "back light" to Hardman to pick up No. 2 from Hardman to Terra Alta, W. Va. Photo taken Sept. 28, 1941 by Bruce D. Fales

Tractive Force	63,200 lbs.
Driver Diameter	64 in.
Weight on Drivers	245,580 lbs.
Total Weight	327,430 lbs.
Steam Pressure	220 lbs.
Tender Capacity	12,000 gals.
	17½ tons

1931
May 12th
P. R. R.

Harrisburg—Jersey City

Train RJ-10 Renova, Jersey, milk

Engine 958 K4s, 11 cars out of Harrisburg plus hack, 17 out of Lancaster plus hack, 18 out of Christiana. Ran 37 miles in 30 minutes Harrisburg, Conestoga tower—Lancaster. 76 miles in 69 minutes N. Phila.—Newark. Took train Jersey City milk track returning to Manhattan Transfer with light engine to ride Train 24 to Penn Station, N.Y. which had run around us while picking up car of milk at Christiana. 24 went into Broad St. Phila.

Very fine run, never saw any K4 run better, light rain

Engineman—Schaller

Fireman—Duncan

1931
May 13th
D. L. & W.

Hoboken—Scranton
Train #5 Chicago Limited
10 cars
Engine 1503 4-8-4 type
O.T. all the way, raining
Engineman—Talmadge

Lackawanna No. 1503, 4-8-4 type, Q1 class

Tractive Force	64,500 lbs.
Drivers Diameter	77 in.
Weight on Drivers	269,000 lbs.
Total Weight	421,000 lbs.
Steam Pressure	250 lbs.
Tender Capacity	12,000 gals.
	14 tons

One of the first 4-8-4 type. Also a pioneer with high driving wheels. Photo taken by Bert Pennypacker at Hoboken, N.J., Nov. 1946

1931
May 14th
D. L. & W.

Scranton—Hoboken

Train 54—73 cars, 3100 tons or 6200 MS as the Lackawanna used at that time instead of tons. The S.P. did likewise.

Engine 1620 4-8-4 type, class Q2

Pusher 2133 to Nay Aug 2-8-2 type

Helper 2230 4-8-2 type to Lehigh

Ice cars at Goldsboro, retainers up at Pocono Summit, retainers down at Stroudsburg. Dover to Patterson 20 miles in 21 minutes.

Very foggy on the mountain, good run.

Lackwanna No. 2215, 4-8-2, 3 cylinder

Tractive Force	77,600 lbs.
Tractive Booster	10,220 lbs.
Drivers Diameter	63 in.
Weight on Drivers	276,500 lbs.
Total Weight	397,500 lbs.
Steam Pressure	200 lbs.
Tender Capacity	12,000 gals.
	14 tons

Photo taken by Bert Pennypacker at Scranton, Pa.

Opposite page:

Long Island No. 310, 2-8-0 type, H-6sb class

Tractive Force	42,168 lbs.
Drivers Diameter	56 in.
Weight on Drivers	180,900 lbs.
Total Weight	204,800 lbs.
Steam Pressure	205 lbs.
Tender Capacity	7,200 gals.
	17 tons

These engines were bought from the P.R.R. and were built at Altoona, Pa. Photo taken at Morris Park, Jamaica, N.Y.

1931
October 1st
Long Island Railroad

Greenport, L.I.—Holban Yard, Hollis, N.Y.
Train extra No. 312 west Greenport freight, Big Bertha with fall Potato move
Engine 312, 2-8-0 type, H6sb class

LV	Greenport	8:20 a.m.	After No. 205 has gone with 6 empties.
LV	Southold SH	10:10	Pick up 10 cars.
LV	Cutchogue	11:40	Pick up 12 cars. Met No. 204
LV	Mattituck K	1:17 p.m.	Pick up 13 cars.
LV	Jamesport	2:10	Pick up 8 cars.
LV	Riverhead	3:27	Pick up 15 cars. Water.
LV	Calverton AH	4:10	Pick up 3 cars.
LV	Manorville MR	5:35	Take water. Head in for No. 20, The Cannonball.
LV	Yaphank YA	6:40	Pick up 4 cars.
LV	Ronkonkoma	8:05	Left train on main track, cut off to take water.
ARR	Holban Yard	11:37	Just 48 minutes under the law with 61 loads, all potatoes and 6 empties. Never did find out the tonnage.

Engineman—William Squires
Fireman—Clarence Carter
Conductor—Charlie Noe

Engine crew and train crew and myself all ate lunch at Riverhead, supper at Ronkonkoma, in lunch rooms opposite depots.

Weather clear, full moon. A lousey hot, dirty day, particularly for Carter having to fire by hand. The long delays in picking up cars were caused by the switching in and out of the potato houses' spur tracks. Never ran more than 25 mph all the way. Good thing it was a typical Long Island fall day with N.W. breeze otherwise it would have been worse.
Total Mileage 82.7

1931
November 10th
P. R. R.

Enola-Altoona
Train E.D.1
Engine 6941—M1—88 cars, 3340 tons, 1 car explosives
Engine had exhaust steam injector
Signed up 6:50 a.m., made up train and left N.C. 9:30, arrived Antis 1:40
Engine lagged all the way. VC1 went around us at Mifflin, he had pusher.
Took coal at Denholm at 11:10. Lots of eastbound freight due to derailment on Pittsburgh division day before. Slipped them all the way through Birmingham Tunnel.
Clear warm day.
Engineman—Hoffman
Fireman—Lighter

P.R.R. M-1a, 4-8-2 type.

Tractive Force	64,550 lbs.
Drivers Diameter	72 in.
Weight on Drivers	271,000 lbs.
Total Weight	390,000 lbs.
Steam Pressure	250 lbs.
Tender Capacity	24,000 gals.
	31½ tons

P.R.R. 2-10-0 type, class I-1s

Ready to leave East Altoona with train Ed-1 and 103 cars.

Tractive Force	90,024 lbs.
Drivers Diameter	62 in.
Weight on Drivers	352,500 lbs.
Total Weight	386,100 lbs.
Steam Pressure	250 lbs.
Tender Capacity	10,300 gals.
	8½ tons

Photo by S. K. F., Jr.

1931
November 10th
P. R. R.

Altoona-Sharpsburg
Train ED1, 103 cars out of Altoona, 105 cars out of Conemaugh, 4100 tons
Engine 6331 I-1s, 2 pushers and helper, all I-1s to Gallitzin
LV BO 2:30
UN 3:30
LV Conemaugh 4:55
LV JD 5:15
ARR Sharpsburg 8:30
Stopped Torrance, Avonmore, Kiski Jct. for water, Avonmore for coal
Cooled hot pin Avonmore, Kiski Jct.
Very hard runner from UN to Conemaugh typical I-1s, dirty ride, ran around VC1 at UN. #15 went around us on hill. Gas in Gallitzin Tunnel #3 track very bad. Socked her hard Kiski Jct. to Sharpsburg.
Clear and warm
Engineman—Lieb
Fireman—Redpath

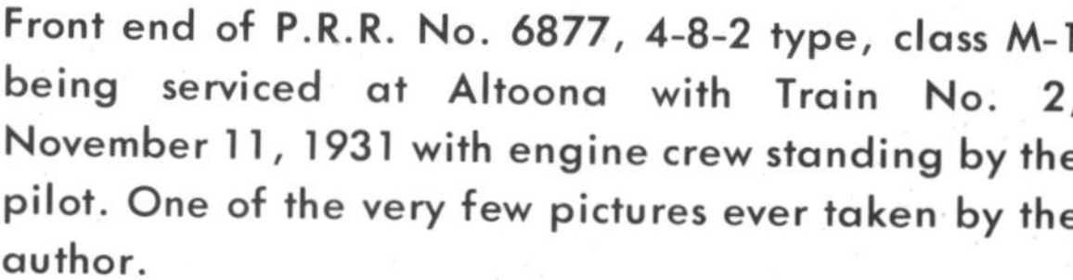

Front end of P.R.R. No. 6877, 4-8-2 type, class M-1 being serviced at Altoona with Train No. 2, November 11, 1931 with engine crew standing by the pilot. One of the very few pictures ever taken by the author.

1931
November 11th
P. R. R.

Pittsburgh—Altoona

#2 Pennsylvania Limited, 16 cars, 1 RF, 3 B60, 1 PB70, 1 P70, 1 D70, 7 SLs, 1 Obs SL

Engine 6877, M1 4-8-2

O.T. all the way, very foggy, then clear then foggy. Engine worked hard all the way, good engine and fine crew

Engineman—Hoover

Fireman—McConnell—one of the 6 McConnell brothers working in engine service out of Altoona on the P.R.R.

1931
November 11th
P. R. R.

Altoona-Harrisburg
Train #24, 9 cars
Engine 3858 K4s
O.T. all the way with extra stops. Ran around I-1 with 176 cars EB
Clear and warm.
Engineman—Marsh
Fireman—Wood

N&W

2 unit Baldwin-Westinghouse Electric Locomotives were in service between Bluefield and West Vivian, W. Va. on the Elkorn Grade. 2 units were rated for 3250 tons up a 2% grade at 14 mph or twice the speed formerly required by three of their steam engines. 4 new locomotives with 30% greater capacity were put in service in 1924.

1931
December 5th
P. R. R.

Greenville, N.J. —Bay View, Md.
Train NE1, 72 cars, left 14 at Ford, 3275 tons
Engine 6845 M1
LV Greenville 2:25 a.m.
N.K. 2:50
LV Holmes 4:01
Ford 4:50
Brill 5:12
ARR North Point 7:04
Excellent run.
Clear and cold.

P. R. R. crack stock train F.W.-8 with M-1 Engine scooping water from track tank at Wilmore, Pa., Pittsburgh Div.

B&O 4-6-2 type, class P-7C No. 5317 crossing the Tigart Valley Bridge at Grafton, W. Va. with the Cincinnatian.

Photo by R. H. Kindig

1932
January 30th
P. R. R.

Harrisburg—N.Y.
Train #28, Broadway Limited—9 cars, 1 M70, 1 PLB, 1 D70, 5 SL (1 lounge) 1 OBS SL
Engine 3737 K4s
LV Hbg. 6:17 a.m.
ARR OB 8:00
N. Phila. 8:12
Man.Tran. 9:37
Good coal, clear cold morning, excellent sunrise, O.T. all the way, road motor into N.Y.
Engineman—J. A. Shunk
Fireman—Arnsberger

Seaboard Air Line 2-6-6-4 type, class R-1

Tractive Force	82,300 lbs.
Drivers Diameter	69 in.
Weight on Drivers	330,000 lbs.
Total Weight	480,000 lbs.
Steam Pressure	230 lbs.
Tender Capacity	16,000 gals.
	24 tons

These locomotives were all sold to the B & O and served out their miles on that railroad. The author rode them on both properties.

1932
February 14th
Seaboard Airline

Camden, S.C.—Raleigh, N.C.

Train 192, 8 cars out of Camden, 11 out of Aberdeen

Engine 254 4-8-2, cut off Hamlet, bad wedges

Engine 262, Hamlet—Johnson Street—Raleigh. Met #3 Sanford

Very clean ride, good crew

Road Foreman on Engine—O. C. Branch

Engineman—Stogner

Conductor—Bowen

How the tender looks when the coal gets low and back. This is when the dirt really blows into the cab regardless of the curtain as the coal gates must be open to make sure the coal is feeding correctly into the conveyor. Photo taken by author from top of Engine 6719 tank while stuck behind Extra west, taking coal and water, at Howelville, Pa., Trenton cutoff, Phila. Div. This will eliminate stop at Thorndale on main line for coal. Note engine was popping off.

1933
January 29th
P. R. R.

Greenville—Enola via Trenton cutoff PG and low grade
Train B3, 32 cars and hack
Engine 6719 M1a
Very poor coal
Signed up 3:45 a.m.
LV Meadows 4:35
Greenville 7:15
NK 7:32
CF 8:42
Howelville 10:00
Glenloch 10:15
Thorndale 10:35
PG 10:49
Shocks Mills 12:15—5 minutes for water
DY 1:00
Went around extra at Howelville with 125 empty battleships out of coal. Stoker trouble repaired at Meadows before leaving. 7 machinists were on the engine.

Very high wind from northwest and 10° temperature
Engineman—A. A. Seifert
Fireman—J. F. Carroll

Lackawanna No. 1641, 4-8-4 type, Q4 class

Tractive Force	72,000 lbs.
Drivers Diameter	74 in.
Weight on Drivers	274,000 lbs.
Total Weight	447,000 lbs.
Steam Pressure	250 lbs.
Tender Capacity	16,000 gals.
	26 tons

A very fine engine except for the small tank which was the largest ever used on D.L.&W. due to never lengthening turntables. Photo taken at Hoboken, N.J., Nov. 10, 1948 by Bert Pennypacker.

1934
January 13th
D. L. & W.

Hoboken—Scranton

Train #1, 14 cars, 12 milk, 1 combine, 1 coach

Engine 1641 4-8-4 24

Signed up 6:30 a.m., left Hoboken 8:00 a.m., arr. Scranton 1:35 p.m. via Rockaway Branch, Hackettstown and Washington.

Empty milk cars being returned to Binghamton.

Heavy snow and sleet on the Poconos. Made all stops. OT all the way.

Engineman—H. F. Bickhorn

Fireman—W. F. Holzwith

1934
January 13th
D. L. & W.

Scranton—Hoboken
Train #6 Lackawanna Limited, 10 cars
Engine 1505 4-8-4, no helper

Left Scranton 10 minutes late, Stroudsburg 10 minutes late, Dover 4 minutes late, Hoboken O.T. 1 RPO, 3 coaches, 1 diner, 5 Pullman
Engineman—L. Harle
Fireman—R. Stahl

Lackawanna No. 1152, 4-6-4 type

Tractive Force	52,800 lbs.
Drivers Diameter	80 in.
Weight on Drivers	198,000 lbs.
Total Weight	377,000 lbs.
Steam Pressure	245 lbs.
Tender Capacity	15,800 gals.
	26 tons

One of the truly great 4-6-4 type built. A little higher steam pressure and tender capacity would have made them perfect. Photo taken at Hoboken, N.J. on Feb. 18, 1951 by Bert Pennypacker.

Florida East Coast Engine 430, 4-8-2 type with No. 75 the Havana Special arriving at Key West, Fla. in Feb. 1929.

Photo by: S.K.F., Jr.

1934
February 17th
Florida East Coast

Jacksonville—Fort Pierce, Fla.
Train #1st-87, Florida Special, 11 SL, 1 diner, 1 express, 13 cars
Engine 423 4-8-2 type to New Smyrna
Engine 437 to Miami
O.T. all the way

1934
March 12th
R. F. & P.

Richmond, Va.—Washington
Train #1st-88, Florida Special, 13 cars; 12 SL, 1 diner
Engine 325 4-6-2 type
LV Richmond 11:00 a.m. O.T.
ARR Washington 18 minutes late
Stoker failed leaving Richmond, lost 5 minutes with steam, would not hold water with both injectors on, 13 minutes. Steam pressure 150 lbs.
Poor coal, weather clear and warm.

R.F.&P. No. 325, 4-6-2 type

Tractive Force	48,580 lbs.
Drivers Diameter	75 in.
Weight on Drivers	205,300 lbs.
Total Weight	332,600 lbs.
Steam Pressure	210 lbs.
Tender Capacity	10,000 gals.
	16 tons

R.F.&P. No. 503, 4-8-2 type

Tractive Force	61,620 lbs.
Drivers Diameter	73 in.
Weight on Drivers	262,000 lbs.
Total Weight	381,000 lbs.
Steam Pressure	225 lbs.
Tender Capacity	12,000 gals.
	16 tons

1934
May 28th
R. F. & P.

Richmond, Va.—Washington
Train 1st 76, Havana Special, 16 cars;
1 PRR MS60
1 PRR B60
1 PRR RF
1 ACL RPO
1 FEC storage
1 RFP storage
1 RFP combine
1 ACL Coach
1 ACL Diner
6 SL
1 OBS sleeper
Engine 504 4-8-2 type
LV Richmond 10:25 a.m., 10 minutes late
ARR Fredericksburg 11:36 O.T., took water
LV Fredericksburg 11:46, 10 minutes late
ARR Alexandria O.T.

Slow order, highway bridge Franconia, also regular slow orders through Ashland, Doswell, Quantico
Weather clear, good engine, fine crew, 5 transients on tank put off Fredericksburg.

P.R.R. No. 1372, 2-8-2 type, class L-1s

Tractive Force	61,465 lbs.
Drivers Diameter	62 in.
Weight on Drivers	240,200 lbs.
Total Weight	320,700 lbs.
Steam Pressure	205 lbs.
Tender Capacity	9,100 gals.
	16 tons

A very old photograph—note the oil burning headlight.

Photo from H. L. Broadbelt collection

1934
October 20th
P. R. R.

Altoona—Pittsburgh
Train 3rd #5, Pennsylvania Limited, 11 cars
Engine 3853 K4s, L1s helper, Altoona, to Gallitzin
Went around 2nd #5 on hill twice. He ran around us at Johnstown.
Poor coal, weather clear, full moon
Engineman—C. J. Rabuck
Fireman—C. A. Robb

C&O 2-6-6-2 type No. 1560, class H-7 with eastward coal train just east of Hinton, W. Va.

1934
October 22nd
P. R. R.

Chicago—Pittsburgh
Train #22, Manhattan Limited, 11 cars
Engine 5344 K4s Chicago Crestline
Extra stop at Warsaw.
Road Foreman—M. A. Vaughn road engine. Very hard worker firing and running her. Scooped water Hanna-Dola
Engineman—B. J. Krull—Chicago—Ft. Wayne
Fireman—C. C. Ekelbury
#52 ahead of us hit monkey car smashing pilot at Upper Sandusky, ran opposing track Dunkirk—Upper Sandusky. 10 minutes late at Crestline.

P.R.R. No. 54 doubleheaded with 2-K-4's coupled, descending the Alleghenys on Horseshoe Curve, Pittsburgh Div. at Kittitanning Point.

Photo by H. W. Pontin, Allston Rail Road Photographs

1934
October 22nd
P. R. R.

Crestline—Pittsburgh

Engine 3887, 8854 4-6-2 type, K-4s class, No. 22 Manhattan Limited, 11 cars,

Rode 1st engine to Orrville, 2nd to Pittsburgh. Very fast run Homewood to Pittsburgh. Took water at Alliance 3887 only. Scooped water, Grafton-Millbrook

1 PB70, 2 P70, 1 D70, 7 SL

Fine crew, good as I ever rode with on P.R.R., O.T. all the way. Engineman, B. P. Faulds.

Fireman—C. J. McCormick, 2nd engine

N.Y.C. No. 5272, 4-6-4 type, class J-1b

Tractive Force	42,300 lbs.
Drivers Diameter	79 in.
Weight on Drivers	184,500 lbs.
Total Weight	346,500 lbs.
Steam Pressure	225 lbs.
Tender Capacity	12,500 gals.
	24 tons

Shown scooping water at Tivoli, N.Y. on the Hudson Div. with train No. 39—the North Shore Limited.

Photo by: H. W. Pontin, Allston Railroad Photographs.

1935
February 9th
N. Y. C.

Harmon—Buffalo
Train #39, North Shore Limited, 13 cars
Engine 5243 J1 4-6-4 type
Good engine, took coal at Brighton, good coal all the way
LV Syracuse 9 minutes late
LV Rochester 3 minutes late
ARR Buffalo 3 minutes late
Had to take slack with Booster only at Schenectady and Fonda. Pusher up Albany hill, never saw a freight train until west of Utica. Met BNY 2 at Rochester. Fastest speed 80 mph, clear and cold, about 15°

1935
February 10th
P. R. R.

Buffalo—Harrisburg via Renovo

Train #570, Buffalo—Washington Day Express, 7 cars

Engine 1488 K4s with 11,000 gallon tank

Took water at Olean and Williamsport, coal at Linden. Met #577 at Machus 20 minutes late, met 571 at Jersey Shore, BNY 14 right in back of us with 6400 tons and 2 M1s, plus L1 and 11 pushers over Keating Summit, snowing hard to the top. Signal out at North Bend. On weekdays we would have had all of RJ10 cars, run extra on Sundays. Were cut off at Williamsport by mistake, went to engine house and back to train

1 RF
1 PB70
2 P70
1 Cafe coach
1 P70
1 PL

C&O No. 602 4-8-4 type, class J-3 with train No. 1st-47 The Sportsman at White Sulphur, W. Va. on June 11, 1943

Tractive Force	64,450 lbs.
Drivers Diameter	74 in.
Weight on Drivers	278,300 lbs.
Total Weight	477,000 lbs.
Steam Pressure	255 lbs.
Tender Capacity	22,000 gals.
	25 tons

P.R.R. No. 4856, 2-C+ C-2 class GG-1 electric.

Tractive Force	72,800 lbs.
Drivers Diameter	57 in.
Weight on Drivers	303,000 lbs.
Total Weight	477,000 lbs.
Rating Continuous at rail 4,620	
Maximum speed 100 mph	

1935
November 24th
P. R. R.

N. Y.—Washington
Train 111, 14 cars
Engine 4833 GG1 1st run on one and took Mrs. Farrington with me. Snowing hard to Bristol. GG1s look fine throwing snow on eastbound trains, probably 4 inches on the ground.
Lost 4 minutes to Trenton getting new steam hose between last two Pullmans. O.T. N. Phila., O.T. Baltimore, O.T. Washington. Got 5 whistles at Nassau (Princeton Jct.) for heat.

1 PB70 D4
3 P70 D4
1 MS 60
1 B60
1 PB70
2 P70
1 D70
2 PL
1 SL (C&O)
Engineman—A. E. Davis
Fireman—N. R. Calkins

P.R.R. No. 4843, class GG-1
Running under 3 position automatic block position light signals on the New York Div.

1935
November 24th
P. R. R.

Washington—Newark
Train #152, Congressional Limited, 10 cars
Engine 4817 GG1
Lost contact under N.Y. Avenue bridge leaving Washington, Panograph not fouled, 3 minutes detention, O.T. Baltimore, 4 minutes detention at Wilmington, station master wanting to know what trouble was at Washington. O.T. at Trenton, received message from J. A. Appleton at N. Phila. General Manager in N. Y. inquiring how I liked GG1, also Mrs. Farrington's opinion. O.T. Newark.
1 PB70
1 P70
1 D70
6 P1
1 OBS lounge
Weather clearing, fine crew,

Engineman—D. J. Keleher
Fireman—F. M. Quinn
Road train 230 Newark—Sunnyside around loop on GG1 following 152. They had come from Broad St., Phila. in 1 hour and 40 minutes making up 10 minutes with 10 stops.

1936
May 17th
P. R. R.

N. Y.—Washington
Train 129, 11 cars
Engine 4836 GG1
O.T. all the way

B&O Diesel No. 64, A1A-A1A type, DP-4 class

4,000 HP—E.M.D.—E7

Wheels	36 in.
Weight on Drivers	428,000 lbs.
Tractive Force	107,000 lbs.

Hauling No. 4, The Diplomat, at 45 mph east of North Takoma, Md. on the west end of the Baltimore Div. Descending Silver Spring Grade with 10 cars.

Photo by Bruce D. Fales.

B&O No. 7153, 2-8-8-0 type, class EL-3a with a 54 car coal train
Grafton to Keyser—Climbing Cranberry Grade east of Salt Lick Curve, West of Terra Alta, W.Va. Nov. 1948

Photo by Bruce D. Fales

1936
July 29th
P. R. R.

Broad St., Phila.—Delmar, Va.
Train #417, 5 cars; I-PB 70, 4 P70
Engine 3347 K2sa
Met. #462 at Dover, O.T. all the way

U.P. No. 3805, 2-8-8-0 type, class MC pushing train No. 257 near Leonard, Oregon—Oregon Div.
Photo by: R. H. Kindig

Tractive Force	123,700 lbs.
Drivers Diameter	57 in.
Weight on Drivers	465,000 lbs.
Total Weight	495,500 lbs.
Steam Pressure	210 lbs.
Tender Capacity	12,000 gals.
	20 tons

1936
August 18th
C. N. R.

Halifax, N.S.—Truro, N.S.
Train #7, 9 cars
Engine 6017 4-8-2 type
Met #2 Windsor Junction, met #6 Shubenacdie, O.T. all the way

R.F.&P. No. 309, 4-6-2 type

Tractive Force	42,800 lbs.
Drivers Diameter	75 in.
Weight on Drivers	199,000 lbs.
Total Weight	293,300 lbs.
Steam Pressure	200 lbs.
Tender Capacity	10,000 gals.

Built by the Baldwin Locomotive Works in 1924 and modernized by the railroad in 1931.

1937
February 3rd
P. R. R.

N. Y.—Washington

Train Advance #133, Florida Special, 11 SLs, 2 diners

Engine 4809 GG1

15 minutes ahead of time at Perryville, then followed L1 with 85 cars Aberdeen to Bengies, lost 25 minutes. L1 had exceptionally big train because of floods in West.

Left Washington as RF & P. 2nd 87, Engine 302, RF & P 93 broke down at Alexandria, everything plugged. Trains were extra 309, 1st 87, #7, 2nd 87, 3rd 87, 4th 87, 307, 73, Southern Railway 31, C & O #3. Left engine and went back to eat. 3 hours and 20 minutes late at Richmond.

C&O No. 502, 4-8-0-4-8-4 type, M-1 class Steam Turbo Electric. Leaving Clifton Forge, Va., Clifton Forge Div. Allegheny sub-Div. on test run with new equipment for the much talked-of streamliner Chessie which fortunately was never put into service. These engines were built because of the coal industry and luckily only three were put into use. They required special coal docks, still had to be turned and were highly expensive in operating costs as were the N&W's turbine attempt some years later. The author rode both several times when they were in service on the C&O with passenger train and freight on the N&W.

Tractive Force	98,000 lbs.
Drivers Diameter	40 in.
Weight on Drivers	533,012 lbs.
Total Weight	857,200 lbs.
Steam Pressure	310 lbs.

Built by the Baldwin Locomotive Works—1947-48.

1937
March 15
P. R. R.

N. Y.—Washington

Train 2nd 131, 12 cars; 1 PB 70, 9 P70s, 1 cafe coach, 1 D70

Engine 4805 GG1 cut off at Wilmington, getting Engine 4821 GG1. 4805 developed motor trouble at Torresdale, failed at Zoo and was cut off at Wilmington after 70 minute detention.

1937
March 23rd
P. R. R.

Washington—N. Y.
Train 1st-152, Advance Congressional Limited, 12 cars, 10 P70, 1 D70, 1 cafe coach
Engine 4187
O.T. all the way
Engineman—D. J. Keleher

N&W No. 1160, 4-8-0 type, M-2c class

Tractive Force	52,457 lbs.
Drivers Diameter	56 in.
Weight on Drivers	239,530 lbs.
Total Weight	279,000 lbs.
Steam Pressure	200 lbs.
Tender Capacity	15,000 gals. 20 tons

This was the heaviest and most powerful Mastodon type ever built and few were used on other railroads. After WW II the N&W rebuilt 2 for switching service to try to economically compete with the Diesels. Note the old and original Baker Valve Gear. The author, needless to say, only rode a few back in the old days with local freights to Radford, Va. and the modernized switching attempts in the Roanoke yards.

B&O No. 6162, 2-10-2 type, class S-1a with train No. 97 east of Brunswick, Md.—Baltimore Div.

Tractive Force	84,300 lbs.
Drivers Diameter	64 in.
Weight on Drivers	346,350 lbs.
Total Weight	440,340 lbs.
Steam Pressure	220 lbs.
Tender Capacity	15,800 gals.
	23 tons

Photo by: Henry M. Tischler

1937
July 31st
C. N. R.

Halifax—Truro
Train #7, 10 cars
Engine 6017, 4-8-2 type
O.T. all the way, same crew and engine as the year before.

1938
February 2nd
P. R. R.

Altoona—Detroit

Train #69, the Red Arrow, 11 cars; 3 DH, 1 PB70, 1 P70, 1 D70, 1 lounge, 4 sleepers

Pittsburgh Division Engine 5467 K4s

LV Altoona 11 minutes late, Arr Pittsburgh 2 minutes early.

Finest K4 I ever rode, I-1 helper on the hill. Passenger tunnel through Gallitzin, fog, light rain

Engineman—Frank Smith, second trip

Fireman—H. F. Berger—X man

Road Foreman—K. L. Roberts

Eastern Division, 9 cars

Engine 5339 K4s, 1 PB70, 1 P 70, 1 D 70, 6 SLs

Engineman—Charles Kelly

Fireman—M. K. Bertoletti

O.T. all the way. Fog and heavy rain

Toledo Division, 10 cars

Engine 3767 K4s

Very fast ride to Mansfield, just missed hitting car west of Tiffin, fast ride Mansfield—Toledo. Took water Toledo. Run over AA railroad. Met ED2 leaving Olive Yard, made full stop Miami River Bridge—Toledo. Got BM70 making 10 cars out of Mansfield

Engineman—J. A. Thomas

Fireman—W. H. Callahan

Road Foreman—M. W. DeWitt

O.T. all the way, excellent coal on all 3 locomotives, all stoker fired.

Two P.R.R. I-1s, 2-10-0 type pushing a westward Preference Train up the Allegheny Grade of 1.8% rounding Horseshoe Curve.

Photo by: H. W. Pontin, Allston Railroad Photographs

Wabash No. 2921, 4-8-4 type, class O-1

Tractive Force	70,750 lbs.
Drivers Diameter	70 in.
Weight on Drivers	275,390 lbs.
Total Weight	459,290 lbs.
Steam Pressure	250 lbs.
Tender Capacity	15,000 gals.
	18 tons

These were very fine 4-8-4's ridden many times by the author. This picture is used here because very naturally there were none available of Engine 523 4-4-2 type built in 1904.

1938
February 3rd
Wabash

Adrian—Fort Wayne
Train #7, 5 cars
Engine 523 4-4-2 type, 85 inch wheels built in 1904, took water at Adrian, very poor coal, O.T. all the way.

N&W No. 129 Streamlined 4-8-2 type, class K-1 at Roanoke, Va.—August 1947—Photo by Bruce D. Fales

Tractive Force	62,920 lbs.
Drivers Diameter	70 in.
Weight on Drivers	240,700 lbs.
Total Weight	353,900 lbs.
Steam Pressure	220 lbs.
Tender Capacity	22000 gals.
	30 tons

16 of these engines were in service, all N&W design.

1938
February 5th
P. R. R.

Chicago—Logansport, Ind.

Train 216—13 cars; 2 B60, 1 PB70, 1 P70, 1 D70, 2 P1, 1 B60, 2 P70, 1 B60, 1 P70, 1 Cafe parlor

Engine 3730 K4s

LV 5 minutes late bridge open, worked her hard all the way, injectors broke at Sandy Hook, took coal and water at Kouts, tough job, poor coal, OT at Van.

P.R.R. No. 460, 4-4-2 type, E6s class

Tractive Force	31,275 lbs.
Drivers Diameter	80 in.
Weight on Drivers	136,000 lbs.
Total Weight	243,000 lbs.
Steam Pressure	205 lbs.
Tender Capacity	7,150 gals.
	16 tons

This was the famous E6 that hauled the 2-car Lindbergh films from Washington to Manhattan Transfer 216 miles in 175 mins., average speed 74 mph including a stop at West Yard, Del. due water scoop trouble in 1927. These engines and C.M. St. P.&P. class A oil burners were the author's favorites.

Photo taken at Ocean City, N.J., Aug. 27, 1955. From collection of Harold K. Vollrath.

1938
February 5th
P. R. R.

Logansport—Indianapolis

Train No. 316—3 cars, 1 B60, 1 Cafe Parlor, off rear end No. 216

Engine 779 4-4-2 type E6s class

Took coal and water at Kraft, poor coal, O.T. all the way.

Some E6's were in service lines west at that time.

1938
February 5th
P. R. R.

Indianapolis—Columbus, Ohio
Train #30, The Spirit of St. Louis, 12 cars, 1 MS60, 1 B60, 1 PB70, 1 P70, 2 D70, 6 SL
Engines 1329, 5378 K4s coupled
Engineman—Sam Corbin
Fireman—George Moore
Assistant Road Foreman—Bill Shields
Left 2 minutes late, arrived Columbus 4 minutes early, stopped Richmond, Greenville, Piqua and Urbana. Took water at Richmond and helper at Urbana, excellent run, fine crew, Corbin wonderful runner. Foggy.

N.Y.C. Engine 3130, 4-8-2 type, class L-4 eastbound oil for New England. The engine is scooping water at East Palmyra, N.Y.—Buffalo Div.

P.R.R. M-1, 4-8-2 type climbing the Allegheny grade rounding the Horseshoe Curve with I-1s helper.

Photo by H. W. Pontin, Allston Railroad Photographs

1938
February 6th
P. R. R.

Columbus—Altoona
Train 2nd VL8, 76 cars, 3810 tons
Pan Handle Division Engine 6729 M1a
Columbus—Pitcairn
Engineman—Dempsey
Fireman—Steve Brody
LV Col. Frog Eye 8:20 a.m.
ND 9:04
Dennison 11:04
Mingo Jct. 12:30
Wierton Jct. 12:38
Bulger 1:34
Carnegie 2:02
Esplen 2:25
Pitcairn 3:20 p.m.
Raining, very wet rail, ran her very hard, slipping all the way, excellent crew
I1s Pushers
Columbus—Summit
Dennison to Cadiz Jct.
Collier—Bulger
Took water at Conesville and Collier, 21,000 gallon tank, about 1 ton of coal left. Had breakfast with Supt. Ridgley Columbus who took me to yard.

1938
February 6th
P. R. R.

Train 2nd VL8, 76 cars, 3810 tons, through from Columbus
Pittsburgh Div. engine 6751 M1 Pitcairn—Altoona
Engineman—J. F. George
Fireman—L. H. Younger
LV SZ 3:30 p.m. Pitcairn
ARR C 5:40 Connemaugh
LV C 6:30
ARR BO 8:20 Altoona
I-1s pusher to Derry
I-1s pusher Connemaugh to Gallitzin
Made fine run to JD "Blairsville Intersection" where CS8 plugged us. Could not get moving again with very wet rail and sand would not run. Engineman went out to sand box 4 times.
Took coal, water and sand at Connemaugh, brake beam down leaving on 41st car. Attention called to broken rail under coal dock, CS8 got out ahead of us. Engine steamed well, good crew, ran her well on hill.
Streamlined K4 on #15, #25 doubleheader with 2 K4s met VC1-2-7 all with I engines. Saw St. Paul engine going west from Baldwin.
25,000 gallon tank K4s on 29 and 59, 49 had 2 K4s with 15 cars. Good westward move.
Raining, blowing, sleeting, coal fair.
3 VL8s came over

P.R.R. Engine H. No. 6765C, 4-8-2 type, class M-1a rounding the horseshoe curve as it climbs the Allegheny grade with Florida fruit received through Potomac yard on the head end.

Photo by H.W. Pontin, Allston Railroad Photographs

R.F.&P. Engine 552, 4-8-4 type, 551 class, The General T. J. Jackson.

Tractive Force	66,500 lbs.
Drivers Diameter	77 in.
Weight on Drivers	277,245 lbs.
Total Weight	466,040 lbs.
Steam Pressure	275 lbs.
Tender Capacity	20,000 gals.
	22 tons

1938
March 1st
R. F. & P.

Potomac Merchandise

Acca Yard, Richmond, Va.—Potomac Yard

Engine 552, General J. T. Jackson, 79 cars out of Acca with 2900 tons, 87 cars out of Fredericksburg with 3200 tons.

Engineman—J. W. Johnson

Fireman—G. O. Allen

LV NA 7:25 p.m.

ARR WH 8:49

LV Fredericksburg 9:44

ARR AF 11:00

Put train over hump, left engine on pit at 12:00. Excellent crew, fine engine, good steamer, easy on coal, took water at Fredericksburg. Engine never worked hard. Clear and warm.

1938
June 4th
C. R. I & P.

Chicago—Eldon

Train #3, Golden State Limited, 14 cars; 1 RPO, 1 Express, 1 Coach, 1 Deluxe coach, 2 Tourist S1, 1 Lounge, 1 Diner, 4 SL, 1 OBSL

Engine 4052 4-8-2 type, class M50A

1 sleeper with Callaway's band cut off at Bureau for Peoria

Terrible coal, shaking her down hard all the way. Chief of Motive power, Jerry Trachta rode with me.

OT all the way

C.R.I.&P. No. 4061, 4-8-2 type, class M-50a

Tractive Force	50,400 lbs.
Drivers Diameter	74 in.
Weight on Drivers	255,500 lbs.
Total Weight	378,000 lbs.
Steam Pressure	200 lbs.
Tender Capacity	10,000 gals.
	16 tons

C.R.I.&P. No. 5027, 4-8-4 type, class S-436

Tractive Force	66,000 lbs.
Drivers Diameter	69 in.
Weight on Drivers	266,500 lbs.
Total Weight	436,000 lbs.
Steam Pressure	250 lbs.
Tender Capacity	15,000 gals.
	20 tons

1938
June 4th
CR I & P

Kansas City—Delhart, Okla.
Train #3, Golden State Limited, 13 cars
Crew changes at Liberal and Dalhart
Engine 5039 4-8-4 type, class R67B
OT all the way

1938
June 5th
C. R. I. & P.

Dalhart—Tucumcari
Train #3, Golden State Limited, 13 cars
Engine 4044 4-8-2 class M50A

Through the dust bowl, over rails, in cab everything white in 20 minutes, lost 35 minutes meeting #4 and 44 at Guymon. Only oil burner I ever rode that would not steam. Could not get her over 170 lbs. My impression was poor engine crew. Arrived Tucumcari 30 minutes late. Putting in new rail all the way over.

So dirty walked back outside of train to rear car, was getting on when S. P. cop put gun on me being so dirty. Tried to tell me RI engine pass no good now, my S. P. pass in my clothes in compartment. Mrs. Farrington and porter had a good laugh as train started and I wrenched away from cop very foolishly thinking it was a joke and engine crew had put him up to it. S. P. conductor informed me enroute Alamogoroo hobo had shot S.P. agent there 3 months previously.

C.R.I.&P. Golden State Limited No. 3 with Engine No. 4060

4-8-2 type, class M-50 west of Bureau, Ill. Illinois Div.

1938
June 6th
S. P. of Mexico

Nogales—Empalme
Train #10, the El Costeno
Engine 907 4-6-0 type, Class T-28, helper 603 2-8-0 type, class C-9
Rode helper out Nogales to top of hill, plenty of Mexicans hanging on all along train, very rough, cattle on track all the way.
1 EX
1 RPO
1 Second Cl. coach
1 First Cl. coach
1 Restaurant sleeper
3 SL
1 OBSSI
OT all the way
Water at Magdalena, Carbo
Engine 904 T-28, 4-6-0 type Hermosillo, San Blas

S.P. of Mexico No. 2103, 4-6-0 type, class T-28

Engines formerly numbered in the 900 series were brought back from Mexico and scrapped in Los Angeles in May 1947. Photo taken March 15, 1947 by H. L. Kelso

Tractive Force	34,580 lbs.
Drivers Diameter	63 in.
Weight on Drivers	118,000 lbs.
Total Weight	153,000 lbs.
Steam Pressure	190 lbs.
Tender Capacity	10,000 gal.
	4,500 gal oil

This engine built in Oct. 1902 by Alco.

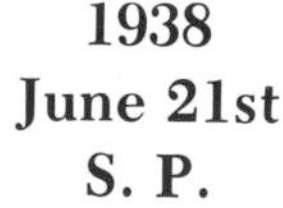

1938
June 21st
S. P.

Tucson—Lordsberg
Train #2, Sunset Limited
Engine 4355 4-8-2 type, MT4, 11 cars, 2 Ex, 1 Postal, 1 coach, 1 chair, 1 diner, 1 lounge, 4 SL
OT all the way

S.P. No. 4350, 4-8-2 type, class Mt-4

Tractive Force	57,510 lbs.
Drivers Diameter	73½ in.
Weight on Drivers	246,000 lbs.
Total Weight	386,000 lbs.
Steam Pressure	210 lbs.
Tender Capacity	16,152 gals. water
	4,692 gals. oil

S.P. No. 2488, 4-6-2 type, class P-10

Tractive Force	45,850 lbs.
Drivers Diameter	73 in.
Weight on Drivers	183,000 lbs.
Total Weight	274,800 lbs.
Steam Pressure	210 lbs.
Tender Capacity	16,152 gals.
	4,692 gals. oil

This engine duplicate of 613 on the Texas Lines

1938
June 22nd
S. P.

El Paso—Sanderson
Train #2, Sunset Limited
Engine 633 4-6-2 P13, 10 cars
OT all the way, weather clear all the way, very hot.

1938
June 24th
T & P

Longview Jct.—Texarkana
Train #16, The Texan, 10 cars
Engine 906 4-8-2 type
OT all the way

C.R.I.&P. No. 4026, 4-8-2 type, class M-50 with a Main Train east of Denver on April 4, 1943, Denver Div.

Photo by: Otto C. Perry

N&W 1st No. 4, The Pocahantas, with Engine No. 600, 4-8-4 type, class J, passing the Peaks of Otter at Bedford, Va. on the Norfolk Div.

1939
May 1st
C R & I P

Chicago—Silvas
Train #91, Time Freight west
Engine 5027, class R67B, 4-8-4 type, 75 cars, 4920 tons
LV Chicago 10:00 a.m.
ARR Silvas 3:15 p.m.
Water at Ottawa, Bureau.
Coal at Bureau.

1938
June 25th
L & N

Louisville—Cincinnati
Train 98 Pan American, 11 cars
Engine 276 Ks 4-6-2 type
Coal, water at Worthville
OT all the way

L&N No. 275, 4-6-2 L type, class K-5 Streamlined for use on the Dixie Flagger and South Wind.

Tractive Force	42,735 lbs.
Drivers Diameter	73 in.
Weight on Drivers	277,000 lbs.
Total Weight	369,000
Steam Pressure	210 lbs.
Tender Capacity	20,000 gals.

These were the most successful Pacific-type locomotives the L&N ever had in service. They were U.S.R.A. design. Built in 1919.

B&O 2-8-8-4 type, class EM-1, Nos. 7621-7607 Running "Light"
Coupled, Keyser to Grafton. Need of Power at Grafton to move coal east.
Climbing 17 mile grade near Swanton, Md. Sept. 1948

Photo by: Bruce D. Fales

1938
June 25th
L & N

Paris, Tenn.—Bowling Green, Ky.
Train 198 Pan American, 5 cars
Engine 228 K-4 4-6-2 type
Water at Clarksville.

1938
June 25th
P. R. R.

Cincinnati—Columbus
Train #202, Pennsylvania Limited
Engine 5354 K4s, stoker fired
Took water at Xenia. Behind 102 at Xenia. OT all the way

C&O No. 541, 4-8-2 type, class J-1

Tractive Force	58,100 lbs.
Drivers Diameter	62 in.
Weight on Drivers	239,000 lbs.
Total Weight	330,000 lbs.
Steam Pressure	180,000 lbs.
Tender Capacity	9,000 gals.
	15 tons

This engine and two others built in 1911-12 by the Richmond Locomotive works were the first mountain-type built and put in service in the U.S. Shown here with second No. 47 at White Sulphur.

Lackawanna No. 1452, 4-8-2 type, 3 cylinder

Tractive Force	61,100 lbs.
Drivers Diameter	73 in.
Weight on Drivers	256,600 lbs.
Total Weight	382,000 lbs.
Steam Pressure	200 lbs.
Tender Capacity	12,000 gals.
	14 tons

3rd cylinder removed at Scranton Shops in 1940. Photo taken at Hoboken, N.J. with Train No. 5, Chicago Limited, in March 1945 by Bert Pennypacker.

1938
September 3rd
D L & W

Scranton—Elmira

Train #5, Chicago Limited

Engine 1452 4-8-2 type, 12 cars, 13 out of Scranton to Binghamton

Rode engine 1606 4-8-4 type helper to Clarks Summit. 40 minutes late out of Binghamton.

1938
September 4th
Michigan Central

Detroit—Chicago
Train#17—The Wolverine
Engine 5323 4-6-4 type J1E, 13 cars Detroit to Ann Arbor, 11 cars Ann Arbor to Chicago, 45 minutes late out of Detroit, 25 minutes late into Chicago. Went into LaSalle Street, Chicago only MC train to use it. PRR #23 doubleheaded with 2 K4s at Englewood OT. Changed fireman at Niles and Jackson, engineman only at Jackson. First engineman very much afraid of me, second man ran her very hard.

N.Y.C. No. 5274, class J-1a, 4-6-4 type

Scooping water at Yosts Mohawk Div. with train No. 8 Wolverine

Tractive Force	42,360 lbs.
Drivers Diameter	79 in.
Weight on Drivers	184,500 lbs.
Total Weight	346,500 lbs.
Steam Pressure	225 lbs.
Tender Capacity	12,500 gals.
	24 tons

1938
September 4th
C. M. St. P. & P.

Chicago—Minneapolis
Train #1st 101, Hiawatha, 10 cars
Engine 2, 4-4-2 type, class A
Ran 105 miles per hour
2nd 101 Milwaukee—Portage 9 cars
Popped off at 93 mph running as fast as 102 mph
2nd 101 St. Paul—Minneapolis
OT all the way.

C.M.St.P.&P. No. 2, 4-4-2 type, class A Oil Burner Shown with the original Hiawatha when it first was put into service.

Tractive Force	30,700 lbs.
Drivers Diameter	84 in.
Weight on Drivers	144,300 lbs.
Total Weight	200,000 lbs.
Steam Pressure	300 lbs.
Tender Capacity	13,000 gals.
	4,000 gals. oil

Four of these engines were built but as the Hiawathas grew heavier they were replaced by the new F-7 4-6-4 type engines which entered service in 1938.

C.M.St.P.&P. No 126, 4-6-4 type, F-6a class

Tractive Force	45,820 lbs.
Drivers Diameter	79 in.
Weight on Drivers	189,720 lbs.
Total Weight	375,850 lbs.
Steam Pressure	225 lbs.
Tender Capacity	15,000 gals.
	20 tons

1938
September 5th
C. M. St. P. & P.

Aberdeen, S.D.—Marmouth, N.D.
Train #15, The Olympian, 11 cars
Engine 116 4-6-4 type—F6a
OT all the way
Hard head wind.

1938
September 6th
C. M. St. P. & P.

Harlowton—Avery
Train #15, Olympian, 11 cars
Motor 10301 Class 3 0-3, 2-C-1 + 1-C-2
OT all the way.

C.M.St.P.&P. No. 17, The Olympian, on the Clear Creek Bridge showing upper tracks in the Bitter Root Mts. east of St. Paul's Pass Tunnel with motor No. 10 300 class EP-3, 2-C-1 + 1-C-2 type. Sixth sub div of the Rocky Mt. Div.

Tractive Force	153,000 lbs.
Weight on Drivers	378,000 lbs.
Total Weight	600,000 lbs.
Max. Spd.	65 mph.

1938
September 6th
C. M. St. P. & P.

Avery—Spokane
Train #15, Olympian, 11 cars
Engine 251 4-8-4 type, oil burner S-1
Engineman—Emerson, great friend of Mr. Gillick O.V.P. of Milwaukee.
Fine crew, fine engine, OT all the way, clear and cool.

C.M.St.P.&P. No. 251, 4-8-4 type, class S-1
This was the first 4-8-4 type built for the railroad by Baldwin
Originally No. 9701

Tractive Force	62,130 lbs.
Drivers Diameter	74 in.
Weight on Drivers	265,700 lbs.
Total Weight	446,530 lbs.
Steam Pressure	230 lbs.
Tender Capacity	20,000 gals.
	25 tons

1938
September 7th
U. P.

Seattle—Portland
Train—Portland Rose, #18, 15 cars
Engine 7017 4-8-2 type, oil burner
OT all the way.
#18 left Portland with 14 cars and 2-8-2 type on UP.

U.P. Engine No. 7854, 4-8-2 type, class MT-73

Tractive Force	54,840 lbs.
Drivers Diameter	73 in.
Weight on Drivers	224,000 lbs.
Total Weight	338,000 lbs.
Steam Pressure	200 lbs.
Tender Capacity	15,000 gals.
	5,480 gals. oil

The L.A. & S.L. engines were numbered 7,800. Here train No. 14, the Pacific Limited, crosses the Rio Hondo west of Pico, Cal.-Cal. Div. Photographed Apr. 1940 by Walter H. Thrall.

1938
September 7th
S. P.

Eugene to Klamath Falls
Train #15, The Oregonian
Engine 4401 4-8-4 Gs1
Helper 3756 2-10-2 type F5, Oak Ridge to Cascade Summit
Rode the helper, very foggy and raining, they pulled hard
Met #16 and 24.

S.P. No. 700, 4-8-4 type, class G-S1

Tractive Force	62,200 lbs.
Drivers Diameter	73 in.
Weight on Drivers	262,000 lbs.
Total Weight	400,700 lbs.
Steam Pressure	250 lbs.
Tender Capacity	16,150 gal.
	4,690 gal oil

This engine carries the numbers used on the Texas Lines and is the duplicate of Engine No. 4403.

1938
September 9th
S. P.

San Jose—Glendale
Train #98, Daylight, 14 cars
Engine 4412 4-8-4 type, GS2, helper 3727 Santa Margarita to San Luis Obispo 2-10-2 F5
OT all the way, fine run, fine crew, fine engine. Started her without booster, used new electric brake.

S.P. No 4410, 4-8-4 type, Class G-S-2

Tractive Force	62,200 lbs.
Drivers Diameter	73 in.
Weight on Drivers	266,500 lbs.
Total Weight	405,900 lbs.
Steam Pressure	250 lbs.
Tender Capacity	23,300 gals.
	5,880 gals. oil

S.P. No. 4114, 4-8-8-2 type, class AC-5

Tractive Force	116,900 lbs.
Drivers Diameter	63 in.
Weight on Drivers	482,500 lbs.
Total Weight	563,400 lbs.
Steam Pressure	235 lbs.
Tender Capacity 16-C-2p	16,152 gal.
	4,662 gal. oil

1938
September 19th
S. P.

Glendale—Fresno

Train—The Owl, #25, 16 cars

Engine 4118 AC5 4-8-8-2 type, Los Angeles Bakersfield

Helper 3739 2-10-2 type. From Mojave to Tehachapi Summit

LV L.A. 20 minutes late, lost 20 more with slow order in the canyon.

3 EX

2 coaches

7 DH

1 Diner lounge

1 Tourist

1 SL

1 OBS S1

Had booster 4-6-2 class P11 Bakersfield to Fresno

Warm and clear. Same night as headender nos. 5 and 44 at Tortuga heard bad news at Bakersfield.

S.P. No 4159, 4-8-8-2 type, class AC-7

Tractive Force	123,400 lbs.
Drivers Diameter	63½ in.
Weight on Drivers	514,800 lbs.
Total Weight	639,800 lbs.
Steam Pressure	250 lbs.
Tender Capacity	22,000 gals.
	6,100 gals. oil

1938
September 21st
S. P.

Roseville—Sparks

Train #14, Pacific Limited, 11 cars, 1 RPO, 1 storage, 2 Ex., 2 deluxe coaches, 1 coach, 1 tourist SL, 1 diner, 1 SL, 10BS, SL

Engine 4163 AC-7 4-8-8-2 type

OT all the way, fine run, fine crew, fine day. Took water at Colfax and Truckee.

Reported rock on westward track at Floriston. At Reno—Boy selling *Reno Evening Gazette* with headline "East Hampton, New York 3 p.m. wind was blowing 110 mph." My home village, the 1938 hurricane.

ON THE HEAD END EASTBOUND OVER THE SIERRA GRADE

The territory described is that portion of the Sacramento Division known as the Sierra Nevada Mountains extending from Roseville, California, on the western slope, to Sparks, Nevada, on the eastern slope, a distance of 137 miles on the eastward, and 139 miles on the westward track.

From Roseville to Norden, the summit where the maximum tonnage moves by eastward direction, the distance from Roseville to Colfax is 36 miles and gradient 1.5, Colfax to Emigrant Gap 30.1 miles, gradient 2.4, and Emigrant Gap to Norden 22 miles, gradient 1.8. The elevation at Roseville is 200 feet above sea level, at Norden 7000 feet, a tonnage lift of 6800 feet.

On arrival at the roundhouse the engineer registers out on the Roundhouse Register, compares time with standard clock, checks Engineer Work Report. He then proceeds to his engine, where he tries the boiler gauge cocks and water glasses to find true level of water in boiler. He then turns steam on lubricator, examines fire box as to cleanliness, looks for leaks, and then inspects and oils those parts of his engine that require it. He sets the lubricator feeds, tries the engine brakes and train control.

On the way from the roundhouse to the train yard he blows out the boiler. On his arrival at train yard engine is coupled to train and he charges air brake system to standard pressure. When he receives the proper signal from carmen he sets the brakes by making a 15 lb. brake reduction, and as soon as the brake valve exhaust closes, notes the brake pipe reduction, which must not exceed 3 lbs. in 30 seconds. He then releases the brakes and adjusts the brake system to standard pressure.

Upon signal to proceed, he starts train by taking slack out gently. After train has started, he moves at a speed not to exceed 8 miles per hour for a distance sufficient to permit running inspection by trainmen. He then increases the speed of train to the maximum permitted under the speed restrictions prevailing, or the speed that engine will handle train. This is done by changing the position of reverse lever as indicated by mechanical instruments on engine. By these instruments he is able to develop maximum draw bar pull with economy.

During the course of his trip, the position of the reverse levers is changed so as to set the valve travel to meet changed grade conditions, and this procedure is followed Roseville to Norden.

Before leaving Norden he makes an air brake test to be sure the air goes through the train and that brakes are working properly. He then re-charges the train to standard pressure. While this is taking place, the trainmen turn up the retainers. After train has been charged to standard pressure, he starts train by releasing the driver brake cylinder pressure gradually, permitting train to move out slowly with slack bunched, until running inspection has been made. Speed is then allowed to pick up to the maxiumum allowable speed, and just before that maximum is reached, a brake pipe reduction, not to exceed 8 lbs., is made, followed by another light reduction, if necessary.

When the engineer feels the speed retarding, he notes the brake pipe reduction on his air gauge—then recharges the brake system. As speed again starts to increase, he applies the brake by making one reduction of brake pipe pressure, bringing it down to where it was on the previous application, and as speed is retarded, he again recharges the brake system. This process is continued to Truckee where retainers are turned down. The braking procedure from Truckee to Sparks is somewhat different, due to the fact that retainers are not used.

After starting the train at Truckee and speed picks up close to the maximum allowable speed, he makes a brake pipe reduction not to exceed 6 lbs. and if necessary follows it with another light reduction. With driver brakes released and working a drifting throttle, as the speed of the train starts to decrease, he builds up sufficient driver brake cylinder pressure on engine to prevent a run out of slack. He then charges the brake system, after which he graduates the driving brake cylinder pressure off, permitting the slack in train to move out gently. This procedure is continued to the foot of the hill, or upon arrival at Sparks. It is necessary that he exercise careful handling to control the slack on the different variations in the grade that prevails Truckee to Sparks.

On arrival at Sparks, engine is uncoupled from train and proceeds to roundhouse, where engineer registers in and fills out Engine Work Report, indicating any work that is necessary which has come to his attention during the trip.

It is the function of the Dispatcher to inform the Yardmaster at Roseville of the consist of the various trains coming into Roseville, which will be made up into trains moving over the Mountain and handled as outlined in the trip above. The Chief Dispatcher also has supervision over the trick dispatcher, who records the movement of this train over the Mountain on his train sheet.

The function of the Trainmaster, under the Assistant Superintendent, is to supervise trainmen and enginemen on these trains and to see that the units moving on the railroad, do so with the least possible delay and the greatest economy.

The Road Foreman of Engines rides with the enginemen and instructs them as to proper braking methods. It is his responsibility to get the greatest efficiency possible out of the power that is provided.

1938
September 22nd
D. & R. G.

Salt Lake City—Denver

Train #2, Scenic Limited, 14 cars to Grand Junction, 13 cars to Pueblo, 11 cars to Denver, besides dynamometer car on head end, Grand Junction to Denver in operation.

Engine 3705 4-6-6-4 type, Salt Lake City to Helper. Class L-105

Made up 15 minutes going up Soldier Summit, fine engine, fine run.

D.&R.G. No. 3750, 4-6-6-4 type, class L-105

Tractive Force	105,000 lbs.
Drivers Diameter	75 in.
Weight on Drivers	437,939 lbs.
Total Weight	641,900 lbs.
Steam Pressure	255 lbs.
Tender Capacity	20,000 gals. 26 tons

1938
September 22nd
S. P.

Sparks—Imlay—Montello—Ogden

Train #28, Overland Limited, 14 cars

Engine 4366 4-8-2 type, MT 4

OT all the way, good crews, loads of ducks flying over the lake.

S.P. No. 4300, 4-8-2 type, MT-1

Tractive Force	57,510 lbs.
Tractive Force Booster	10,100 lbs.
Drivers Diameter	73 in.
Weight on Drivers	246,000 lbs.
Total Weight	329,100 lbs.
Steam Pressure	210 lbs.
Tender Capacity	12,000 gals. 4,000 gals. oil

1938
September 22nd
D. & R. G.

Engine 1700 4-8-4 type. Helper to Grand Junction

Engine 1803 4-8-4 type. Grand Junction to Denver

Helper 3602 2-8-8-2 type. Minturn to Tennessee Pass

OT all the way, rode dynamometer car Glenwood-Salida. Drawbar pull on Tennessee Pass 80,000 lbs. Mrs. Farrington rode engine Salida-Pueblo

40 minutes late out of Malta

OT at Denver

D.&R.G. No. 1800, 4-8-4 type, class M-68

Tractive Force	67,200 lbs.
Drivers Diameter	73 in.
Weight on Drivers	279,172 lbs.
Total Weight	479,360 lbs.
Steam Pressure	285 lbs.
Tender Capacity	20,000 gals. 26 tons

Shown with train no. 2, the Scenic Limited, into Pueblo, Col.

Photo by Otto C. Perry 2/4/38

C.B.&Q. No. 5621, 4-8-4 type, class O-5a
Arriving St. Paul with trains No. 47-57 combined

Tractive Force	67,500 lbs.
Drivers Diameter	74 in.
Weight on Drivers	280,500 lbs.
Total Weight	473,700 lbs.
Steam Pressure	250 lbs.
Tender Capacity	18,000 gals.
	27 tons

Built by C.B.&Q. at West Burlington Shops.
Photo by H. W. Pontin, Rail Photo Service

1938
September 23rd
C. B. & Q.

Brush to Ft. Morgan
Train #6, The Aristocrat, 12 cars
Engine 5617 4-8-4 type
OT all the way.

September 24th

Lincoln to Creston
Train #6, The Aristocrat, 10 cars
Engine 3006 4-6-4 type
OT all the way.

1938
September 25th
Michigan Central

Detroit—Buffalo
Train #40, North Shore Limited—14 cars
Engine 5273 J1B 4-6-4 type
Cutoff St. Thomas slipping at high speed
Engine 5374 J1B 4-6-4 type
St. Thomas—Buffalo
Could not make up time—20 minutes late.

C&O No. 490, 4-6-4 type, L-1 class
Rebuilt from 4-6-2 type, F-19 equipped with Poppet Valves

Tractive Force	49,200 lbs.
Drivers Diameter	74 in.
Weight on Drivers	202,900 lbs.
Total Weight	388,700 lbs.
Steam Pressure	210 lbs.
Tender Capacity	21,000 gals.
	30 tons

Photo taken at east end of Stevens Yard, Ohio with No. 3 the F.F.V.

Lackawanna No. 1153, 4-6-4 type at Binghamton, N.Y. with first No. 2, The Pocono Express. Photo by Bert Pennypacker, August 13, 1937.

1938
September 25th
D L & W

Buffalo—Hoboken
Train #6, Lackawanna Limited
Engine 1151 4-6-4 type Buffalo—Scranton
OT Freight wreck Factoryville were first through EB
Engine 1505Q1 4-8-4 type Scranton—Hoboken
Helper 1622Q3 4-8-4 type Scranton—Lehigh
Fast ride up the hill making up 10 minutes, Sunday crowd, extra stops, made up 20 minutes, Hoboken OT.

C.M.St.P.&P. No. 100, 4-6-4 type, class F-7a

Tractive Force	50,300 lbs.
Drivers Diameter	84 in.
Weight on Drivers	216,000 lbs.
Total Weight	415,000 lbs.
Steam Pressure	300 lbs.
Tender Capacity	20,000 gals.
	25 tons

1938
September 29th
C. M. St. P. & P.

Chicago—Marion, Iowa
Train Southwest Ltd. #107, 11 cars
Engine 102 4-6-4 type, class F-7
LV Chicago 6:25 p.m.
Spalding 7:08, ran around #65
Elgin 7:15
Davis Jct. 8:22
Savanna 9:50, water, coal
LV Savanna 10:20
Delmar 11:07
Oxford Jct. 11:30
AAR Marion 12:14 a.m.
Fine engine—all so smooth with 84″ wheel. Coming up out of Savanna from the river bottom she was really working and he was hitting her hard up the easy hill.

C.M.St.P.&P. Engine 206, 4-8-4 type, class S-2

Tractive Force	70,800 lbs.
Drivers Diameter	74 in.
Weight on Drivers	282,320 lbs.
Total Weight	490,450 lbs.
Steam Pressure	285 lbs.
Tender Capacity	20,000 gals.
	25 tons

1938
October 1st
C. M. St. P. & P.

Milwaukee—Muskego Yard—St. Paul Yard
Train #263, Coast Freight, 89 loads, no empties, 3790 tons
Engine 227 4-8-4 type, class S-2
LV Muskego Yard at 4:10 p.m.
ARR Brookfield 5:20, water
LV Brookfield 5:30
ARR Portage 6:40, pick up 9 loads
LV Portage 7:10 pm., coal and water
New Lisbon 8:15, water
ARR LaCrosse 10:00 p.m., coal, water and sand
LV LaCrosse 10:30 p.m.
ARR Red Wing 1:35 a.m., water
LV Red Wing 1:42 a.m..
ARR St. Croix Tower 2:15
ARR St. Paul Yard 2:55 a.m.
Great run—a junior Hiawatha.
Excellent crews and fine engine.

Southern No. 1396, 4-6-2 type, class Ps-4
Painted green with gold trimmings for Crescent Limited Service.

Tractive Force	47,500 lbs.
Drivers Diameter	73 in.
Weight on Drivers	182,000 lbs.
Total Weight	304,000 lbs.
Steam Pressure	200 lbs.
Tender Capacity	14,000 gals.
	16 tons

1938
October 15th
Southern

Atlanta—Charlotte
Train Cresent Limited #38, 10 cars
Engine 1394 4-6-2 type, class Ps-4
LV Atlanta 1:10 p.m.
ARR Tocca 3:10 p.m.
LV Tocca 3:15
ARR Greenville 4:37, water and coal
LV Greenville 4:40
ARR Spartanberg 5:30, water
Gastonia 6:45
ARR Charlotte 7:25 p.m.
Poor coal—hard on water, hooking mail all the way.
1 R P O
1 P L B
4 SL
1 Diner
2 SL
1 OBS SL

N.Y.,N.H.&H. No. 1400, 4-6-4 type, class I-5

Tractive Force	44,000 lbs.
Drivers Diameter	80 in.
Weight on Drivers	193,000 lbs.
Total Weight	365,300 lbs.
Steam Pressure	285 lbs.
Tender Capacity	18,000 gals.
	16 tons

1938
November 18th
N. Y., N. H. & H.

Boston—Penn Station, N.Y.C.

Train #177, Senator

Engine 1403, 4-6-4 type, Class I5, Boston-New Haven, 14 cars

Took water at Providence, fine engine, hard runner, excellent crew

Sept. 21st hurricane damage still in great evidence

New Motor New Haven to Penn Station—forgot to write down number, 9 cars

OT all the way.

B&O No. 7600, 2-8-8-4 type, class EM-1, starting up Cranberry Grade at McMillan W.Va., with eastward extra. 7032-7109 pushing 54 cars, 20 mph. July 26, 1949
Photo by R. H. Kindig

1938
November 22nd
P. R. R.

Pittsburgh—Cleveland
via Salem
Train No. 303—4 cars
Engine 5409 4-6-2 type, K4s class
OT all the way, fine engine and crew.

D.&R.G.W. No. 3406, 2-8-8-2 type, class L-95 drifting down grade at Coal Creek with 25 D.H. troop pullmans 5 of which are out of sight around 2nd curve.

Tractive Force	95,000 lbs.
Drivers Diameter	57 in.
Weight on Drivers	394,000 lbs.
Total Weight incl. loaded tender	639,200 lbs.
Steam Pressure	200 lbs.
Tender Capacity	9,000 gals.
	20 tons

Photo taken Sept. 6, 1942 by Preston George

1938
November 23rd
P. R. R.

Cleveland—Pittsburgh
via Youngstown
Train No. 332, 4 cars
Neglected to write engine number, a very rough K4.
OT all the way.

1938
December 9th
Lehigh Valley

Buffalo—Wilkes Barre, Pa.
Train No. 10, Black Diamond Express, 8 cars
Engine No. 2061, 4-6-2 type, K4 class
Buffalo—Sayre. Water, coal—Towanda
Engine No. 2096 4-6-2 type, K6b class
Sayre—Newark
Rode R1 helper out of Ithaca to North Spencer where they cutoff. Engine No. 4007 2-10-2 type. 13 miles

Lehigh Valley No. 4000, 2-10-2 type, R1 class

Tractive Force	72,620 lbs.
Drivers Diameter	63 in.
Weight on Drivers	293,560 lbs.
Total Weight	374,100 lbs.
Steam Pressure	200 lbs.
Tender Capacity	10,500 gals.
	15 tons

Nos. 4060-4069 were sold to Hocking Valley and then to C&O becoming their B1 class engines No. 2950-2959 where they were completely modernized. They were used almost entirely between Charlottesville, Gladstone, Strathmore Potomac Yd.
Photo from collection of H. L. Broadbelt.

1938
December 9th
Lehigh Valley

Wilkes Barre—Newark (South Street)
Black Diamond Express, Train No. 10—9 cars
Engine No. 2096, 4-6-2 type, K6b class Wilkes Barre—Newark
Rode T3 helper No. 5128 4-8-4 type, T3 class Wilkes Barre—Mountain Top
Only time I was able to get a seat from Buffalo—Newark was on the two helpers. Snowing hard.
Waited 20 minutes for connection at Mauch Chunk (now Jim Thorpe) from Hazelton, Pa.
Ran opposing track around eastward freight train through Jutland Tunnel.
Fast ride, Three Bridges to Newark. Arriving 25 minutes late having made up only 5 minutes from Bethlehem. Sleeting.

Lehigh Valley No. 5129, 4-8-4 type, T3 class

Tractive Force	66,500 lbs.
Drivers Diameter	77 in.
Weight on Drivers	270,100 lbs.
Total Weight	441,400 lbs.
Steam Pressure	275 lbs.
Tender Capacity	20,000 gals.
	30 tons

Another good one built by Baldwin.
Photo from H. L. Broadbelt collection.

Rock Island No. 5051, 4-8-4 type, class R-67 with No. 91 westbound Gold Ball Freight near Tiskiawa, Ill. Illinois Div

1939
May 1st
C. R. I. & P.

Chicago—Silvis
Train #91, Time Freight west, Gold Ball
Engine 5027, 4-8-4 type, 75 cars, 4920 tons
LV Chicago 10:00
ARR Silvis 3:15
Water at Ottawa—Bureau
Coal at Bureau

1939
June 30th
Atlantic Coast Line

Richmond, Va.—Florence, S.C.
Train #75, Havana Special
Engine 1801 4-8-4 type, 13 cars: 2 EX, 2 storage, 1 RPO, 2 Coaches, 1 Diner, 4 SL, 1 Lounge
Took water at south Rocky Mount and Milan, coal at Milan. Engine was in great shape, very fine smooth, easy run including 35 mph speed limit through several towns. Engine answered throttle beautifully, big tank rode exceedingly well
OT all the way

Atlantic Coast Line No. 1811, 4-8-4 type, class R-1 hauling train No. 75, the Havana Special

Tractive Force	63,900 lbs.
Drivers Diameter	80 in.
Weight on Drivers	263,127 lbs.
Total Weight	460,270 lbs.
Steam Pressure	275 lbs.
Tender Capacity	24,000 gals.
	27 tons

R.F.&P. No. 602, 4-8-4 type hauling No. 73, the A.C.L. Champion passing A.F. Tower south of Alexandria, Va. running 40 mph in January 1948. Photo by Bruce D. Fales

1939
July 5th
Atlantic Coast Line

Jacksonville—Florence, S.C.
Train #76, Havana Special
Engine 1805 4-8-4 type, class R1
Took water Savannah, Bennett, coal at Bennett
17 cars:
2 RPo
2 storage
4 Express
2 Coaches
1 Diner
5 SL
1 Lounge
OT all the way

1939
July 5th
R. F. & P.

Richmond—Washington
Train 1st #76, Havana Special
Engine 602 4-8-4 type, Thomas Jefferson
Easy run on time all the way making up 10 minutes to Fredericksburg
11 cars:
9 SL
1 Diner
1 Lounge
Taking Richmond—New York sleepers with ACL coaches on 2nd 76

R.F.&P. No. 602, 4-8-4 type, Governor Thomas Jefferson

Tractive Force	62,800 lbs.
Drivers Diameter	77 in.
Weight on Drivers	260,486 lbs.
Total Weight	406,810 lbs.
Steam Pressure	260 lbs.
Tender Capacity	15,500 gals.
	17 tons

1939
July 29th
Santa Fe

Chicago—Shopton
Train #19, Chief
Engine 3426 4-6-2 type—14 cars, 1 mail storage to KC
Marceline—Rothville
Train #19, Chief
Engine 3430 4-6-2 type—14 cars
1st #12 derailed Rothville with engine 3429. Lost 2 hours and 30 minutes Shopton to Marceline.

Santa Fe No. 3431 modernized 4-6-2 type, class 3400 coming off the Missouri River Bridge at Sibley with train No. 24, the Grand Canyon Limited former Missouri Div.

Tractive Force	41,400 lbs.
Drivers Diameter	79 in.
Weight on Drivers	193,054 lbs.
Total Weight	319,794 lbs
Steam Pressure	220 lbs.
Tender Capacity	20,000 gals
	7,107 gals. oil

Santa Fe No. 3458, 4-6-4 type, 3451 class modernized

Tractive Force	43,300 lbs.
Drivers Diameter	79 in.
Weight on Drivers	206,000 lbs.
Total Weight	352,600 lbs.
Steam Pressure	230 lbs.
Tender Capacity	15,000 gals.
	5,488 gals. oil

With No. 5, the Ranger, north of Ponca City, Okla. with 11 cars on February 22, 1946.
Photo by Preston George

1939
July 30th
Santa Fe

Syracuse—La Junta
Train #19, Chief—11 cars
Engine 3456 4-6-4 type modernized
Ran 90 minutes late.
La Junta—Las Vegas
Train #19, Chief—11 cars
Engine 3753 4-8-4 type modernized
Ran 90 minutes late.
Las Vegas—Albuquerque
Train #17, Super Chief—11 cars
Diesel 3
Ran around 19 at Bernalillo—OT all the way.
Albuquerque—Seligman
Train #19, Chief
Engine 3753 4-8-4 type
Ran 75 minutes late, used approximately 2000 gallons water Albuquerque to Gonzales.

Santa Fe No. 3753, 4-8-4 type, 3751 class modernized

Tractive Force	64,834 lbs.
Drivers Diameter	80 in.
Weight on Drivers	280,600 lbs.
Total Weight	464,700 lbs.
Steam Pressure	226 lbs.
Tender Capacity	20,000 gals.
	7,107 gals. oil

1939
July 31st
Santa Fe

Barstow—Los Angeles
Train #19, Chief, 11 cars
Engine 3753 4-8-4 type
Ran 25 minutes late.

1939
September 7th
Santa Fe

Los Angeles—Barstow
Train #20, The Chief, 12 cars
Engine 3774 4-8-4 type
No helper San Berdo—Summit, left 30 minutes late, 25 minutes late at Barstow
Barstow—Los Angeles via 3rd district
1st #7, Fast Mail, 12 cars
Engine 3769 4-8-4 type
OT all the way.

Santa Fe No. 3770, 4-8-4 type, 3765 class climbing Cajon Pass at Pine Lodge, Ca. with No. 20, The Chief.

Tractive Force	66,000 lbs.
Drivers Diameter	80 in.
Weight on Drivers	286,890 lbs.
Total Weight	499,600 lbs.
Steam Pressure	300 lbs.
Tender Capacity	20,000 gals.
	7,107 gals. oil

1939
September 8th
Union Pacific

Los Angeles—Ogden
Train #8, Los Angeles Limited, 11 cars
Engine 3939 4-6-6-4 type Los Angeles—Las Vegas
Rode top of tank up Cajon Pass. The famous UP road foreman and much admired Mr. Peacock rode with me. He was as popular as the father of the great tennis player Jack Kramer was on the same division.
OT all the way.

U. P. No. 3940, 4-6-6-4 type, $\frac{21\text{-}21}{69\text{-}32}$—406 MB class

Tractive Force	97,350 lbs.
Drivers Diameter	69 in.
Weight on Drivers	403,000 lbs.
Total Weight	582,000 lbs.
Steam Pressure	255 lbs.
Tender Capacity	25,000 gals.
	28 tons

Starts down Sherman Hill with an eastward extra, 54 cars, 20mph.
Picture taken August 1947 by R. H. Kindig. Wyoming Div.

U.P. No. 2243, 2-8-2 type, MacA-63-26/28-216-D class heading east from Cheyenne with a mixed train. The car behind the two coaches is a box car converted for use as a caboose. Photo taken November 30, 1941 by Preston George.

Tractive Force	53,628 lbs.
Drivers Diameter	63 in.
Weight on Drivers	216,000 lbs.
Total Weight	288,700 lbs.
Steam Pressure	200 lbs.
Tender Capacity	10,000 gals.
	17 tons

1939
September 9th
Union Pacific

Caliente—Milford

Train #8, Los Angeles Limited, 11 cars

Engine 7851 4-8-2 type

Rode helper 2727 2-8-2 type to Crestline, Road foreman on engine was one of the famous Hemstret UP family from Salt Lake City. Had ridden with his father before.

Met #21 and Santa Fe #19 detouring on account of high water on Santa Fe's Arizona division.

Have already met Santa Fe #7 2117 and 3 Las Vegas—Caliente only about 50 minutes late.

1939
September 9th
Union Pacific

Ogden—Cheyenne
Train #28, Overland Limited
Engine 825 4-8-4 type, first trip in service
17 cars to Green River, 19 cars from Green River to Cheyenne
Helper 2841 2-8-2 type to Wasatch
#38 1st 888, 28, 2nd 888, and 88 came over that night
OT all the way
Took water at Evanston, coal and water at Carter, Hanna.

September 10th

Cheyenne—Omaha
Train #28, Overland Limited, 20 cars
Engine 825 4-8-4 type
Rode train #6 Fast Mail
Engine 811 4-8-4 type Cheyenne—Sidney
Very fast run with 16 cars, lost 5 minutes when engine would not stop popping off with closed throttle
Sidney—Omaha

U.P. No. 825, 4-8-4 type, FEF-80-25/32 class 270-BK

Tractive Force	63,800 lbs.
Drivers Diameter	80 in.
Weight on Drivers	270,000 lbs.
Total Weight	483,000 lbs.
Steam Pressure	300 lbs.
Tender Capacity	23,500 gals.
	25 tons

This was the first of the 820 class the author rode all the way from Ogden—Omaha on her first trip and it was also the last one he rode from Milford to Yermo in 1948 on Train No. 5. None that he rode ever performed better.

Train #28, Overland Limited
Engine 825 4-8-4 type, 20 cars
Made up 50 minutes, took coal Julesburg and Columbus.

U.P. No. 815 with train 818, Los Angeles Challenger, at Archer, Wyoming. Morrison Smith, 1., and Dick Kindig are taking its picture.

Tractive Force	63,500 lbs.
Drivers Diameter	77 in.
Weight on Drivers	270,000 lbs.
Total Weight	465,000 lbs. in working order
Steam Pressure	260 lbs.
Tender Capacity	119,764 gals. 25 tons

This is a new one when the photographer snaps two other good photographers.
Photo by Preston George.

1939
September 10th
Chicago & Northwestern

Omaha—Boone
Train #28, Overland Limited—19 cars
Engine 4001 4-6-4 type, class E4
Good crew, very foggy, lefthand running with their amazing train control and Mars headlight. OT all the way.

Boston & Maine No. 4117, 4-8-2 type, R-1-d class

Tractive Force	67,000 lbs.
Drivers Diameter	73 in.
Weight on Drivers	269,116 lbs.
Total Weight	415,200 lbs.
Steam Pressure	240 lbs.
Tender Capacity	23,000 gals.
	21 tons

1940
February 12th
B & M

Mechanicville, N.Y.—Boston
Train R B 2, 82 cars, 3787 tons
Engine 4113, 4-8-2 type, class R1-a
LV Mechanicville 8:10 a.m.
ARR West Portal (Hoosac Tunnel) 9:57 helper electric engine 5503 1B+B1 type through Hoosac Tunnel, 4.75 miles long 0.5 percent grade, ascending grade from each portal to apex near center.
LV East Portal 10:20
ARR Greenfield 11:30 water
LV Greenfield 11:40
ARR Fitchburg 1:35 water
LV Fitchburg 1:40
ARR Boston 3:10 p.m.
Engine did remarkably well—practically 40 miles of 0.95% grade from mile post 188 to mile post 142.

1940
April 10th
S P

Colton—Yuma

Train # Colton Block, Extra 5041 East, 52 loads, 3670 tons, 1835 M

Engine 5041 4-10-2 type, class SP-3, helper 3614 2-10-2 type, class F-1

LV Colton 7:25 p.m.

ARR Beaumont 8:30, cut off helper—Cabazon 9:10 water

Palm Springs 9:52

ARR Indio Yard 11:07

LV Indio Yard 11:40 water and meeting 839

ARR Niland 2:05 water and oil train inspection met #5 one hour and 25 minutes late

LV Niland 2:30

ARR Yuma 5:15 a.m.

Lost about 35 minutes waiting on 43 and 3 both over 2 hours late.

Full moon—fairly cool for the Salton subdivision. Three cyl engines are never my favorite.

S.P. No. 5043, 4-10-2 type, 3 cylinders SP-3

Tractive Force	83,500 lbs.
Booster	12,200 lbs.
Drivers Diameter	63½ in.
Weight on Drivers	317,500 lbs.
Total Weight	445,000 lbs.
Steam Pressure	225 lbs.
Tender Capacity	116,000 gals.
	4,912 gals. oil

Southern Pacific No. 3800, 2-8-8-4 type, AC-9 class

Tractive Force	124,300 lbs.
Drivers Diameter	63½ in.
Weight on Drivers	531,200 lbs.
Total Weight	689,900 lbs.
Steam Pressure	250 lbs.
Tender Capacity	22,120 gals.
	28 tons

1940
April 15th
S P

El Paso, Octavia Street—Tucumcari

Train #994, 45 loads, 12 empties, 1800 M, 3600 tons

Engine 3804 2-8-8-4 type, class AC-9 coal burner

LV Octavia Street 4:10 p.m.

Alvarado 5:07

met 39

Orogande 5:45 water

Alamogordo 6:55 coal and water

LV Alamogordo 7:17

ARR Carrizozo 9:22 coal and water

LV Carrizozo 10:05

met #3 here instead of Robasart

Corona 12:40 a.m.

ARR Vaughn 1:47 coal and water

Met 2 extras west and #43 instead of Pastura

LV Vaughn 2:35

Santa Rosa 4:15 water

ARR Tucumcari 5:37 a.m.

Engine did well over Corona but was very hard on water; on both subdivisions. Fine crew. Train rigidly inspected at Alamogordo, Carrizozo and Vaughn.

Santa Fe No. 5000 first of the 2-10-4 type on that railroad, helping No. 17, The Super Chief, up Raton Pass on the 3.3 grade with diesel No. 13 just below Wooten, Colorado, 1st District N.M. Div., now 2nd District, Colorado with 12 cars. Photo taken on May 19th, 1946 by Preston George.

Tractive Force	93,000 lbs.
Drivers Diameter	69 in.
Weight on Drivers	327,000 lbs.
Total Weight	502,600 lbs.
Steam Pressure	300 lbs.
Tender Capacity	20,000 gals.
	7,324 gals. oil

This engine only one of the 5,000 class built was nicknamed the Madam Queen but was so successful, the 5001 class followed.

1940
April 18th
Santa Fe

Chicago—Wichita
Train #11, Kansas Citian, 8 cars Chicago—Kansas City, 6 cars KC to Wichita
2 cars going on #211 to Tulsa
Diesel #1
Could hardly haul train and make up time.

1940
April 18th
Santa Fe

Wichita—Clovis
Train #23, Grand Canyon Limited
Engine 3715 modernized 4-8-2
12 cars to Amarillo, 11 Amarillo—Clovis
OT all the way.

Santa Fe Engines 1797, 2-8-8-2 type and 3719 and 3713 coupled climbing Raton Pass.

Tractive Force	136,985 lbs.
Drivers Diameter	57 in.
Weight on Drivers	485,200 lbs.
Total Weight	539,000 lbs.
Steam Pressure	270 lbs.
Tender Capacity	18,000 gals.
	20 tons

Bought from N&W, sold to Virginian after war.

Photo by Otto C. Perry

Tractive Force	56,800 lbs.
Drivers Diameter	69 in.
Weight on Drivers	238,800 lbs.
Total Weight	351,700 lbs.
Steam Pressure	210 lbs.
Tender Capacity	15,000 gals.
	20 tons

Santa Fe No. 5010, 2-10-4 type, 5001 class

Tractive Force	93,000 lbs.
Drivers Diameter	74 in.
Weight on Drivers	371,900 lbs.
Total Weight	538,520 lbs.
Steam Pressure	310 lbs.
Tender Capacity	21,000 gals.
	7,000 gals. oil

1940
April 20th
Santa Fe

Clovis—Belen
Train #43, extra 5005 west
Engine 5005 2-10-4 type
101 cars to Vaughn, 3800 tons
107 cars to Belen, 3950 tons
Good run Clovis—Vaughn.
Called 12:30 a.m.
LV Clovis 3:40
ARR Vaughn 7:40, coal, water; water also Mountainair.
LV Vaughn 8:30
ARR Belen 3:32
Brake sticking Yeso, brake beam down Willard, undesired quick action, Mountainair
11 hours 52 minutes including dead time
My old friend, road foreman, Carraway rode with me. He is nicknamed Mr. 5000 as he has broken in and brought these locomotives to where they are today. He felt very badly about the detentions which were of course no fault of the 5005.

1940
April 21st
Santa Fe

Winslow—Los Angeles
1st #7 Fast Mail—12 cars
Engine 3771 4-8-4 type
OT all the way, great engine as usual.
106° at Needles as usual.

Santa Fe No. 3773, 4-8-4 type, 3765 class descending Cajon Pass with No. 19, The Chief passing Cantilever Signal 712 just west of Ono, Cal., first district Los Angeles Div.

Santa Fe No. 5000, 2-10-4 type, 5,000 class helping Diesel No. 7 with No. 17, The Super Chief on June 19th, 1946 climbing Raton Pass, 1st District, N.M. Div., now 2nd District, Colorado District.

Photo by R. H. Kindig

1940
April 22nd
Santa Fe

Los Angeles—San Diego
Train #74, San Diegoan—6 cars
Engine—Diesel 7
OT all the way.
San Diego—Los Angeles
Train #75, San Diegoan—6 cars
Diesel 7
Lost 15 minutes at Bandini sawing by eastward time freight train

S.P. No. 4185, 4-8-8-2 type, AC-8 class

Tractive Force	123,400 lbs.
Drivers Diameter	63½ in.
Weight on Drivers	531,700 lbs.
Total Weight	657,900 lbs.
Steam Pressure	250 lbs.
Tender Capacity	22,000 gals.
	6,100 gals. oil

1940
April 23rd
Southern Pacific

Los Angeles—Bakersfield
Train #59, The West Coast—15 cars
Engine #4188 4-8-8-2 type new AC. 8
OT all the way, great engine as usual.

1940
April 24th
Santa Fe

Seligman—Winslow
Train #20, The Chief—12 cars
Engine 3756 mod. 4-8-4 type
Left Seligman 5 minutes late, left Ash Fork 15 minutes late, OT at Winslow
Met #17 at Ash Fork, #19 on the mountain.

Santa Fe No. 3754, 4-8-4 type, 3751 class coal burner before modernization and conversion to oil.

Tractive Force	66,000 lbs.
Drivers Diameter	73 in.
Weight on Drivers	272,880 lbs.
Total Weight	432,240 lbs.
Steam Pressure	210 lbs.
Tender Capacity	15,000 gals.
	20 tons

Photo taken at Denver, Colo. in 1937 by R. H. Kindig.

Head end and rear end of Santa Fe Freight Train rounding Tehachapi Loop with road engine in background, first pusher in foreground and rear pusher at left coming out of tunnel. With a 70 car train head end is over rear end. The three engines are all Santa Fe 3800 or 3900 class.

Photo by G. M. Best, Railroad Photographic Club.

1940
April 24th
Santa Fe

Bakersfield—Barstow
Train #24, Grand Canyon Limited—6 cars
Engine 3711 4-8-2 type
OT all the way. Met SP freight train on the loop.

Santa Fe No. 3897, 2-10-2 type, 3800 class

Tractive Force	85,360 lbs.
Drivers Diameter	63 in.
Weight on Drivers	316,660 lbs.
Total Weight	402,470 lbs.
Steam Pressure	220 lbs.
Tender Capacity	15,000 gals.
	5,000 gals. oil

1940
April 25th
Santa Fe

Albuquerque—La Junta
Train #20, Chief—12 cars
Engine 3756 mod. 4-8-4 type
Helper Glorieta 976 old 2-10-2 type
Helper Raton 3881 2-10-2 type
OT all the way.

1940
April 26th
N. Y. C.

Chicago—Buffalo
Train #26—20th Century Limited—12 cars
Engine 5453 J3A 4-6-4 type Chicago—Collinwood
Engine 5408 J3A 4-6-4 type Collinwood—Buffalo
Lost 40 minutes following 1st and 2nd 68 Sandusky to Dunkirk
ARR Buffalo 37 minutes late.

N.Y.C. No. 5405, 4-6-4 type, J-3a class

Tractive Force	43,440 lbs.
Booster	12,100 lbs.
Drivers Diameter	79 in.
Weight on Drivers	196,000 lbs.
Total Weight	360,000 lbs.
Steam Pressure	275 lbs.
Tender Capacity	14,000 gals.
	30 tons

Western Pacific No. 259, 2-8-8-2 type, M-137-151 class

Tractive Force	137,000 lbs.
Drivers Diameter	63 in.
Weight on Drivers	549,656 lbs.
Total Weight	663,100 lbs.
Steam Pressure	235 lbs.
Tender Capacity	22,000 gals.
	6,000 gals. oil

1940
May 25th
W. P.

Oroville—Portola
Train Extra 257 east—54 cars, 3470 tons
Engine 257 M137-151 2-8-8-2 type
LV Oroville 8:15 a.m.
LV Keddie 12:30
ARR Portola 4:50 p.m.
Took water at Keddie, engine performed beautifully.

1940
May 29th
W. P.

Salt Lake City—Elko
Train Extra 402 west
Engine 402 4-6-6-4 type—57 cars, 25 empties, 2780 tons
LV Roper 2:20 p.m.
ARR Wendover 7:10
LV Wendover 8:35
ARR Elko 2:15 a.m.

Took water at Burmester, Wendover and Wells. Engine serviced at Wendover, caboose changed. Engine ran extremely well taking the Wendover hill 68 miles of 1% with ease. Good crew. Coal burner.

Western Pacific No. 402, 4-6-6-4 type

Tractive Force	99,600 lbs.
Drivers Diameter	70 in.
Weight on Drivers	399,000 lbs.
Total Weight	590,000 lbs.
Steam Pressure	265 lbs.
Tender Capacity	22,000 gals.
	25 tons

C&O No. 2341, 2-8-2 type, K-3 class

Tractive Force	67,700 lbs.
Drivers Diameter	63 in.
Weight on Drivers	273,000 lbs.
Total Weight	358,500 lbs.
Steam Pressure	200 lbs.
Tender Capacity	16,000 gals.
	20 tons

These engines, the author considers, are the finest 2-8-2 type he has ever ridden.

Photo by G. Grabill, Jr. Railroad Photographic Club.

1940
September 21st
P. R. R.

Columbus—St. Louis
Train 1st 31—Spirit of St. Louis—12 cars
Engine 5484 K4s 4-6-2 type
Engine very hard on water. Lost 10 minutes in back of VC 1 New Paris
ARR Union Station 35 minutes late.

Missouri Pacific No. 1729, 2-10-2 type

Tractive Force	81,500 lbs.
Booster	13,180 lbs.
Drivers Diameter	63 in.
Weight on Drivers	326,080 lbs.
Total Weight	420,650 lbs.
Steam Pressure	210 lbs.
Tender Capacity	12,000 gals.
	16 tons

1940
September 22nd
M. P.

St. Louis—Kansas City
Train #11, Exposition Flyer, 9 cars
Engine 2107 4-8-4 type. Rebuilt from 2-8-4 type.
OT all the way.

D&R.G. No. 1702, 4-8-4 type, M-64 class with No. 6, Exposition Flyer, near Tolland, Colo. James Peak, under which the Moffat Tunnel passes is shown in background.

Tractive Force	63,700 lbs.
Drivers Diameter	70 in.
Weight on Drivers	264,900 lbs.
Total Weight	696,750 lbs. Incl. Loaded Tender
Steam Pressure	240 lbs.
Tender Capacity	14,000 gals. 20 tons

Photo by R. H. Kindig in November 1941

1940
September 23rd
D & R G

Denver—Salt Lake City
Train #5, Exposition Flyer
Engine 1703 4-8-4 type—Denver to Grand Junction—7 cars
Engine 1709 4-8-4 type—Grand Junction—Salt Lake City—7 cars
No helper at Helper
Heavy lightning storm at Soldier Summit. Met an extra there, #6 at Thistle, #2 at Provo
OT all the way.

1940
September 23rd
Western Pacific

Winnemucca—Portola
Train #39, Exposition Flyer—11 cars
Engine 177 4-8-2 type ExFEC
Portola to Orrville

Train #39, Exposition Flyer—11 cars
Engine 323 2-8-2 type
Met eastward preference train at Keddie with no water
Orrville—Oakland

Train #39, Exposition Flyer—11 cars
Engine 179 4-8-2 type ExFEC
Hit by truck at Del Paso lost 55 minutes. Driver not hurt.

Western Pacific Extra 253 east with green fruit gets a red order board at Belden

Photo by Ed. W. Bewley, Allston Railroad Photographs

Five engine Eastward Southern Pacific Freight Train rounding the Horseshoe Curve at Goldtree, Cal. on the Coast Division. These engines are all F-4's or F-5's, 2-10-2 type.

Tractive Force	75,150 lbs.
Drivers Diameter	63 in.
Weight on Drivers	304,400 lbs.
Total Weight	390,400 lbs.
Steam Pressure	200 lbs.
Tender Capacity	10,060 gals.
	2,940 gals. oil

1940
September 24th
S. P.

San Francisco—San Luis Obispo
Train No. 374, Overnight—54 cars
Engine 4414 4-8-4 type, GS2 class, Helper 3757 2-10-2 type Santa Margarita—San Luis Obispo
OT all the way allowing me to catch No. 76 to L.A.

1940
September 25th
Santa Fe

Los Angeles—Barstow
Train #20—The Chief—11 cars
Engine 3769 4-8-4 type
Helper 1226 4-6-2 type San Berdo-Summit A C main track blocked on mountain we went up passing track.
Parted air hose leaving L.A. Union station
OT all the way.

Santa Fe No. 24, Grand Canyon Limited with engine 3761, 4-8-4 type modernized and helper 1226, 4-6-2 type.

Tractive Force	36,000 lbs.
Drivers Diameter	73 in.
Weight on Drivers	166,300 lbs.
Total Weight	256,900 lbs.
Steam Pressure	200 lbs.
Tender Capacity	9,000 gals.
	3,398 gals. oil

Photo by W. H. Thrall, July 1940.

Santa Fe No. 3775, 4-8-4 type, 3765 class running 70 mph with No. 19, The Chief, West of Ayer, Colo. N.M. Div., now Colorado Div., 2nd District.

Photo taken Feb. 22, 1939 by Otto C. Perry.

1940
September 25th
Santa Fe

Barstow—Los Angeles
Train #7—Fast Mail—9 cars
Engine 3772 4-8-4 type
Dead head pullman on rear end.
Met #4 at Highland Park.
OT all the way.

S.P. No. 4454, 4-8-4 type, GS-4 class

Tractive Force	64,760 lbs.
Booster	13,000 lbs.
Drivers Diameter	80 in.
Weight on Drivers	275,700 lbs.
Total Weight	475,000 lbs.
Steam Pressure	300 lbs.
Tender Capacity	23,300 gals.
	5,880 gals.oil

1940
September 26th
S. P.

Los Angeles—San Jose
Train #99—Morning Daylight—15 cars
Engine 4456 Gs4 4-8-4 type 2-10-2 Helper 3721
F-4 San Luis Obispo—Santa Margarita
Met #26 60 76 Los Angeles to Glendale
Circus train at Santa Barbara.
OT all the way.

S.P. No. 2715, 2-8-0 type, C-5 class

Tractive Force	45,470 lbs.
Drivers Diameter	57 in.
Weight on Drivers	197,900 lbs.
Total Weight	224,500 lbs.
Steam Pressure	210 lbs.
Tender Capacity	7,000 gals.
	2,940 gals. oil

This engine built in June 1904. If still in service it would be one month younger than the author.

1940
September 27th
S. P.

Roseville—Sparks
Train #482
Engine 4177 AC8 4-8-8-2 type
Two helpers 2811 2-8-0 Class C9 to Norden cut in four cars ahead of waycar. Only 3970M, 1985 tons, 60 empties, 7 loads. Got 2 more at Truckee, lost 30 minutes behind work train at Towle, 45 minutes for lunch at Emigrant Gap. Weather clear and warm. Fine crew.
Engineman—G. N. Mattick
Fireman—E. R. Cook
LV Rooseville 6:55 a.m.
LV Newcastle 7:40
ARR Colfax 8:15—took water
LV Colfax 8:35
LV Towle 9:10
Worktrain
ARR Emigrant Gap 10:55
Lunch
LV Emigrant Gap 11:40
LV Crystal Lake 12:00. Train inspected
ARR Norden 12:45 Retainers up—took water, helper cut out
LV Norden 1:10
LV Stanford 1:45 Inspection
Arrive Truckee 2:05
LV Truckee 2:20—got 2 cars
ARR Sparks 3:40

S.P. No. 4159, 4-8-8-2 type, AC-7 class

Tractive Force	123,400 lbs.
Drivers Diameter	63½ in.
Weight on Drivers	514,800 lbs.
Total Weight	639,800 lbs.
Steam Pressure	250 lbs.
Tender Capacity	22,000 gals.
	6,100 gals. oil

1940
September 28th
S. P.

Sparks—Oakland Pier
Train #21—Pacific Limited
Engine 4161 AC7 4-8-8-2 type to Roseville
Engine 4329 Roseville—Oakland Pier—4-8-2 type
17 cars:
1 RF
1 EX
1 Baggage
1 RPO
3 Coaches
3 Tourists
1 Diner
1 Lounge
4 SL
1 OBS SL
2 88's with 18 and 21 cars and 3 24's came over that night. Lost 15 minutes on east slope to Summit.
OT at Roseville, lost 8 minutes at Davis taking water, OT at Berkeley, went in 7 minutes late.

S.P. No. 3769, 2-10-2 type, F-5 class

Tractive Force	75,150 lbs.
Booster	10,970 lbs.
Drivers Diameter	63 in.
Weight on Drivers	306,100 lbs.
Total Weight Loaded	397,900 lbs.
Steam Pressure	200 lbs.
Tender Capacity	16,152 gals.
	4,692 gals. oil

1940
September 29th
S. P.

Redding—Eugene
Train #20, Klamath—12 cars
Engine 4336 4-8-2 type Redding—Dunsmuir
Engine 4357 4-8-2 type Dunsmuir—Klamath Falls
Helper 3667 2-10-2 type Dunsmuir—Grass Lake
Engine 4404 4-8-4 type Gs1 Klamath Falls—Eugene
OT all the way, weather warm and clear except Cascade Summit with usual fog and rain. My good friend, road foreman Young, rode with me Dunsmuir—Grass Lake.

Northern Pacific No. 2667, 4-8-4 type, A-3 class

Tractive Force	69,800 lbs.
Drivers Diameter	77 in.
Weight on Drivers	294,000 lbs.
Total Weight	491,800 lbs.
Steam Pressure	260 lbs.
Tender Capacity	20,000 gals.
	27 tons

1940
September 30th
Northern Pacific

Sand Point—Livingston
Train #2, North Coast Limited, 12 cars to Butte, 13 Butte to Livingston
Engine 2607 4-8-4 type to Missoula, Class A
Engine 2661 4-8-4 type—Missoula—Livingston, Class A3
Helper 1730 2-8-2 type at De Smet, Class W3
Pusher on rear end at Homestake and Bozeman 2-8-2
OT all the way.

Southern Pacific No. 3811, 2-8-8-4 type, AC-9 class Leaving Tucumcari, New Mexico, with a 101 Car Westward Extra.

Photo taken May 1940 by R. H. Kindig, Rio Grande Div.

1940
October 1st
Northern Pacific

Jamestown—Staples
Train #2, North Coast Limited—13 cars out of Jamestown, 15 out of Manitoba Jct.
Engine 2666 4-8-4 type A3
OT all the way.

C&O No.1572, 2-8-8-2 type, H-7-A class

Tractive Force	103,500 lbs.
Drivers Diameter	57 in.
Weight on Drivers	491,840 lbs.
Total Weight	569,830 lbs.
Steam Pressure	205 lbs.
Tender Capacity	16,000 lbs.
	20 tons

1941
April 13th
P. R. R.

New York—Harrisburg
Train #29, Broadway Limited—8 cars
Engine 4891 G-G-1
Ran around #31, #41, #69
OT all the way.

1941
November 7th
C & O

Louisville—Ashland
Train #4—46, The Sportsman—8 cars
Engine 462 4-6-2 type F-16
Helper 1210 2-8-2 type, Olive Hill—Mt. Savage K-3 class

C&O Passenger Trains at Huntington, W.Va. On left No. 473, 4-6-2 type, F-17 class, right No. 432 4-6-2 type, F-15 class

Tractive Force	46,900	32,400 lbs.
Drivers Diameter	74 in.	73 in.
Weight on Drivers	199,830 lbs.	157,200 lbs.
Total Weight	334,420 lbs.	237,400 lbs.
Steam Pressure	200 lbs.	180 lbs.
Tender Capacity	16,000 gals.	9,000 gals.
	20 tons	15 tons

C&O No. 494, 4-6-2 type, F-19 classs

Tractive Force	46,900 lbs.
Drivers Diameter	74 in.
Weight on Drivers	200,000 lbs.
Total Weight	331,500 lbs.
Steam Pressure	200 lbs.
Tender Capacity	18,000 gals.
	28 tons

1941
November 8th
C & O
Ashland—Hinton

Train #46 Sportsman
Engine 491—10 cars
4-6-2 type F-19 class
OT
Water—Handley

C&O No. 600 "Thomas Jefferson" 4-8-4 type, J-3 class called Greenbrier on the C&O.

Tractive Force	66,450 lbs.
Booster	14,355 lbs.
Drivers Diameter	74 in.
Weight on Drivers	273,500 lbs.
Total Weight	477,000 lbs.
Steam Pressure	255 lbs.
Tender Capacity	22,000 gals.
	25 tons

Photo taken at Charlottesville, Va. Sept. 9, 1937 by Bruce D. Fales.

1941
November 8th
C & O
Hinton—Charlottesville

Train #46 Sportsman

Engine 603 4-8-4 type, J-3 class "James Madison," 10 cars

C&O No. 546, 4-8-2 type, J-2A class

Tractive Force	60,850 lbs.
Drivers Diameter	69 in.
Weight on Drivers	246,850 lbs.
Total Weight	363,550 lbs.
Steam Pressure	210 lbs.
Tender Capacity	16,000 gals.
	22 tons

This engine built by Baldwin in 1919 and modernized.
Photo taken at Charlottesville, Va. Clifton Forge Div. Mountain Sub-Division by Bruce D. Fales, Sept. 9, 1937.

1941
November 18th
C & O
Charlottesville—Washington

Train #6 F.F.V.
Engine 543 4-8-2 type, J-2A class, 8 cars OT all the way.

R.F.&P. No. 265, 4-6-2 type

Tractive Force	34,700 lbs.
Drivers Diameter	73 in.
Weight on Drivers	151,200 lbs.
Total Weight	240,000 lbs.
Steam Pressure	185 lbs.
Tender Capacity	12 tons
	10,000 gals.

1941
December 20th
R. F. & P.
Richmond—Washington

Train #88, Florida Special—16 cars
Engine 308 4-6-2 type
Helper 262 4-6-2 type
OT all the way.

1942
February 20th
N. Y. C.

Buffalo—Albany
Train #50, Empire State Express—15 cars
Engine 5428 J3A
LV Buffalo 15 minutes late engine would not steam, 25 minutes late out of Rochester, 35 minutes late out of Syracuse, second stop for water 10 minutes, ARR Albany 55 minutes late
Cold and snowing.

N.Y.C. No. 5426, J-3A class, 4-6-4 type. Semi-streamlined hauling Train No. 50, the Empire State Express.

1942
March 11th
Santa Fe

Dodge City—La Junta   Colorado Div.
Train No.17-J, The Super Chief, nine cars, 530 tons, diesels 12-11-4

	MPH	*Arr.*	*Late*	*Departed*	*Late*	*Delay*
Dodge City				6:59 a.m.	26″	
18.7	59.0					
Cimarron				7:18 a.m.	28″	
31.1	93.3					
Garden City				7:38 a.m.	25″	
51.3	78.9					
Syracuse				8:17 a.m.	29″	
21.0	90.0					
Holly				8:31 a.m.	25″	
27.4	91.3					
Lamar				8:49 a.m.	22″	
34.0	97.1					
Las Animas				9:10 a.m.	17″	
18.9	75.6					
La Junta		9:25 a.m.	13″			

First Dist.   83.2
Miles 202.4—146 mins.

Engineer: C. Peairs
Conductor: F. Simmons

Santa Fe No. 18, The Super Chief with diesel 13 1-B-1B type at Ayer, Col. 1st Dist., N.M. Div. now 2nd Dist. Col. Div.

Tractive Force	53,925 lbs.
Drivers Diameter	36 in.
Weight on Drivers	215,700 lbs.
Total Weight	316,000 lbs.
Horsepower	2,000
Water Capacity-Heating Boiler	1,100 gals.
Fuel Capacity	1,200 gals.

Photo by Otto C. Perry.

C&O No. 3004, 2-10-4 type, T-1 class

Tractive Force	91,584 lbs.
Booster	15,000 lbs.
Drivers Diameter	69 in.
Weight on Drivers	373,000 lbs.
Total Weight	566,000 lbs.
Steam Pressure	260 lbs.
Tender Capacity	23,500 gals.
	30 tons

This was truly one of the greatest locomotives ever built and the P.R.R. J-1 was a copy of it, the finest engine they ever had.

1942
April 25th
C & O

Russell—Waldbridge
Train Extra 3029 West, 160 loads, 13,500 tons
Engine 3029 2-10-4 type, class T-1
LV Russell 2:10 p.m.
N.J. Cabin 2:50
Greggs 4:10
Scipio 6:27 water
C.H. Cabin 7:50
ARR Parsons 8:40
Parsons—Waldbridge
Train Extra 3029 West, 160 loads, 13,500 tons
Engine 3029 2-10-4 type, class T-1
LV Parsons 10:15
M.D. Cabin 12:50 a.m. water
C Cabin 2:10
Fostoria 3:55
ARR Waldbridge 5:25 a.m.
#46 was in Columbus for us. This is the 7th run I have made on these engines with their 160 loads and I have always considered it one of the top one-half dozen moves in the U. S. and the engine is one of the all around finest 2-10-4.
Raining all the way on Hocking Division.

1942
August 12th
Santa Fe

La Junta—Dodge City, Colorado Div. Train No. 18-K, The Super Chief, 12 cars, 660 tons
Diesels 15-15-A

	MPH	*Arr.*	*Late*	*Departed*	*Late*	*Delay*
La Junta				9:36 p.m.	1′14″	
18.9	66.7					
Las Animas				9:53 p.m.	1′14″	
34.0	97.1					
Lamar				10:14 p.m.	1′09″	
27.4	96.7					
Holly				10:31 p.m.	1′04″	
21.0	96.9					
Syracuse				10:44 p.m.	59″	
29.4	98.0					
Lakin				11:02 p.m.	50″	
21.9	73.0					
Garden City				11:20 p.m.	50″	
31.1	93.3					
Cimarron				11:40 p.m.	45″	
18.7	93.5					
Dodge City		11:52 p.m.	40″			

First Dist. 89.3
Miles 202.4—136 mins.
Engineer: J. H. Horning
Conductor: B. C. Jones

Santa Fe No. 18, The Super Chief, Diesel No. 15 at Abajo, N.M. a mile and one half west of Albuquerque, N.M. on the 3rd District of N.M. Div., now 4th District, Colo. Div.

Photo by Edward W. Bewley, Railroad Photographic Club.

L&N No. 1954, 2-8-4 type, M-1 class

Tractive Force	65,290 lbs.
Drivers Diameter	69 in.
Weight on Drivers	268,200 lbs.
Total Weight	447,200 lbs.
Steam Pressure	265 lbs.
Tender Capacity	22,000 gals.
	24 tons

1942
November 1st
L & N

Covington, Ky—Nashville, Tenn.
Train—The Silver Bullet #71—62 cars, 3550 tons
Engine 1961 2-8-4 type M1
LV Covington 11:35 a.m.
ARR Louisville—Strawberry Yard 5:15 p.m.
Coal and water at Worthville
LV Louisville 9:45—55 cars, 3420 tons
ARR Bowling Green 1:35 a.m.
LV Bowling Green 2:00—coal and water
ARR Nashville—Radnor Yard 6:00 a.m.

C&O No. 305, 4-6-4 type, L-2 class

Tractive Force	52,000 lbs.
Drivers Diameter	78 in.
Weight on Drivers	217,500 lbs.
Total Weight	439,500 lbs.
Steam Pressure	255 lbs.
Tender Capacity	21,000 gals.
	30 tons

1942
November 14th
Chesapeake & Ohio

Handley—Russell

Train #5, Sportsman Cincinnati Section, 12 cars

Engine 305 4-6-4 type L2

LV Handley 10:45 p.m.

Cabin Creek Jct. 10:56

Marmet 11:03

Between Marmet and South Ruffner 7.3 miles hit large 7 passenger Buick that had been run off crossing between rails and deserted. Attempt made to stop us at Cabin Creek Jct. but too late.

Went 39 rail lengths with engine truck on ground tearing up railroad, knocking steam heat connections off entire train and flat wheeling 11 cars. Road foreman shut off stoker and feed water pump as calmly as this is written. Fireman went up on top of tank. I stood up. Fire was really flying while we were sure we had hit automobile. I thought engine had stripped herself and something would probably be coming through cab. When finally got stopped I was first on ground and could not believe engine truck on ground and we had come all that distance without upsetting. Engine crew were numb. Speed was 70 mph. Short flagged 2nd 90 Eastward manifest flatwheeling a lot of his cars. Engine 1572 2-8-8-2 type Class H7 sent from Handley, pulled train back to Cabin Creek Junction. Wreckers sent from Handley and Huntington. Engine re-railed in aproximately 5 hours. LV South Ruffner, Engine 1572—5:10 a.m., ARR Huntington 7:10 a.m., LV Huntington 7:47 a.m. Engine 464 4-6-2 type F17 ARR Russell 9:02 a.m. 5 hours and 58 minutes late. This run is placed in this book to show the hazards the U. S. railroads are constantly up against with vehicle traffic at highway and road crossings.

Duluth, Missabe & Iron Range No. 222, 2-8-8-4 type, M-3 class

Tractive Force	140,000 lbs.
Drivers Diameter	63 in.
Weight on Drivers	560,257 lbs.
Total Weight	695,040 lbs.
Steam Pressure	240 lbs.
Tender Capacity	25,000 gals.
	26 tons

1942
November 20th
Duluth, Missabe & Iron Range

Hibbing—Proctor
Train Extra 224 East, 90 loads, 6300 tons
Engine 224 2-8-8-4 type, class M-3
LV Hibbing 3:45 p.m.
ARR Proctor 8:10 p.m., water Coleraine junction
Proctor to Ore Docks down 2.18 grade 7 miles; 25 miles per hour, all retainers up.

Santa Fe 4-unit diesel No. 104, B-B type, No. 100 class

Tractive Force	230,500 lbs.
Drivers Diameter	40 in.
Weight on Drivers	922,000 lbs.
Total Weight	922,000 lbs.
Horsepower	5,400
Fuel Capacity	4,800 gals. of oil

1943
January 10th
Santa Fe

Needles—Seligman
Train CTX
Engine, diesel 116—4 units
LV Needles 2:41 p.m.
LV Topock 3:20—5 minutes detention behind work train
Passed Yucca 4:15
Passed Harris 5:17
Passed Kingman 5:35
Passed Louise 5:47
LV Berry 5:55—inspection
Passed Walapai—6:16
Passed Hackberry 6:36
Passed Truxton 7:10
ARR Peach Spring 7:32—inspection
LV Peach Spring 7:40
Passed Yampai 8:30
ARR Seligman 9:05 p.m.

Great performance with no stops for fuel or water, no helpers on the longest steam helper district in the country Needles to Yampai 135 miles. Practically 1.42 all the way. Elevation at Needles 476 feet, Seligman 5234 feet.

Santa Fe 4-unit 5,400 hp diesel No. 110 climbing Cajon Pass with a solid GFX train.

1943
January 17th
Santa Fe

Seligman—Winslow
Train GFX, 66 cars to Ash Fork, 3690 tons, dropped 11 cars of oil at Ash Fork
Diesel 109—4 units, Ash Fork to Winslow 3542 tons
LV Seligman 6:10
ARR Ash Fork 7:15—Helper 3829 2-10-2 type
LV Ash Fork 7:42
ARR Supai 9:05—cut off helper
LV Supai 9:10
ARR Williams 9:30—crew ate. Inspected train.
LV Williams 9:50
Passed Riordan 11:00—met 19, 16 minutes late
ARR Angell 11:37
LV Angell 11:45
Stop Canyon Diablo 12:05—red home signal
LV Canyon Diablo 12:11
ARR Winslow 1:05
With steam engines this train would have required the additional service of helpers Seligman to Crookton and the 28 miles from Williams to Riordan.

1943
April 12th
U. P.

Ogden—Omaha
Train Extra 4015 east, 69 cars, 3190 tons
Engine 4015 4-8-8-4 type, class 1-68-32-540 MB 23¾-23¾
LV Ogden 1:15 p.m.
ARR Echo 2:51—coal and water
LV Echo 3:14
ARR Evanston 4:50—engine serviced
LV Evanston 5:10
ARR Carter 6:26—coal and water
LV Carter 6:37
ARR Green River 7:50—removed two short loads and 1 bad order
LV Green River 9:40
Engine 3961 4-6-6-4 type, class 3-69-32-404-MB
ARR Bitter Creek 11:40—coal and water
LV Bitter Creek 11:51 p.m.

Union Pacific No. 4002, 4-8-8-4 type, $\frac{23\frac{3}{4}\text{-}23\frac{3}{4}}{68\text{-}32\text{-}540\text{-MB}}$ class

Tractive Force	135,375 lbs.
Drivers Diameter	68 in.
Weight on Drivers	540,000 lbs.
Total Weight	762,000 lbs.
Steam Pressure	300 lbs.
Tender Capacity	24,000 gals.
	28 tons

These engines performed a great job particularly during the war. They were hard to fire and in my opinion would have been better with a feedwater heater rather than exhaust steam injector.

1943
April 13th
U. P.

ARR Rawlins 2:15 a.m. in the yard at 2:35. Held 2 hours and 45 minutes for fleet of eastward passenger trains.
LV Rawlins 5:20—60 cars, 3050 tons
ARR Hanna 6:31—coal and water
LV Hanna 6:47
ARR Rock River 8:00—water, only 2 minute detention, fast work
LV Rock River 8:02
ARR Laramie 9:05—Pacific fruit express inspection, no cars require icing.
LV Laramie 11:10 with 45—18 cars, 3000 tons
ARR Buford 1:15—air test
LV Buford 1:20
ARR Cheyenne 3:00
LV Cheyenne 5:20
Train RV36—40 loads, 23 empties are foreign cars en route home, 2785 tons

Engine 9056 4-12-2 type, class UP-67-$\frac{27}{31\text{-}32}$-369-BK
ARR Pine Bluffs 6:28—coal, water and inspection. Engine serviced
LV Pine Bluffs 6:42
Pass Kimball 7:15—running inspection
ARR Sidney 8:10—caboose changed
LV Sidney 8:30
Pass Julesburg 9:46
Head in Ogallala for #102, take coal at 10:30
LV Ogallala 10:57
Running inspection passing O'Fallons
ARR North Platte yard 11:50 p.m.
Train spotted at the ice dock at 12:20 a.m.

Union Pacific No. 9085, 4-12-2. The famous U.P. 3-cylinder type built only for them.

UP-67-$\frac{27}{31\text{-}32}$-372-BK

Tractive Force	96,650 lbs.
Drivers Diameter	67 in.
Weight on Drivers	372,000 lbs.
Total Weight	515,000 lbs.
Steam Pressure	220 lbs.
Tender Capacity	18,000 gals.
	22 tons

Opposite page:

U.P. No. 5306, 2-10-2 type, TTT-63-29½/30-308-D class

Crossing the Snake River east of Huntington, Oregon with a westward extra, 74 cars, Idaho Div. Photo by R. H. Kindig

Tractive Force	70,450 lbs.
Drivers Diameter	63 in.
Weight on Drivers	308,000 lbs.
Total Weight	397,100 lbs.
Steam Pressure	200 lbs.
Tender Capacity	12,000 gals.
	20 tons

1943
April 14th
U. P.

Train is now combined with RO 12, fast stock from Denver, 31 cars of stock and 2 manifest cars placed on head end to fill us out. Train and engine crews called for 4:10 to leave North Platte at 4:40 a.m.

Engine 5060 2-10-2 type, class TTT 63-29½/30-311 D.

LV North Platte 5:30 a.m. 60 loads and no empties

Passed Gothenburg 6:37

ARR Lexington 7:05—take water, walking inspection made of train

LV Lexington 7:17

Passed Kearney 8:06

Passed Gibbon 8:25

Passed Wood River 8:40

ARR Grand Island yard 9:10—cabooses changed Class C inspection

LV Grand Island 9:45, 60 leads, no empties, 2597 tons

Engine 5032 2-10-2 type, class TTT-63-29½/30-286-D.

Approaching Chapman they swing us down from rear end thinking they see a smoking journal, make walking inspection but find nothing.

Passed Central City 10:35

ARR Columbus 11:10—coal and water, 3 cars of livestock behind the engine set out

LV Columbus 11:45

Passed Fremont 12:45

ARR Valley 1:02, 14 cars of stock set out for feed and water

LV Valley 1:18

ARR Summit 1:57—set out 5 cars for South Omaha and 1 for C. St. P. M. & O.

LV Summit 2:03

ARR Council Bluffs 2:20 p.m. ice dock

G.N. No. 2024, 2-8-8-0 type, N-3 class

Tractive Force	108,400 lbs.
Drivers Diameter	56 in.
Weight on Drivers	459,200 lbs.
Total Weight	489,200 lbs.
Steam Pressure	275 lbs.
Tender Capacity	21,500 gals.
	24 tons

This engine was built by the G.N. and modernized with the help of the Baldwin Loco. Works. They handle single 180 cars—16,740 tons, the longest and heaviest train the author ever rode hauled by a steam locomotive.

1943
November 17th
Great Northern

Kelly Lake—Allouez
Train—Extra 2014 East, 180 cars, 16,740 tons
Engine 2014 2-8-8-0 type N3
Coupled to train 10:15
Brake test 10:26—Two stickers
Leave Kelly Lake 10:37
Pass Riely 10:58
Pass Casco 11:31
Pass Baden 12:13
Pass Arlberg 12:28
ARR Brookston 12:42
LV Brookston 1:19
Cloquet 2:07
Scanlon 2:13
Carlton 2:20
Bridge 6 2:35
State Line Tower 2:45
Dewey 2:54
Boylston 3:07
Saunders 1:16
Bridge A-8 3:19
ARR Allouez 3:32

All cars equipped with new Westinghouse AB brake, 110 lb. rail, excellent crew, engine does a beautiful job. Train rigidly watched and inspected, 30 mph speed limit, retainers up on first 40 cars all the way down. No bad slack action.
Engineman—Fosig
Fireman—LeBlanc
Conductor—Barilani

Great Northern Railway Company

1943

IRON ORE OPERATIONS

THE ORE OPERATION—GENERAL

The Great Northern transports iron ore from the Mesabi Range to the Allouez Ore Docks for about 12 mining companies. These companies mine iron ore from over 100 different properties and load ore at approximately 55 loading points on our trackage.

The transportation of ore is more complex than picking up the cars at mines, moving them to the docks and dumping ore into boats. The mining companies make up about 55 different grades of ore. Because of the varied chemical and physical properties of the Mesabi, Cuyuna and Vermilion Range ores, the blending of these ores to attain a grade most suited to a particular blast furnace is of great importance. After ore is loaded into cars, samples are taken from groups of three to seven cars. The samples are analyzed so the mining companies can tell how many cars from different mines should be mixed to make up a grade. They then advise us which cars go into which boats. This is done by assigning a block number to groups of cars. This block number designates a boat and it also has a suffix letter, either A, B, C, or D, which designates the dumping order in the dock pocket. Each road train usually contains cars for about 15 blocks and generally has to be cut 21 times during classification. Some cars don't fit any block being accumulated, so they are set aside and classified later when a block is assigned. After ore is classified by blocks, it is shoved to the dock in cuts averaging 38 cars.

Good communications between themselves and the mining companies are essential. There are teletype installations at the assembly points on the range at Nashwauk, Canisteo and Calumet, at Kelly Lake, at the Hanna Office in Hibbing for handling Hanna, Cleveland-Cliffs, Inland and Jones & Laughlin business; in Duluth for handling Pickands Mather; in the Superintendent's Office in Superior, and on the Ore Docks. A primary use of teletype is to transmit train consists as soon as a train departs the Range, and to transmit back grade messages so block numbers can be assigned the cars. In ore operations, radio is used extensively. All engines in ore service, whether mine run, road haul or yard, are radio equipped. All road haul and mine run cabooses also have radio. In addition, there are a number of wayside stations in the ore territory.

The movement of iron ore from the Range to the Docks can be separated into three coordinated but different segments:

A. Mine Transfer Service
B. Road Haul
C. Classification and Boat Loading

A. *MINE TRANSFER SERVICE*

Under the direct supervision of the Trainmaster and Chief Dispatcher, this part of the operation includes the movement of empty cars from the points where set out by road trains to the mines, and the return of loaded cars to the build up points for movement by road train back to Allouez. We build up road trains at Canisteo, Calumet and Nashwauk primarily and serve mines from Gunn to east of Buhl. Currently, no mines in the Grand Rapids or Virginia areas are operating. The Chief Dispatcher's main function is to work with the mining companies allocating empties to the various mines. The over-all daily allotment of cars to the mining company is initially given the Chief Dispatcher by the Dock Superintendent. Mine run transfers are handled by single units of SD-7 or SD-9 power.

B. *ROAD HAUL*

Road trains consist of 205 cars, loaded or empty. The crews begin their trip at Allouez and work in a turnaround, accomplishing the round trip of over 200 miles in about ten hours. The Chief Dispatcher at Superior is responsible for the road movement and coordinates the need for empties or loads with the Range on one hand and the Docks on the other. The line from Saunders to Brookston is double track and from Brookston to both Kelly Lake and Gunn is CTC controlled from Superior. Normal locomotive consists for road trains are three F-7 class units.

C. *YARD CLASSIFICATION AND BOAT LOADING*

This operation begins when the road train stops in Allouez Yard. The Yard has a capacity of 9000 ore cars and consists of a 19 track receiving yard, a 9 track departure yard and an 89 track classification yard with tracks of 25 to 45 cars in length. There are also two smaller yards mainly for handling interchange ore with the Northern Pacific. The DM&IR interchange is at Saunders.

The road trains are humped and classified at the yard tower under supervision of the General Yardmaster. While being humped they are weighed automatically. A console operator punches on a key board the car number. The electronic computer pulls the tare weight of the car out of its memory and a tape is produced in the dock office showing net weight of ore in the car. This tape is fed into machines on the dock to produce punch cards used for a number of records including block lists, abstracts, boat cargo reports, mine waybills, etc.

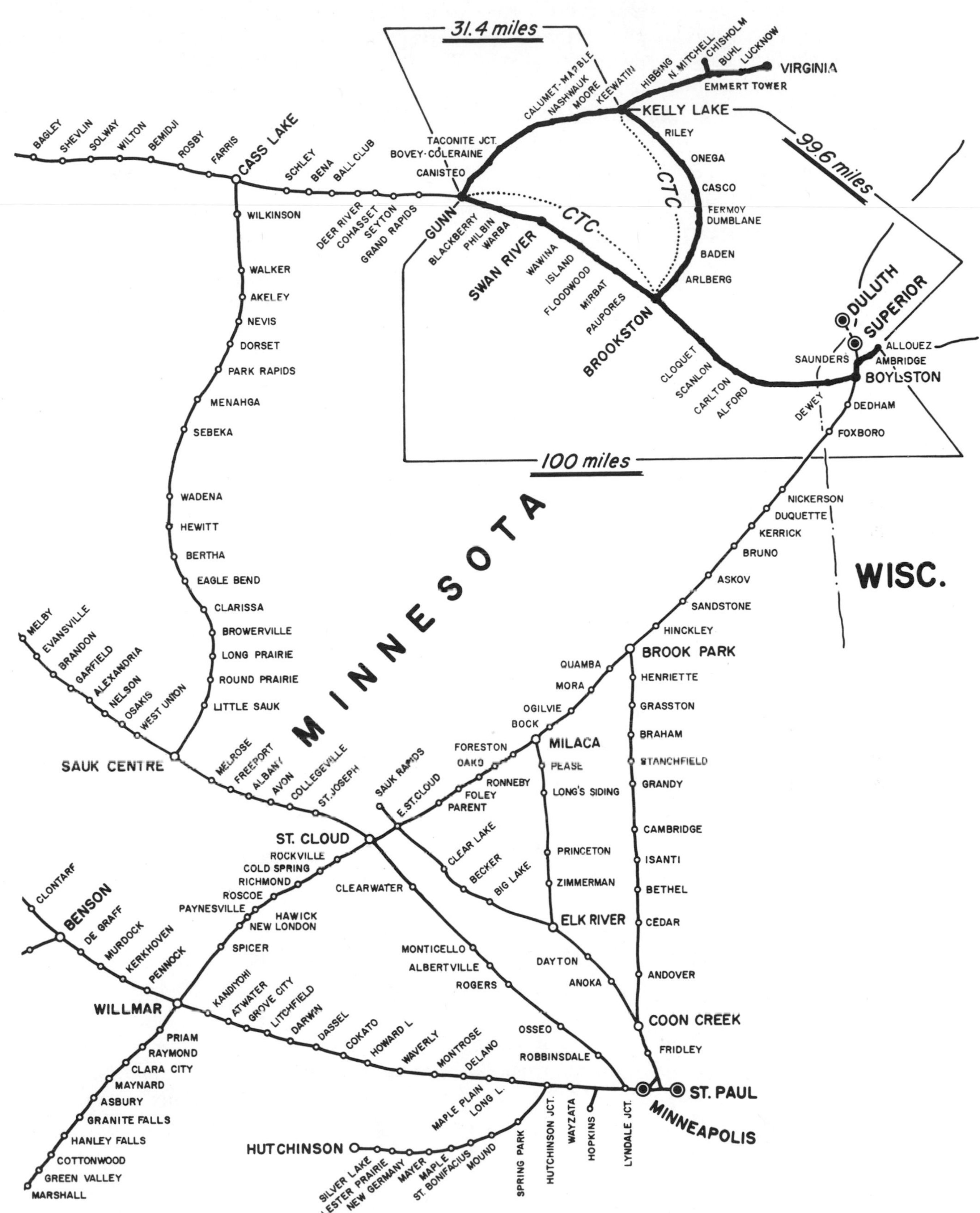
31.4 miles
99.6 miles
100 miles
CTC
CTC
MINNESOTA
WISC.
VIRGINIA
LUCKNOW
BUHL
CHISHOLM
N. MITCHELL
HIBBING
EMMERT TOWER
KELLY LAKE
KEEWATIN
MOORE
NASHWAUK
CALUMET-MARBLE
TACONITE JCT.
BOVEY-COLERAINE
CANISTEO
RILEY
ONEGA
CASCO
FERMOY
DUMBLANE
BADEN
ARLBERG
BAGLEY
SHEVLIN
SOLWAY
WILTON
BEMIDJI
ROSBY
FARRIS
CASS LAKE
SCHLEY
BENA
BALL CLUB
DEER RIVER
COHASSET
SEYTON
GRAND RAPIDS
GUNN
BLACKBERRY
PHILBIN
WARBA
SWAN RIVER
WAWINA
ISLAND
FLOODWOOD
MIRBAT
PAUPORES
BROOKSTON
CLOQUET
SCANLON
CARLTON
ALFORD
DULUTH
SUPERIOR
SAUNDERS
ALLOUEZ
AMBRIDGE
BOYLSTON
DEWEY
DEDHAM
FOXBORO
NICKERSON
DUQUETTE
KERRICK
BRUNO
ASKOV
SANDSTONE
HINCKLEY
BROOK PARK
WILKINSON
WALKER
AKELEY
NEVIS
DORSET
PARK RAPIDS
MENAHGA
SEBEKA
WADENA
HEWITT
BERTHA
EAGLE BEND
CLARISSA
BROWERVILLE
LONG PRAIRIE
ROUND PRAIRIE
LITTLE SAUK
MELBY
EVANSVILLE
BRANDON
GARFIELD
ALEXANDRIA
NELSON
OSAKIS
WEST UNION
SAUK CENTRE
MELROSE
FREEPORT
ALBANY
AVON
COLLEGEVILLE
ST. JOSEPH
SAUK RAPIDS
E. ST. CLOUD
QUAMBA
MORA
OGILVIE
BOCK
MILACA
FORESTON
OAKS
PEASE
RONNEBY
FOLEY
PARENT
LONG'S SIDING
HENRIETTE
GRASSTON
BRAHAM
STANCHFIELD
GRANDY
CAMBRIDGE
ISANTI
BETHEL
CEDAR
ANDOVER
COON CREEK
FRIDLEY
ST. CLOUD
ROCKVILLE
COLD SPRING
RICHMOND
ROSCOE
PAYNESVILLE
HAWICK
NEW LONDON
SPICER
CLEARWATER
CLEAR LAKE
BECKER
BIG LAKE
PRINCETON
ZIMMERMAN
ELK RIVER
DAYTON
ANOKA
MONTICELLO
ALBERTVILLE
ROGERS
OSSEO
ROBBINSDALE
CLONTARF
BENSON
DE GRAFF
MURDOCK
KERKHOVEN
PENNOCK
WILLMAR
KANDIYOHI
ATWATER
GROVE CITY
LITCHFIELD
DARWIN
DASSEL
COKATO
HOWARD L.
WAVERLY
MONTROSE
DELANO
PRIAM
RAYMOND
CLARA CITY
MAYNARD
ASBURY
GRANITE FALLS
HANLEY FALLS
COTTONWOOD
GREEN VALLEY
MARSHALL
MAPLE PLAIN
LONG L.
HUTCHINSON
SILVER LAKE
LESTER PRAIRIE
NEW GERMANY
MAYER
MAPLE
ST. BONIFACIUS
MOUND
SPRING PARK
HUTCHINSON JCT.
WAYZATA
HOPKINS
LYNDALE JCT.
MINNEAPOLIS
ST. PAUL

The yard classification is coordinated with dock requirements by the Dock Superintendent who is responsible for the dumping of ore into the dock, the build up of cargoes in anticipation of vessel arrivals, and the loading of ore into boats. Shove engines, normally SD-7 or SD-9 power working as single units, spot their cuts over specific pockets upon direction of the Dock Office. After spotting loads the shove crew normally gathers up available empties and returns them to the departure yard. There foreign cars are switched out for return to interchanges and system cars are made up into 205 car trains and readied for return to the Range.

ALLOUEZ YARD FACILITIES

Cars needing repair are switched to the repair track at Allouez. Previous to 1963 a repair track was also in operation at Kelly Lake, but now all work is centralized here. During the winter months the scheduled major repair programs are carried out in the buildings located toward the west end of the yard.

In this area also is the new automatic oiling device which lubricates the journal boxes as westbound trains of empties are pulling out of the yard. The trains are pulled through the oiler at about 5 MPH, the journal box covers are raised by a horizontal bar and simultaneously 4–6 OZ of oil is injected by pressure into the journal box. In the early part of the season the oiler is set to place 8 OZ into each box, but this is cut down after each car has had a chance to make two or more round trips to the Range. Present car fleet consists of 7600 ore cars of 150,000 lbs. capacity.

Adjacent to the Classification Yard is the steam plant and yard. Prior to 1943, steam to thaw frozen ore was supplied by locomotives spotted around the Classification Yard. In 1943 the original stationary plant was built and it was remodeled in 1951–1953. The facility now consists of two boilers each capable of producing 48,000 lbs. of steam per hour. In addition, there is a supplemental battery of six locomotives each of which can produce 24,000 lbs. of steam per hour. The steam yard will hold 12 cuts of 30 cars each, or 360 cars at a time.

Steam lines run along the tracks and hoses are attached to outlets on the lines and to threaded fittings on the cars. All cars have ten fittings each. Fall steaming is almost an annual event and on occasions spring steaming has been necessary. The 1962 season was the first in 28 years that no steaming was required.

ALLOUEZ ORE DOCKS

Cars are shoved from the Classification Yard to one of the three operating docks (Dock #3 having been retired in 1958) in 35 to 40 car cuts, depending on the weight and availability of ore. The maximum grade of the dock approach is 1.044% for 1500 feet. On the dock cars are spotted to fit every other pocket, or every 24 feet. This conforms with the boat hatches, most of which are on 24 foot centers. The average car load has been about 63 tons and four cars are put in a pocket. Cargoes vary from 10,000 to 25,000 tons and during 1962 averaged 14,600; a figure that is steadily rising as larger and fewer carriers replace the smaller ones. The average time a boat is at our dock is around 5½ hours.

During 1962 the newer boats loaded to a depth of 25′ 9″ when the 27 foot channel was completed in the St. Mary's River. Boats vary in width from 50 to 75 feet, the longest is 730 feet, which is maximum for boats going through the Soo Locks and also the St. Lawrence Seaway.

They have three docks operating with a total of 1026 ore pockets for a storage capacity of 344,000 tons. The distance between docks is about 200 feet and each dock is long enough so we can load two boats on a side simultaneously. Plans are being made to remove retired Dock #3 which will give us a boat basin 1900 feet long and 400 feet in width between Docks #2 and #4 to accommodate increasingly longer and wider boats.

The car dumping procedure is mostly mechanized. Cars are opened and closed by mobile trapping machines and when necessary are unloaded by gantry cranes and car shake-out machines. Ore dock forces work seven days a week on all shifts because of the around-the-clock demands of boat arrivals.

More detailed information about the individual docks is shown on the attached appendix.

RECORD OF ORE LOADING DOCKS AT ALLOUEZ

	Dock 1	*Dock 2*	*Dock 3*	*Dock 4*
Length of Dock	2244′	2100′	1956′	1812′
Number of Pockets	374	350	326	302
Capacity Per Pocket, Cars	7 cars at 50 ton	7 cars at 50 ton	6 cars at 50 ton	6 cars at 50 ton
Storage Capacity Gross Tons	130900	122500	97800	90600
Cu. Ft. Per Pocket to Bottom of Stringers	5620	5620	5100	5035
Height Water to Center of Hinge Hole	41′–2″	41′–0″	38′–9″ 38′–9½″	40′–2″
Height Water to Deck of Dock	80′–8″	80′–6″	77′–0″	75′–0″
Width of Dock Outside to Outside of Partition Posts	56′–0″	56′–0″	59′–8″	62′–6″
Length of Spouts	36′–0″	36′–0″	34′–0″	34′–6″
Angle of Pocket	47°–30′	47°–30′	47°–30′	47°–30′

HISTORY—Construction of Docks

Dock 1—Original construction of timber 1892. Rebuilt with timber 1906–07. Rebuilt with concrete and steel inner 1/3, 1925–26. Middle 1/3, 1926–27. Outer 1/3, 1927–28. Gantry Crane & floodlights installed 1952–53.

Dock 2—Original construction in timber, 250 pockets 1899 & 1900. Original construction in timber 100 pockets 1901–02. 250 pockets rebuilt in timber 1909–10. 100 pockets rebuilt in timber 1911–12. Entire dock rebuilt with concrete & steel 1922–23. Floodlights installed 1952–53. Gantry Crane installed 1953–54.

Dock 3—Original construction in timber, 160 pockets 1902–03. Original construction in timber 166 pockets 1905–06. Inner 160 pockets rebuilt in kind 1917–18. Outer 166 pockets rebuilt in kind 1920–21. 60 inner pockets rebuilt in spring 1942. Next 86 pockets rebuilt spring of 1944. 80 pockets rebuilt 1952–53. Taken out of service in 1958.

Dock 4—Constructed with concrete and steel in 1911.

1944
July 17th
N. Y. C.

Harmon—Syracuse
Train 20th Century Limited, 1st #25, 11 cars
Engine 3136 4-8-2 type, L4b class
On time Rensselaer, Utica, Syracuse
Engine did very well as they have right along making 25 and 26's time with 72″ wheels.
No pusher on Albany Hill, like the J engines always got with over 7 cars. Scooped water all the way. Will coal at Wayneport next division.

N.Y.C. No. 3135, 4-8-2 type, L-4B

Tractive Force	59,850 lbs.
Drivers Diameter	72 in.
Weight on Drivers	266,500 lbs.
Total Weight	401,100 lbs.
Steam Pressure	250 lbs.
Tender Capacity	15,200 gals.
	42 tons

1944
September 5-6
Santa Fe

La Junta-Dodge City
Train Super Chief #18E, 12 cars, 660 tons
Engine 3461 4-6-4 type, 3460 class

	MPH	*ARRIVED*	*LATE*	*DEPARTED*	*LATE*	*DELAY*
La Junta						
18.9	56.7			11:40 p.m.	3′28″	
Las Animas						
34.0	85.0			12:00 m.n.	3′21″	
Lamar						
27.4	78.3			12:24 a.m.	3′19″	
Holly						
21.0	84.0			12:45 a.m.	3′18″	
Syracuse						
29.4	84.0			1:00 a.m.	3′15″	
Lakin						
21.9	93.8			1:21 a.m.	3′09″	
Garden City						
31.1	81.1			1:35 a.m.	3′05″	
Cimarron						
18.7	80.1			1:58 a.m.	3′03″	
Dodge City		2:12 a.m.	3′00″			
First Dist.	79.9					

Miles 202.4—152 mins.
Engineer C. H. Townsend, Conductor B. B. Jones
18's diesel had failed losing 3′18″ to La Junta. The fastest ride I have ever had on a steam locomotive was engine 3465 on this division and it is also the fastest diesel ride I have ever had, on the Colorado division.

Santa Fe No. 3465, 4-6-4 type, class 3460

Tractive Force	49,300 lbs.
Drivers Diameter	84 in.
Weight on Drivers	213,440 lbs.
Total Weight	412,380 lbs.
Steam Pressure	300 lbs.
Tender Capacity	20,000 gals.
	7,107 gals. oil

Erie No. 2936, 4-6-2 type, K-5A class

Tractive Force	43,800 lbs.
Drivers Diameter	79 in.
Weight on Drivers	198,960 lbs.
Total Weight	307,860 lbs.
Steam Pressure	200 lbs.
Tender Capacity	10,000 gals.
	16 tons

1944
November 28th
Erie

Salamanca—Jersey City
Train Erie Limited #2, 12 cars
Engine 2938 4-6-2 type, class K5a
LV Salamanca 11:30 a.m.
LV Hornell 1:33 p.m., water
LV Elmira 2:51 p.m., water
Binghamton 4:11, water, pick up Express Car.
Susquehanna 4:49, helper 3361 2-8-4 type, Class S3
LV Susquehanna 4:54
ARR Gulf Summit 5:12
LV Gulf Summit 5:17, cut off helper
ARR Port Jervis 7:23, water
LV Port Jervis 7:27
ARR Jersey City 9:30 p.m.
On business car Chicago Salamanca amazingly good engine-stoker fired. Also stops at Tuxedo and Patterson.
3 EX, 1 Storage, 2 RF's, 1 RPO, 3 Coaches, 1 Diner, 1 Lounge, SL, 1 SL.

1945
May 10th
Santa Fe

La Junta—Raton
Train, Main running as second #3. 14 cars
Engine 3784 4-8-4 type, 3776 class
LV Raton 1:15 a.m.
ARR Thatcher 2:05, head in meet #4, engine 3785
LV Thatcher 2:20
ARR Trinidad 3:15, water, get helper 1794 2-8-8-2 type, Ex N & W Y 3 then sold to Virginian after War was over.
LV Trinidad 3:25
LV Lynn 3:55, cut off helper
ARR Raton 4:20, meet #8
Engine great as always—so are roller bearing rods.

Santa Fe No. 3785, 4-8-4 type, class 3776

Tractive Force	66,000 lbs.
Drivers Diameter	80 in.
Weight on Drivers	281,900 lbs.
Total Weight	494,350 lbs.
Steam Pressure	300 lbs.
Tender Capacity	24,500 gals.
	7,107 gals. oil

First of two delivered with roller bearing rods shown descending Glorieta Pass with 4th #3 running as a Main Train west of Glorieta 3rd Dist. N.M. Div. now 5th Dist. Colo. Div.

Photo by R. H. Kindig.

C&O No. 2730, 2-8-4 type, K-4 class called Kanawha type by C&O.

Tractive Force	69,350 lbs.
Booster	14,400 lbs.
Drivers Diameter	69 in.
Weight on Drivers	292,000 lbs.
Total Weight	460,000 lbs.
Steam Pressure	245 lbs.
Tender Capacity	21,000 gals.
	30 tons

This was one of the author's three favorite 2-8-4 types in the U.S. and he rode them all. Also in passenger service.

1945
August 31st
C & O

Stevens, Ky.—Hinton W. Va.
Train #92—Stevens to Russell, 95 loads, 4,845 tons, Russell to Hinton, 61 loads, 3170 tons
Engine 2741 2-8-4 type K4

Station	*Arrived*	*Departed*	*Delay*	*Remarks*
Stevens (Called)	3:00 a.m.	3:30 a.m.	30 min.	Put engine on train, test brakes, clear yard
MS Cabin	7:06 Clear	7:13		
Russell (Called)	7:13	9:41	2 hr. 28 min.	Service locomotive, reclassify train, cutting out short manifest and adding through manifest from Northern and Big Sandy Divisions and clear yard.
Russell (Called)	9:00	9:41		
NC Cabin	9:46	9:55	9 min.	Waiting for Extra 1249 west, troop train, before crossing to freight main.
Ashland	10:03	10:12	9 min.	Pick up one load
Elk Yard (Charleston)	12:19 p.m.	12:34	15 min.	Pick up three loads
Handley	1:16	1:30	14 min.	Water and clean fire.
CS Cabin	2:55	3:05	10 min.	Stopped for caretaker to inspect 14 cars of horses on which it was reported some of the horses were down.
Hinton	4:01	4:32	31 min.	Pulled train in upper yard. Bring engine back to passenger station.
Total time:		13 Hours 2 Min.		Consumed 49,500 gallons water, 25 tons of coal
Delays:		4 Hours 26 Min.		
Running time:		8 Hours 36 Min.		

te Fe No. 2919, 4-8-4 type, class
0

:tive Force	66,000 lbs.
ers Diameter	80 in.
ght on Drivers	293,860 lbs.
l Weight	510,150 lbs.
m Pressure	300 lbs.
der Capacity	24,500 gals.
	7,000 gals. oil

1945
September 15th
Santa Fe

Dodge City—La Junta
Train 1st #7, fast mail, 13 cars—975 tons
Engine 2921 2900 class, 4-8-4 type

	MPH	*ARRIVED*	*LATE*	*DEPARTED*	*LATE*	*DELAY*
Dodge City						
18.7	53.4			3:46P	1′46″	
Cimarron						
6.1	73.2			4:07P	1′8″	
Ingalls						
12.7	76.2			4:12P	1′47″	
Pierceville						
12.3	73.8			4:22P	1′46″	
Garden City						
6.6	56.5			4:32P	1′46″	
Holcomb						
8.0	96.0			4:39P	1′47″	
Deerfield						
7.3	73.0			4:44P	1′44″	
Lakin						
29.4	73.5			4:50P	1′43″	
Syracuse						
21.0	66.3			5:14P	1′36″	
Holly						
27.4	82.2			5:33P	1′34″	
Lamar						
34.0	81.6			5:53P	1′28″	
Las Animas						
14.7	80.1			6:18P	1′22″	
Casa						
4.2	63.0			6:29P	1′18″	
La Junta		6:33P	1′13″			
First Dist.	72.7		202.4 miles in 167 minutes			

Engineer F. P. Balch. Weather cloudy, hard head wind from West.

B&O No. 7450, 2-6-6-2 type, KK-2 class

Tractive Force	90,000 lbs.
Drivers Diameter	70 in.
Weight on Drivers	373,000 lbs.
Total Weight	466,000 lbs.
Steam Pressure	250 lbs.
Tender Capacity	18,000 gals.
	20 tons

These engines were not a success. Only two were built, one with a water tube firebox. They were a forerunner of the famous 2-6-6-4 type and 4-6-6-4 type that were soon to be built.

1946
February 18th
B. & O.

Cumberland—Connellsville

Train Chicago #97, 47 loads, 1 empty, 3380 tons

Engine 6208 2-10-2 type, class S-1a

LV Cumberland 4:18 p.m.

LV Hyndman 4:50, Helper 7451 2-6-6-2 type, class K-K2

FO Tower 5:23

Sand Patch 6:03, Cut off helper, water

Meyersdale 6:33

HK Tower 7:50

ARR Connellsville 9:00 p.m.

Snowing, slippery rail—fine run, good crew. This engine still one of the top two Santa Fe type in my opinion.

B&O No. 7602, 2-8-8-4 type, EM-1 class

Tractive Force	115,000 lbs.
Drivers Diameter	64 in.
Weight on Drivers	485,000 lbs.
Total Weight	628,700 lbs.
Steam Pressure	235 lbs.
Tender Capacity	22,000 gals.
	25 tons

One of the really best 2-8-8-4's ever built.

1946
February 20th
B. & O.

Keyser—East Grafton

Train St. Louis #97, 38 loads, 3 empties, 3155 tons

Engine 7715 2-8-8-4 type, class EM-1, helper 4442-2-8-2 type, class Q4

LV Keyser 6:55 p.m.

ARR Altamont 8:27, cut off helper, water

LV Altamont 8:40, did fine on the 17 mile grade

ARR Terra Alta 9:35

ARR M & K Junction 9:55, get helper 7208 2-8-8-0 type, class EL2-a

LV M & K Junction 10:07

ARR West End W. S. Tower 10:21, cut off helper

LV West End 10:31

ARR East Grafton 11:05 p.m.

Great engine—foggy and low clouds as usual. Train inspected at Altamont and West End.

B&O No. 7208, 2-8-8-0 type, EL-3a

Tractive Force	121,700 lbs.
Drivers Diameter	58 in.
Weight on Drivers	470,800 lbs.
Total Weight	493,000 lbs.
Steam Pressure	210 lbs.
Tender Capacity	12,000 gals.
	20 tons

1946
February 21st
B. & O.

East Grafton—Cumberland

Train Extra 7607 East, 71 cars, all loaded coal, 5120 tons

Engine 7607 2-8-8-4 type, class EM-1, helper 7704 2-6-6-4 type, class KB-1

LV East Grafton 9:15 a.m.

ARR Hardman 9:37

LV Hardman 9:45 Get two El-5 Pushers

Tunnelton 10:27

M & K Junction 11:02

ARR Terra Alta 12:27, cut off helper, both pushers, water

LV Terra Alta 12:55

ARR Altamont 2:31, retainers up

LV Altamont 2:56

ARR West Keyser 4:44

All moves perfectly handled; Raining, sleeting, low clouds.

P.R.R. No. 6110, 4-4-4-4 type, T-1 class

Tractive Force	65,000 lbs.
Drivers Diameter	80 in.
Weight on Drivers	268,200 lbs.
Total Weight	497,200 lbs.
Steam Pressure	300 lbs.
Tender Capacity	19,500 gals.
	41 tons

1946
April 5-6th
P. R. R.

Altoona—Pittsburgh
Broadway Limited #29, 11 cars
Engine 6114 4-4-4-4 type, class T-1, helper 6792 4-8-2 type, class M1a
LV Altoona 10:50 p.m.
ARR Gallitzan 11:25, cut off helper
LV Gallitzan 11:28
ARR Pittsburgh 1:33 a.m. O.T., wet, raining—all water scooped

April 6th

Fort Wayne—Chicago
Broadway Limited #29, 11 cars
Engine 6114 4-4-4-4 type, class T-1
LV Fort Wayne 6:05 a.m. CST
ARR Englewood 8:30
ARR Chicago 8:45 a.m.
Weather clear—engine rode well, but very slippery at speed. I much prefer any good 4-8-4. All water scooped.

N&W No. 2156, 2-8-8-2 type, class Y6a

Tractive Force	152,206 lbs.
Drivers Diameter	57 in.
Weight on Drivers	522,850 lbs.
Total Weight	582,900 lbs.
Steam Pressure	300 lbs.
Tender Capacity	22,000 gals.
	26 tons

Built by N&W at Roanoke Shops.

1946
May 19th
N & W

Roanoke—Bluefield
Train Time Freight #99, 68 cars, no empties, 3980 tons
Engine 2161 2-8-8-2 type, class Y6-a
LV West Roanoke 6:10 a.m.
ARR Arthur 7:05, went in for #15
LV Arthur 7:20
ARR Walton 8:20, water
LV Walton 8:32
Glen Lyn 10:07
ARR East Bluefield, yard limit, 11:20

N&W No. 1212, 2-6-6-4 type, class A

Tractive Force	114,000 lbs.
Drivers Diameter	70 in.
Weight on Drivers	432,350 lbs.
Total Weight	573,000 lbs.
Steam Pressure	300 lbs.
Tender Capacity	22,000 gals.
	26 tons

Built by N&W at Roanoke Shops.

1946
May 19th
N & W

Bluefield—Williamson

Train Time Freight #99, 68 cars, no empties, 3980 tons

Engine 1208 2-6-6-4 type, class A, helper electric engine 2508, class LC-1

LV Bluefield 12:20 p.m.

ARR Elkhorn 1:24, cut off helper

LV Elkhorn 1:32

ARR Wilmore 2:36, water

LV Wilmore 2:41

Devon 3:25

ARR East Williamson 4:57

Fine Engine—best on the N & W, I have always said, OT all the way.

Sorry I cannot go to Portsmouth with her. Weather clear and warm—never slipped once. Good rail.

Met by operating vice-president, R. H. Smith, to go back with him on #4 sleeping on business car until #4 left.

N&W No. 604, 4-8-4 type, J-1 class

Tractive Force	73,300 lbs.
Drivers Diameter	70 in.
Weight on Drivers	288,000 lbs.
Total Weight	494,000 lbs.
Steam Pressure	275 lbs.
Tender Capacity	22,000 gals.
	26 tons

This engine was built at Roanoke by the N&W and is shown here in August 1947 ready for No. 25 westbound "Powhatan Arrow."

Photo by Bruce D. Fales.

1946
May 20th
N & W

Williamson—Bluefield
Train #4 Pocahontas, 11 cars
Engine 603 4-8-4 type, class J
LV Williamson 4:10 a.m. OT
Iaeger 5:19
Welch 5:50
North Fork 6:16, water
Elkhorn 6:28
ARR Bluefield 7:10 a.m. OT
Bluefield—Roanoke
same Train #4 Pocahontas, 12 cars
Engine 603 4-8-4 type, class J
LV Bluefield 7:25 a.m.
Narrows 8:10
Pearsburg 8:16, 100 in for us
Walton 8:55
Christiansburg 9:09, regular stop—so fill tank
LV Christiansburg 9:16
Salem 9:44
ARR Roanoke 10:00 a.m. OT
Engine handled train very well—particularly on Elkhorn grade. But I have never been one of the J class great admirers. Also get tired of standing up. Have done it for too many miles and hours, on too many locomotives in my life time.

1946
July 17th
N. Y. C.

Chicago—Buffalo
Train 20th Century Limited #26, 14 cars
Engine 6002 4-8-4 type, class S1A
LV Chicago 4:00 p.m.
Toledo, Collinwood and Buffalo O.T. Engine serviced at Collinwood, also coal. Ran around 68 at Dunkirk. Thunder storm Collinwood-Erie.
Good to see N.Y.C. have a great engine at last that can go through Chicago Harmon or Harmon Chicago in all weather with high wheel. As I saw this engine class christened, at Schenectady in 1945 was always much interested. Rode them 9 trips in milk, fast freight, mail, and express service all over the railroad and they were excellent. Water scooped all the way over.

N.Y.C. No. 6000, 4-8-4 type, S-1 class

Tractive Force	62,500 lbs.
Drivers Diameter	79 in.
Weight on Drivers	275,000 lbs.
Total Weight	471,000 lbs.
Steam Pressure	275 lbs.
Tender Capacity	18,000 gals.
	46 tons

Because of the track tanks, the N.Y.C. loaded their tenders to very high capacity with 46 tons.

G.N. No. 442, eastward Manifest Train, descending the 1.6 grade near Chumstick, Washington. First Sub-Div. Cascade Div. Class Y-1.

Photo by William J. Pontin, Rail Photo Service.

Weight on Drivers	420,600 lbs.
Total Weight	527,200 lbs.
HP	3,000
Tractive Force	126,180 lbs.
Speed	45 mph

1946
October 17th
Great Northern

Seattle—Wenatchee
Train No. 28, Fast mail, 10 cars, Engine 2535 4-8-2 type, P-2 class
Electric Engine 5014, Skykomish—Wenatchee, Y-1 class
LV Seattle 9:30 p.m.
LV Everett 10:48
LV Skykomish 12:10 a.m., get electric helper
Pass Scenic 12:45
Grade 2.2 Sky to Scenic
8 miles of 1.57 through Cascade Tunnel
Pass Berne 1:05
Chumstick, met No. 27
AR Wenatchee 2:30 a.m. O.T. all the way
Clear and warm.

1946
October 18th
Great Northern

Wenatchee—Interbay
1st, 401 Forwarder, 57 cars, 3,565 tons
Engine No. 2553 4-8-4 type, S-1 class
Electric Helper Engine No. 5011, Class Y-1, Streamlined
LV Wenatchee 11:45 a.m.
Pass Berne 2:10 p.m.
Pass Scenic 2:40 p.m.
AR Skykomish 4:05 p.m. Cut-off Electric Engine Helper
LV Skykomish 4:25 p.m.
AR Everett 6:35 p.m.
LV Everett 7:10 p.m.
AR Interbay 8:57 p.m.
Raining at Berne—usual low clouds. Some difference with the Cascade Tunnel. I was there the day it was opened in 1929 from the old line and the 4% grade. Clear and warm at Everett and Interbay. Retainers not used because of regenative breaking with Electric Engine.

G.N. No. 5, The Cascadian, leaving West Portal of Cascade Tunnel coming into Scenic, Washington with streamlined Electric Engine No. 5011—Class Y-1. The grade is 2.2 descending, the Engine is type B—D+D—B with 119,000 lbs. Tractive Force.

Photo by Wm. J. Pontin, Rail Photo Service.

5011

G.N. No. 2, "The Empire Builder," arriving at Summit, Montana after climbing the 1.6 grade from Walton with helper No. 5900, three unit 4500 hp. EMD diesel with road engine No. 2575, 4-8-4 type, S-2 class.

1946
October 20th
Great Northern

Summit—Whitefish
Train extra 301 west, 51 cars, 3,400 tons
Engine 301, 4 unit Diesel
LV Summit 2:50 p.m.
LV Walton 3:56
Belton 5:04
Columbia Falls 5:40
ARR Whitefish 6:00
No retainers.

1946
October 21st
Great Northern

Whitefish—Summit
Train Apple Knockers Special, extra 2517 East
Engine 2517 4-8-2 type, class P-2, 8 cars
LV Whitefish 9:15
Columbia Falls 9:30
Coram 9:50
Belton 10:00
Red Eagle 10:10
ARR Walton 10:35, water
LV Walton 10:55
ARR Summit 12:30
LV Summit 2:00 p.m. Train extra 3208 Dozer, Engine #3208 2-8-2 type, class 03
ARR Blackfoot 4:50 after splitting switch with Dozer, at Browning
LV Blackfoot 5:15, Train 1st 472 Diesel 404, 84 cars, 1 empty, 4,800 tons
ARR Sundance 5:35, get two cars of stock
LV Sundance 6:08
Cut Bank 6:30
Baltic 6:40, snowing hard
Ethridge 6:53
ARR Shelby 8 p.m. Was getting on short time for #2 which I was going to ride to Havre.

G.N. No. 2508, 4-8-2 type, P-2 class with No. 2 "The Empire Builder" along Kootenai River east of Troy, Montana on the Kalispell Div.

Tractive Force	57,580 lbs.
Drivers Diameter	73 in.
Weight on Drivers	242,000 lbs.
Total Weight	365,600 lbs.
Steam Pressure	210 lbs.
Tender Capacity	15,000 gals. wtr. 5,800 gals. oil

Photo by Otto C. Perry, Aug. 1, 1938.

1946
October 24th
Great Northern

Whitefish—Summit
Train 1st 436, 50 loads, 45 empties, 3,600 tons
Engine 304, 4 unit Diesel
LV Whitefish 10:25
Columbia Falls 10:43
Coram 10:57
ARR Belton 11:18, met #27
LV Belton 11:19
ARR Walton 12:50, get helper, #2175 2-10-2 type, class Q2
LV Walton 1 p.m.
Single Shot 1:35
Blacktail 1:45
ARR Summit 2:15
At that time there were in service on the Kalispell Division 4 rotary plows, 3 dozers, one spreader and five wedge plows on pilots of 2-8-2 type engines.

G.N. No. 2577, 4-8-4 type, S-2 class

Tractive Force	58,300 lbs.
Drivers Diameter	80 in.
Weight on Drivers	247,300 lbs.
Total Weight	420,900 lbs.
Steam Pressure	225 lbs.
Tender Capacity	17,000 gals.
	5,800 gals. oil

First 4-8-4 type built with 80 inch driving wheels.

G.N. No. 2552, 4-8-4 type, S-1 class

Tractive Force	67,000 lbs.
Drivers Diameter	73 in.
Weight on Drivers	273,700 lbs.
Total Weight	472,120 lbs.
Steam Pressure	250 lbs.
Tender Capacity	22,000 gals.
	5,800 gals. oil

1946
October 25th
Great Northern

Blackfoot—Whitefish
Train #428, 4 loads, 121 empties, 3,375 tons
Engine 305, four unit Diesel, 5,400 HP
LV Blackfoot 3:30 p.m., Browning 4:05
Triple Divide 4:32, Spotted Robe 4:50
Glacier Park 5:17
ARR Summit 5:50
LV Summit 6:03, no retainers
ARR Nimrod 6:40
LV Nimrod 7:05
Red Eagle 7:59
Coram 8:30
Columbia Falls 8:52
ARR Whitefish 9:05

G.N. No. 2047, 2-8-8-2 type, R-2 class

Tractive Force	146,000 lbs.
Drivers Diameter	63 in.
Weight on Drivers	544,000 lbs.
Total Weight	630,750 lbs.
Steam Pressure	240 lbs.
Tender Capacity	22,000 gals.
	5,800 gals. oil

Engine is just east of Summit, Montana with 49 cars running 15 mph. with an eastward extra on Aug. 6, 1938. Kalispell Div.

Photo by Otto C. Perry. One of the author's favorites of this type.

1946
October 26th
Great Northern

Whitefish—Blackfoot
Train #1-472, 91 loads, 5,000 tons
Engine 2049, class R2 2-8-8-2 type, helper 2554 4-8-4 type, class S1
LV Whitefish 8:00 a.m.
Columbia Falls 8:35
Coram 9:10, met ex-417 West
ARR Belton 9:45, met ex-423 West
LV Belton 9:55
ARR Red Eagle 10:11, train parted
LV Red Eagle 10:52, pass Pinnacle 11:52
ARR Walton 12:10, inspection
LV Walton 12:35
ARR Summit 1:35
LV Summit 1:55, cut off helper, met 1st and 2nd #1
Pass Glacier Park 3:07
Pass Browning 4:10
ARR Blackfoot 5:50 p.m.

1946
October 29th
Great Northern

Shelby—Havre
Train #2 Empire Builder, 13 cars
Engine 2580 4-8-4 type, class S-2
LV Shelby 8:40, running around #446
ARR Chester 9:45
LV Chester 9:50
ARR Pacific Junction 10:58
ARR Havre 11:05 O.T.
Great to ride the S-2. First 4-8-4 built with 80 inch wheels thanks to C. O. Jenks, operating vice-president.
On this trip, he was at Whitefish fighting snow at 2:00 a.m. He must have been nearing 70 years of age. Had dinner there with him on his car. Great man—always wonderful to me.

G.N. No. 2587, 4-8-4 type, S-2 class with No. 1 "The Empire Builder" east of Summit, Montana, August 6, 1938, coming out of snowshed.

Kansas City Southern No. 900, 2-10-4 type, class J

Tractive Force	93,300 lbs.
Drivers Diameter	70 in.
Weight on Drivers	350,000 lbs.
Total Weight	509,000 lbs.
Steam Pressure	310 lbs.
Tender Capacity	21,000 gals.
	4,500 gals. oil

1946
November 20th
Kansas City Southern

Kansas City—Shreveport

Train #77 Merchandise Special, 62 loads, 3120 tons

Engine 904 2-10-4 type

LV Air Line Jct., Kansas City 8:03 p.m.

ARR Pittsburgh, North Yard 12:07

LV North Yard 12:32 a.m.

ARR Watts 4:52

LV Watts 5:15

ARR Heavener 7:57

LV Heavener 8:15

Get Helper 765 2-8-8-0 type, G-2 class

ARR Rich Mountain 9:12—cut off helper

ARR De Queen 12:05 p.m.

ARR Shreveport 3:45

Excellent run, all cars go through, water taken only at the division points, oil at Pittsburg and Heavener, train rigidly inspected from head and rear end, no switching except cabooses. Great engine.

Southern No. 1463, 4-8-2 type, TS class

Tractive Force	50,300 lbs.
Drivers Diameter	69 in.
Weight on Drivers	209,800 lbs.
Total Weight	314,800 lbs.
Steam Pressure	200 lbs.
Tender Capacity	9,000 gals.
	12 tons

NOTE: The Southern Valve Gear first used on and named after this railroad.

1947
September 14th
Southern R. R.

Spartanburg—Ashville
Train Carolina Special #28, 7 cars
Engine No. 1462 4-8-2 type, TS class
LV Spartanburg 2:15 p.m.
LV Melrose 3:30 p.m., helper 4883 2-8-2 type, MS-4 class on rear end, 3 miles of 4.7, 4.4, 4.1
Saluda 3:45, cut off helper
Hendersonville 4:17, water met #27
ARR Ashville 5:10 p.m. OT

Made this round trip 9 times in 1929–30, on freight and coal trains as well as passenger. Much improved with two safety tracks and rigid special instructions. Ride in from Salisbury to Ashville also most interesting with 2% grade to Ridgecrest and many 7 and 8 degree curves. Cannot find transcripts of many runs there.

Southern No. 4885, 2-8-2 type, MS-4 class

Tractive Force	59,900 lbs.
Drivers Diameter	63 in.
Weight on Drivers	239,500 lbs.
Total Weight	326,000 lbs.
Steam Pressure	200 lbs.
Tender Capacity	10,000 gals.

1947
September 16th-17th
Southern R. R.

Ashville—Spartanburg
Train Carolina Special #27, 8 cars
Engine No. 1342 4-6-2 type, PS-2 class
LV Ashville 11:20 a.m.
ARR Hendersonville 12:03
ARR Saluda 12:30 #156 in for us, retainers up
ARR Melrose 12:40 p.m., retainers down
Tyron 12:52, meet 1st 57
ARR Spartanburg 1:55 OT

1947
November 15th
Union Pacific

Ketcham, Sun Valley—Pocatello
Train X B24 East Inspection Car
LV Ketcham 12:40 p.m.
Pass Hailey 12:55
Pass Bellevue 1:02
ARR Priest 1:20
Back in on spur for Extra 561 East to clear us.
Pass Richfield 1:55
ARR Shoshone 2:12
Wait at Shoshone for First no. 18 to leave and follow No. 18 to Pocatello.
LV Shoshone 3:05
LV Minidoka 4:02
LV American Falls 4:35
ARR Pocatello 5:07 Two minutes in back of First no. 18, following his yellow block all the way.

Union Pacific inspection car B24 extra east runs special for the author, left, from Ketchum to Pocatello. Ketchum Agent with uniform cap, Mrs. Farrington, Road Master, Assistant Supt. of Idaho Div. and Engineman.

Missouri Pacific No. 2208, 4-8-4 type

Tractive Force	67,200 lbs.
Drivers Diameter	73 in.
Weight on Drivers	279,400 lbs.
Total Weight	489,000 lbs.
Steam Pressure	285 lbs.
Tender Capacity	19,350 gals.
	20 tons

1947
December 15th
M. P.

St. Louis—Poplar Bluff

Train Sunshine Special 2nd-21, South Texas Section, 14 cars

Engine 2210 4-8-4 type

LV St. Louis 6:30 p.m.

ARR Bismarck 8:30, water, helper 1727 2-10-2 type

LV Bismarck 8:35

ARR Tip Top 9:15, cut off helper

LV Tip Top 9:10

Gads Hill 9:40

ARR Poplar Bluff 10:45 p.m.

Robert R. Young's business car on west Texas section along side of us in St. Louis I beat it for the engine. We had Col. White OVP business car through to Harligen as I was making Field and Stream Pathé Sportescope for the M.P. Engine performed beautifully and handled 14 heavy weight cars with ease. The line change between Tip Top and Gads Hill reduced the maximum grade at this point from 2.45% southward and 2.15% northward to 1.25% compensated for curvature in both directions and replaced one 8-degree curve and several only slightly less severe. Now none is greater than 2 degrees.

This relocation reduced mileage 0.7 and together with other projects cut 3 miles from the total distance over the De Soto subdivision of the Missouri division.

R.F.&P. No. 574, 2-8-4 type, R.R. class None

Tractive Force	64,100 lbs.
Drivers Diameter	69 in.
Weight on Drivers	270,900 lbs.
Total Weight	433,200 lbs.
Steam Pressure	245 lbs.
Tender Capacity	22,000 gals.
	25 tons

1948
May 1st
R. F. & P.

Richmond—Acca Yard—Potomac Yard

Train Fruit Growers Express Extra 575, solid fruit, 55 loads, 3127 tons

Engine 575 2-8-4 type

LV Acca 2:10 p.m.

Ashland 2:41, 30 miles speed limit through town

ARR Fredricksburg 4:14, water and inspection

LV Fredricksburg 4:25

Quantico 5:02

ARR Potomac Yard 6:17, followed yellow blocks

Fine run—cab very smokey with head wind. Excellent crew—weather clear and warm.

Rock Island No. 5042, 4-8-4 type, S4 class with Train No. 91, "California Gold Ball," west of Bureau, Illinois, Illinois Div., on Oct. 22, 1942. Note high car second from engine.

1948
May 7th
C. R. I. & P.

Pratt—Tucumcari
Train #91, Chicago, California Gold Ball
Engine 5021 4-8-4 type, 68 cars, 4750 tons
LV Pratt 9:40 p.m.
Greensburg 10:33, met #94
Mineola 11:35, water
Fowler 11:55, met #92
Kismet 12:50, met #40
ARR Liberal 1:40 a.m.
LV Liberal 2:10, water
Guymon 3:27, water
Texhoma 3:47
ARR Dalhart 5:40
LV Dalhart 6:40
Romero 7:50, met #44
Naravisa 8:10, water
Logan 8:45, met #94
ARR Tucumcari 11:15
Fine run engine performed well all the way—new line change and Cimarron Bridge at Liberal. Beautiful job.

C&O No. 1605, 2-6-6-6 type, H-8 class named Allegheny on the C&O

Tractive Force	110,200 lbs.
Drivers Diameter	67 in.
Weight on Drivers	471,000 lbs.
Total Weight	724,500 lbs.
Steam Pressure	260 lbs.
Tender Capacity	25,000 gals.
	25 tons

1948
September 20th
C & O

Hinton—Clifton Forge
Extra 1611 East, 110 loads, 11,000 tons
Engine 1611 2-6-6-6 type, class H8, helper on rear end 1620 2-6-6-6 type
LV Hinton 7:50 a.m.
Ronceverte 9:45 a.m., water
Pass White Sulphur 11:17 a.m.
ARR Allegheny 12:27 p.m., cut off pusher
LV Allegheny 12:31—O.X. Cabin 1:00 p.m.
B. S. Cabin 1:57 p.m.
ARR Clifton Forge 3:20 p.m.
Fine move over the easiest eastward Allegheny grade of any railroad. Fine engine, usual good C&O crew.

Western Maryland Extra 812 East leaving Hendricks, W. Va. Elkins Division with pushers 828 and 810 on rear end. Two more helpers are on the head end.

Photo taken July 1949 by R. H. Kindig.

LINE UP OF ROAD TRIP—September 28th to October 1st, inclusive 1948. Cars 203 and 204—Baltimore to Elkins—Train Nos. 3 and 9, September 28th.

Car 203's party to go to Cheat Club, upon arrival of Train No. 9 at Elkins and remain there over night.

Wednesday Morning, September 29th—Yard Diesel Engine, with Combine Car, will be run out of Elkins in time to pick up party at Cheat Club 9:00 a.m., then to Webster Springs, and back to Cheat Club. Car 203's party to remain at Cheat Club Wednesday night.

Thursday Morning, September 30th—Mr. and Mrs. Farrington will leave Cheat Club in time to make Train No. 10 out of Elkins at 7:20 a.m. and will ride car No. 204 to Cumberland.

Car No. 204—Train No. 10—Elkins to Cumberland.

Mr. and Mrs. Farrington to ride Train WM-3, Cumberland to Connellsville, and 2-WM6, Connellsville to Cumberland.

Car No. 203 to move from Elkins to Cumberland on Train No. 4, arriving Cumberland 5:55 p.m., September 30th.

Friday, October 1st—Car No. 204 will be put on Train WM-2, Cumberland to Hagerstown. Interval at Hagerstown for Mr. and Mrs. Farrington to look at shops. Mr. Abbott will arrange for 1400 class engine by way of the B.&H. Sub-Division, adjusting the tonnage so that it will arrive at Baltimore between 5 and 6 p.m.

Car No. 203—Train No. 2—Cumberland to Baltimore.

1948
September 28th
Western Maryland

Baltimore—Hagerstown
Train #3, Engine #204 4-6-2 type, 4 cars, 2 business
LV Baltimore 8:25 a.m.
Emory Grove 9:14, met #6, water
Falls, met #302
Union Bridge 10:12, water
Keymar 10:19, met #304
Thurmont 10:40, water
Blue Ridge 11:13, top of the hill
ARR Hagerstown 11:50 a.m. OT

Western Maryland No. 206, 4-6-2 type, K-2 class with Train No. 3

Tractive Force	39,736 lbs.
Drivers Diameter	69 in.
Weight on Drivers	160,500 lbs.
Total Weight	254,300 lbs.
Steam Pressure	200 lbs.

The WM K-2 were all oil burners for their last years in service. This photo was taken at Hillen Terminal, Baltimore, Md. March 1948 by Bruce D. Fales.

Western Maryland No. 810, 2-8-0 type, H-9 class

Tractive Force	68,200 lbs.
Drivers Diameter	61 in.
Weight on Drivers	268,200 lbs.
Total Weight	294,900 lbs.
Steam Pressure	210 lbs.
Tender Capacity	15,000 gals.
	16 tons

Photo from H. L. Broadbelt Collection.

1948
September 29th
Western Maryland

Elkins W. Virginia—Thomas
Train Extra 823 East, 80 loads, 5565 tons
Engine 823 2-8-0 type H9
Called 2:30 p.m.
On train 2:50 p.m.
LV Elkins 3:01
ARR Montrose 3:31 p.m.
LV Montrose 3:49, retainers up
Porterwood 4:17, retainers down
Pass Parsons 4:27
ARR Hendricks 4:40, 6 helpers cut in
Hendricks to Thomas 11 miles running time, 1 hour 13 minutes, very wet and slippery rails. Grade averaging 3% for almost 9 miles then 3.57% for 2 miles.
ARR Thomas 6:09 p.m. One helper continues to Fairfax where there is another slight grade east to Summit.
110 lb. rail, amazing move, Western Maryland figures 1 engine for 800 tons. They also have 14 miles of 3% from Laurel Bank to Spruce, also given 6 helpers there.

Western Maryland No. 1201, 4-6-6-4 type, M-2 class

Tractive Force	95,500 lbs.
Drivers Diameter	69 in.
Weight on Drivers	402,266 lbs.
Total Weight	601,000 lbs.
Steam Pressure	250 lbs.
Tender Capacity	22,000 gals.
	30 tons

Photo from H. L. Broadbelt Collection.

1948
September 30th
Western Maryland

Cumberland—Connellsville
Train WM-3, 12 loads, 78 empties, 2429 tons
Engine 1206 helper 1212 4-6-6-4 type, class M-2
LV Cumberland 12:45 p.m.
ARR Deal East End 1:52, cut off helper
ARR Greenwood 3:50
ARR Connellsville 3:56
Easy run—road engine took water at Deal Tower. Only 3 tunnels. Big Savage 3294.6 feet—plenty hot. Wonderful clearances, excellent crew.

Western Maryland No. 1112, 2-10-0 type, I-2 class

Tractive Force	96,300 lbs.
Drivers Diameter	61 in.
Weight on Drivers	386,800 lbs.
Total Weight	419,280 lbs.
Steam Pressure	240 lbs.
Tender Capacity	22,000 gals.
	30 tons

The author made more than a dozen trips on these engines and considers them by far the finest Decapod Type ever built.

Photo from H. L. Broadbelt Collection.

1948
September 30th
Western Maryland

Connellsville—Cumberland

Train 2nd WM-6, 47 loads, 5 empties, 3390 tons

Engine 1119 2-10-0 type, class I2 helper #1114 to Deal

LV Connellsville 5:42 p.m.

ARR Deal 8:10 p.m.

LV Deal 8:45, water

ARR G. C. Jct. 10:10 p.m.

Engine did excellent job—rode beautifully for a Decapod type.

Western Maryland No. 1403, 4-8-4 type, J-1 class

Tractive Force	70,600 lbs.
Drivers Diameter	69 in.
Weight on Drivers	290,000 lbs.
Total Weight	506,500 lbs.
Steam Pressure	255 lbs.
Tender Capacity	22,000 gals.
	30 tons

This photograph was taken at Baldwin Locomotive Works, Eddystone, Pa. From Collection of H. L. Broadbelt.

1948
October 1st
Western Maryland

Cumberland—Hagerstown
Train #WM2, 82 loads, 11 empties, 1 business car on head end, 5410 tons
Engine 1402 4-8-4 type, class J1
LV Knobmount (Cumberland) 9:13 a.m.
ARR Fairplay 10:00, met extra 11:05
ARR Woodmount Club 10:40, stoker failing
LV Woodmount Club 10:57
Hancock 11:20, water
ARR Williamsport 12:15, helper 817 2-8-0 type, class H9
ARR Yard Office Hagerstown 12:46
LV Hagerstown running as extra 1403 1:15 p.m., 25 loads, 2300 tons, 1 b. car
Engine #1403 4-8-4 type, class J1, helper 723 2-8-0 type, class H7a, to Highfield
ARR Highfield 2:03, retainers up
LV Highfield 2:06
ARR Fairfield 2:38, retainers down
LV Fairfield 2:45
LV Millers 4:35, water
ARR Emory Grove 5:21
LV Emory Grove 5:38
ARR Port Covington 7:02 p.m.

Fine run—amazing clearances over entire railroad. Cross Potomac River 6 times—Little Orleans to Potomac River ten miles. Indigo Tunnel 4350 feet, Stick Pile Tunnel 1706.5 feet, Kessler Tunnel 1843.3 feet, Welton Tunnel 783 feet after 7th crossing of Potomac River Mile post 162, 8th crossing Potomac River mile post 163, 9th crossing Potomac River mile post 164, Knobley Tunnell 1448.3 feet.

D.&R.G. No. 3618, 2-8-8-2 type, L-132 class

Tractive Force	131,800 lbs.
Drivers Diameter	63 in.
Weight on Drivers	572,000 lbs.
Total Weight	665,000 lbs.
Steam Pressure	240 lbs.
Tender Capacity	18,000 gals.
	30 tons

1950
January 17th
D. & R. G.

Helper—Geneva

Train Extra 553, 7200 tons, 80 cars, to Soldiers Summit

Engine 553, 4 unit deisel, 6000 horse power, helper 3615 2-8-8-2 type, class L-132

LV Helper 8:00 p.m.

ARR Soldiers Summit 10:47, cut off helper, get 10 cars, retainers up in light position.

LV Summit 11:35, no inspection

Pass Thistle 1:47 a.m.

ARR Geneva 3:50 a.m.

Diesel will turn and immediately take 120 empties east bound with no helper Thistle—Soldier Summit; 29 miles at 2%.

West bound helper Castle Gate; 4 miles 2.90. Castle Gate—Kyune

9 miles 2.4.

This was all 4% in 1912 when I first rode engine up it on Train #1.

Bessemer & Lake Erie No. 647, 2-10-4 type, H-1-G class

Tractive Force	96,700 lbs.
Drivers Diameter	64 in.
Weight on Drivers	371,359 lbs.
Total Weight	523,600 lbs.
Steam Pressure	250 lbs.
Tender Capacity	23,000 gals.
	25 tons

1950
June 22nd
Bessemer & Lake Erie

Albion—Bessemer Yard
Train Extra 625 East
Engine 625 2-10-4 type, II1D Class, helper 647, class H1G

Station	*Time*	*Speed*	*Remarks*
Albion—called	10:00 a.m.		
RX Tower (south end Albion Yard)	10:42	12	
Springboro	10:56	39	
Conneautville	11.02	34	
Dicksonburg	11:11	23	
Harmonsburg	11:24	14	
Meadville Jct.	11:30	30	
Hartstown	11:41	40	
KO Junction Yard	11:55	19	Set off 13 ore. Took wter on both engines. Made walking and running inspection of train.
KX South End (south end KO Jct. Yard)	12:46	12	
Greenville (North Main St.)	12:56	14	
KY	1:16	26	
Fredonia	1:26	36	
Coolspring (Porter Cut-off)	1:30	42	
Filer	1:50	24	
Grove City	1:56	35	Speed limit over crossing.
Reed	1:59	25	
Harrisville	2:09	30	
Branchton Yard	2:14	19	Set off 4 ore. Took coal and water. Made walking and running inspection of train.

B.&L.E. No. 647, 2-10-4 type, H-1-G class. Hauling heavy ore train single up the 1% grade south of Dicksonburg, Pa.

	2:51		
Claytonia	3:02	29	
Euclid	3:12	22	
Queen Jct.	3:15	33	
Butler (yard limits)	3:48	20	Speed limit over crossing
BD Tower	4:03	40	
Houseville	4:25	16	
Curtisville Yard	4:45	15	
SU Tower (south end of yard)	4:48	29	
Deer Creek	4:55	40	
River Valley	4:58	30	Speed limit over Allegheny River Bridge
East Oakmont	5:03	23	
XB Tower (north end Bessemer Yard)	5:10	18	
Tied up	5:41 p.m.		

B.&L.E. No. 613, 2-10-4 type, H-1-D class. Pushing ore train headed southward, of course, near Rural Ridge, Pa.

On duty 7 hours 41 minutes. Running time between terminals 6 hours 59 minutes. It was necessary to yard this train on two tracks: final terminal time 41 minutes. Had train been yarded on one of the long tracks in ore yard, which would have held entire train, final terminal time would have been approximately 18 minutes. The tonnage leaving Albion was 13,025 tons for 109 loads. Tonnage was reduced at two points—KO Junction and Branchton.

Leaving Albion: 109 ore, 12,044 gross tons, 13,025 rating tons.

Set off 13 ore at KO Junction account heavier grade; leaving there with 96 ore, 10,589 gross tons, 11,453 rating tons.

Set off 4 ore at Branchton account heavier grade; leaving there with 92 loads, 10,152 gross tons, 10,980 rating tons.

9 tons resistance used per car.

The capacity of cars was 55 90-ton; 33 70-ton; 21 50-ton—total 109.

There were 9,510 short tons of ore in the 109 cars.

Weather clear, temperature 80 degrees, good rail.

Engineman—H. A. Engle

Conductor—L. W. Van Dusen

B.&L.E. 4-unit diesel No. 703, 5,400 hp. built by Electro-Motive crossing the Allegheny River Bridge at River Valley, Pa. with 110 loads of ore totaling 11,000 tons.

1950
July 22nd
Bessemer & Lake Erie

Albion—Bessemer
Train Extra 701 East, 110 loads, 12,983 tons
Engine—Diesel 701A—701B, 705A, 705B, 5400hp.

Station	*Time*	*Speed*	*Amps*	*Remarks*
RX Tower	3:19 a.m.	11	400	
Springboro	3:37	33	325	
Conneautville	3:42	26	375	
Dicksonburg	3:55	15	560	
Harmsonburg	4:08	12	630	Slowest speed on hill 11 mph; highest amperage 675. No slipping; no sand used.
Meadville Jct.	4:15	25	380	
Hartstown	4:26	37	310	Throttle closed at Patton's Bridge. Dynamic brake applied at Patton's Bridge at 37 mph; released at KO Jct. at 20 mph. Train brakes not used.
KO Jct.	4:36	20	. . .	
KO Jct. Yard	4:39	20	350	
KX South End	4:43	17	520	
Williamsons Rd.	4:48	11	680	
East Ave.	4:55	11	690	Slowest speed on hill 11 mph; highest amperage 690. No slipping; no sand used.
Fredonia Rd.	4:59	11	690	
KY	5:11	20	450	
Fredonia	5:22	28	350	
Coolspring (PCO)	5:27	40	190	
Cornell Viaduct	5:30	32	325	
Kimble Viaduct	5:39	22	425	
Filer	5:51	19	455	
Grove City	5:57	34	300	
Reed	6:00	23	410	Slowest speed on hill 20 mph; highest amperage 450.
Carter	6:08	23	410	
Harrisville	6:12	19	460	Dynamic brake applied at first road crossing south of Harrisville at 23 mph; released just south of Branchton road crossing at 13 mph. Made 6 pound brake pipe reduction at Wick at 31 mph, increased to 11 pounds, graduated off at Branchton station at 16 mph. Moved via northward track Branchton to bridge 1, Butler. Slowest speed on hill 10 mph; highest amperage 725. (Note: This movement was made on a reverse track apparently making no difference as speed was same as though used normal track.) Slipped several times, Sherwin to Euclid; used sand intermittently.
Branchton	6:18	16	. . .	
UN Tower	6:21–6:49			
Hallston	7:06	26	355	
Claytonia	7:09	16	525	
Euclid	7:25	14	525	

B.&L.E. Diesel No. 704 with 11,000 tons of ore passing Rockdale, Pa.

Station	*Time*	*Speed*	*Amps*	*Remarks*
Queen Jct.	7:30 a.m.	30	. . .	Dynamic brake applied 1 mile south of Euclid at 20 mph, released at Calvin Yard 1000-foot board at 12 mph. Made 5-pound brake pipe reduction at Tasa Mine, released at Sunbury undergrade a 6-pound reduction at old
Oneida	7:39	29	. . .	Oneida, followed by a 2-pound
Calvin	7:45	13	150	reduction, released at 16 mph 1/2
Butler	7:56	12	175	mile north of Calvin yard 1000-
Nigger Cut 8 deg.				foot board
curve	8:04	24	390	
BD Tower	8:11	33	315	
Rockdale	8:19	12	630	
West Saxonburg	8:34	10	700	
Houseville	8:45	10	700	Slowest speed on hill 9 mph;
Ivywood	8:51	24	375	highest amperage 750. Dynamic brake applied 1/2 mile south of Ivywood at 28 mph, released 1 mile north of Culmerville at 30 mph.
Culmerville	8:58	27	. . .	Made 5-pound brake pipe reduction at Refractory at 36 mph, released at Red Hot Coal Co. track at 32 mph.

Station	*Time*	*Speed*	*Amps*	*Remarks*
Curtisville	9:04	14	. . .	
SU Tower	9:08	17	. . .	Dynamic brake applied in south end of Culmerville cut at 16 mph, released at Republic Jct. 20 mile slow order Curtisville to south switch of Russellton storage tracks.
Republic Jct.	9:15	24	. . .	
Deer Creek	9:18	36	. . .	Made 5-pound brake pipe reduction 1/2 mile south of Russelton account slow order, releases just north of Republic Jct.
River Valley	9:22	28	375	
East Oakmont	9:27	19	475	
Milltown	9:31	13	580	
XB Tower	9:35	9	750	Slipped several times moving through XB Tower cross-over.

Call Albion 2:30 a.m. tied up North Bessemer 10:10 a.m. On duty 7 hours 40 minutes.

Weather clear 52°, good rail. Conductor reported only one slack action which was when making release of brakes at Branchton station.

North Bessemer yarded train on track 38 East

Engineman—G. W. Burnett operated engine Albion—Branchton and Butler—North Bessemer

Shows what the diesels can do with heavy tonnage

N.Y.C. No. 6000, 4-8-4 type, S-1 class returning empty milk cars to upper New York State, Hudson Div. west of Peekskill.

P.R.R. No. 6464, 2-10-4 type, J1-A class built at Altoona in 1943 shown at Chicago in Nov. 1950.

Tractive Force	95,100 lbs.
Tractive Force Booster	15,000 lbs.
Drivers Diameter	69 in.
Weight on Drivers	379,483 lbs.
Total Weight	575,880 lbs.
Steam Pressure	270 lbs.
Tender Capacity	21,000 gals.
	30 tons

The author feels this was by far the finest engine the Pennsylvania ever owned. They performed magnificently on 8 different trips on which the author rode. Photo from collection of Harold K. Vollrath.

1950
August 2nd
P. R. R.

Columbus—Sandusky

Extra No. 6461 west, Engine No. 646 2-10-4 type, J1A class, 150 loads, 12,900 tons

LV Frog Eye—Columbus 4:50 p.m.

ARR Bucyrus 6:55

Coal and water and running inspection

LV Bucyrus 7:10

ARR Sandusky 9:05

Fine run—All railroad crossings green for us including P. R. R. at Bucyrus, Erie and Big Four at Marion, also Big Four at Chatfield. C. & O. at Atlantic Jct. and the Nickel Plate at Belleview. Weather clear.

Nickel Plate No. 730, 2-8-4 type, S-1 class

Tractive Force	64,100 lbs.
Drivers Diameter	69 in.
Weight on Drivers	258,000 lbs.
Total Weight	421,000 lbs.
Steam Pressure	245 lbs.
Tender Capacity	22,000 gals.
	22 tons

1950
August 3rd
Nickel Plate

Train No. NKP12, 77 cars, 4,820 tons
Engine No. 732 2-8-4 type, S-1 class
LV Belleview 8:20 a.m.
ARR East Cleveland 10:50, water and coal
LV East Cleveland 11:12, picking up 4 cars, now have 4,990 tons
ARR Conneaut 12:57 p.m., water and inspection
LV Conneaut 1:17
ARR Buffalo 4:25, 247.8 miles
Fine run, good crew, typical Nickel Plate fast freight. This engine still one of the best and one of the few steam engines left still able to run in the United States. Weather clear, thunderstorm over the lake in afternoon.

Frisco No. 1069, 4-6-2 type, T-45 class

Tractive Force	40,700 lbs.
Drivers Diameter	73 in.
Weight on Drivers	190,700 lbs.
Total Weight	296,000 lbs.
Steam Pressure	200 lbs.
Tender Capacity	10,000 gals.
	18 tons

1950
November 12th
Frisco

St. Louis—Springfield

Train #37 Frisco Flash, 77 cars, no empties, 3825 tons

Engine 4507 4-8-4 type

LV St. Louis 6:50 p.m.—back of #1

ARR Newburg 10:20 helper 1073 4-6-2 type

LV Newburg 10:25

ARR Dixon 11:20, coal and water, cut off helper

LV Dixon 11:35

ARR Springfield 1:45 a.m.

Grade on Dixon Hill is 1.27 maximum for the 15 miles.

Frisco No. 4503, 4-8-4 type

Tractive Force	69,800 lbs.
Drivers Diameter	74 in.
Weight on Drivers	280,000 lbs.
Total Weight	462,500 lbs.
Steam Pressure	250 lbs.
Tender Capacity	18,000 gals.
	24 tons

1950
November 13th
Frisco

Springfield—St. Louis
Train Texas Special #2, 12 cars
Engine 4501 4-8-4 type—oil burner
LV Springfield 5:30 a.m., 20 minutes late
ARR Newburg 8:15, 10 minutes late, water
LV Newburg 8:25
ARR St. Louis 11:30 a.m., OT

THE VIRGINIAN RAILWAY COMPANY

SCHEDULE FOR SPECIAL PASSENGER TRAIN
NOVEMBER 16th AND 17th, 1950

DAY	DATE	LEAVE	ARRIVE	TIME	RUNNING AND LAYOVER TIME	
			FIRST DAY			
Thursday	November 16	Norfolk		5:31 AM		
			Victoria	8:31 AM	3′ 00″	
		Victoria		8:41 AM	10″	
			Roanoke	11:41 AM	3′ 00″	6′ 10″
		Roanoke		11:51 AM	10″	
			Narrows	1:49 PM	1′ 58″	
		Narrows		2:19 PM	30″	
			Princeton	3:06 PM	47″	
		Princeton		4:01 PM	55″	
			Mullens	5:16 PM	1′ 15″	5′ 35″
						11′ 45″
			SECOND DAY			
Friday	November 17	Mullens		5:05 AM		
			Page	6:48 AM	1′ 43″	TURN
		Page		7:13 AM	25″	ENGINE
			D B Tower	7:43 AM	30″	
		D B Tower		7:43 AM	—	
			Page	8:03 AM	20″	
		Page		8:03 AM	—	
			Elmore	9:43 AM	1′ 40″	
		Elmore		9:43 AM	—	
			Princeton	10:53 AM	1′ 10″	
		Princeton		10:53 AM	—	
			Roanoke	1:38 PM	2′ 45″	8′ 33″
		Roanoke		6:59 PM		
			Victoria	10:14 PM	3′ 15″	
		Victoria		10:24 PM	10″	
			THIRD DAY			
Saturday	November 18		Norfolk	1:24 AM	3′ 00″	6′ 25″
						14′ 58″

NOTE: Elmore to Roanoke Motor Generator Locomotive EL2B—

Friday	November 17	Elmore		10:30 AM		
			Ronaoke	5:30 PM	7′ 00″	Tonnage Train 9000 Tons from Clarks Gap.

Virginian #210, 4-6-2 type, class PA hauling Train #4 at Norfolk, Virginia.

Tractive Force	46,634 lbs.
Drivers Diameter	69 in.
Weight on Drivers	189,000 lbs.
Total Weight	298,000 lbs.
Steam Pressure	200 lbs.
Tender Capacity	10,500 gals.
	14 tons of coal

Photo taken by H. Reid, January 15th, 1956.

Special Train Leaving Norfolk at 5:31 A.M., Thursday, November 16, 1950, enroute to New River Division, arriving Roanoke 11:41 A.M. same date, returning leaving Ronaoke 6:59 P.M., Friday, November 17, 1950, arriving Norfolk 1:24 A.M., Saturday, November 18, 1950.

FIRST SUB-DIVISION

Lv- Norfolk	5:31 A.M.
Tidewater	5:41 A.M.
Carolina	5:45 A.M.
South Branch	5:49 A.M.
Algren	5:59 A.M.
Suffolk	6:10 A.M.
Kenyon	6:16 A.M.
Boaz	6:25 A.M.
Burdette	6:35 A.M.
Morgan	6:45 A.M.
Sebrell	6:55 A.M.
Joyner	7:05 A.M.
Gray	7:13 A.M.
Jarratt	7:22 A.M.
Purdy	7:32 A.M.
Adsit	7:42 A.M.
Dolphin	7:49 A.M.
Alberta	7:58 A.M.
Dundas	8:10 A.M.
Kenbridge	8:20 A.M.
Ar- Victoria	8:31 A.M.

SECOND SUB-DIVISION

Lv- Victoria	8:41 A.M.
Nutbush	8:49 A.M.
Meherrin	8:57 A.M.
Briery	9:05 A.M.
Abilene	9:16 A.M.
Cullen	9:25 A.M.
Phenix	9:34 A.M.
Aspen	9:41 A.M.
Brookneal	9:51 A.M.
Keever	10:10 A.M.
Seneca	10:10 A.M. No. 4
Taber	10:19 A.M.
Mansion	10:27 A.M.
Altavista	10:33 A.M.
Leesville	10:42 A.M.
Huddleston	10:52 A.M.
Stone Mountain	11:02 A.M.
Westgate	11:08 A.M.
Goodview	11:18 A.M.
Hardy	11:26 A.M.
Demuth	11:35 A.M.
Ar- Roanoke	11:41 A.M.

Virginian #508, 2-8-4 type, class BA, with Eastward Time Freight at South Norfolk, Va., December 3rd, 1952, First Sub Div. Norfolk Div. Note the excellent track and Ballast.

Photo by H. Reid.

REVISED SCHEDULE
ELMORE EAST ONLY

THE VIRGINIAN RAILWAY COMPANY

SCHEDULE FOR SPECIAL PASSENGER TRAIN
NEW RIVER DIVISION
FROM ROANOKE, VA. TO DB TOWER, W. VA. AND RETURN
NOVEMBER 16th AND 17th, 1950

FIRST DAY—NOVEMBER 16

Lv.	Roanoke	11:51 AM
	Salem	12:02 PM
	Wabun	12:09 PM
	Kumis	12:17 PM
	Fagg	12:29 PM
	Shelby	12:43 PM
	Whitethorne	12:56 PM
	McCoy	1:06 PM
	Eggleston	1:16 PM
	Pembroke	1:26 PM
	Norcross	1:35 PM
	Celco	1:45 PM
Ar.	Narrows	1:49 PM
Lv.	Narrows	2:19 PM
	Rich Creek	2:27 PM
	Kellysville	2:40 PM
	Ingleside	2:57 PM
Ar.	Princeton	3:06 PM
Lv.	Princeton	4:01 PM
	Kegley	4:08 PM
	King	4:13 PM
	Rock	4:18 PM
	MX Tower	4:25 PM
	Algonquin	4:39 PM
	Herndon	4:52 PM
	Alpoca	5:01 PM
	Elmore	5:06 PM
Ar.	Mullens	5:16 PM

SECOND DAY—NOVEMBER 17

Lv.	Mullens	5:05 AM
	Maben	5:17 AM
	Slab Fork	5:32 AM
	Surveyor	5:43 AM
	Harper	5:52 AM
	Pax	6:10 AM
	Oak Hill Jct	6:27 AM
	Hamilton	6:38 AM
Ar.	Page	6:48 AM
Lv.	Page	7:13 AM
Ar.	DB Tower	7:43 AM
Lv.	DB Tower	7:43 AM
Lv.	Page	8:03 AM
	Hamilton	8:10 AM
	Oak Hill Jct	8:22 AM
	Pax	8:39 AM
	Harper	8:54 AM
	Surveyor	9:04 AM
	Slab Fork	9:15 AM
	Maben	9:26 AM
	Gulf Junction	9:38 AM
Ar.	Elmore	9:42 AM
Lv.	Elmore	10:20 AM
	Alpoca	10:26 AM
	Herndon	10:39 AM
	Algonquin	10:59 AM
	MX Tower	11:11 AM
	Rock	11:17 AM
	King	11:23 AM
	Kegley	11:30 AM
Ar.	Princeton	11:40 AM
Lv.	Princeton	12:59 PM
	Ingleside	1:08 PM
	Kellysville	1:23 PM
	Rich Creek	1:36 PM
	Celco	1:48 PM
	Norcross	1:59 PM
	Pembroke	2:09 PM
	Eggleston	2:18 PM
	McCoy	2:27 PM
	Whitethorne	2:36 PM
	Shelby	2:45 PM
	Fagg	2:59 PM
	Kumis	3:14 PM
	Wabun	3:21 PM
	Salem	3:30 PM
Ar.	Roanoke	3:44 PM

Virginian #211, 4-6-2 type, class PA with train #4 in electrified zone in the New River Palisades, Pembroke, Va. 3rd Sub Div. New River Div.

Photo by H. Reid taken on July 26th, 1949.

Virginian No. 904, 2-6-6-6 type, AG class

Tractive Force	110,200 lbs.
Drivers Diameter	67 in.
Weight on Drivers	495,000 lbs.
Total Weight	753,000 lbs.
Steam Pressure	260 lbs.
Tender Capacity	26,500 lbs.
	25 tons

This engine was rated for 19 degree curves. First Sub Div. Norfolk Div.

Photo taken at Suffolk, Va. April 9, 1949 by H. Reid.

1950
December 5th
Virginian

Sewalls Point—Roanoke
Train Extra 907 West with 0 loads, 163 empties, 4411 tons
Engine 907 2-6-6-6, class AG
LV Sewalls Point 8:30 a.m.
Tidewater 9:00
Carolina 9:19
Suffolk 9:58
Walters 10:23
Sedley 10:37
Sebrell 11:05
Joyner 11:18
Jarratt 11:39
Purdy 11:52
Adsit 12:02 P.M.
Alberta 12:21
Dundas 12:36
Kenbridge 12:45
ARR Victoria 1:05
LV Victoria 2:50 P.M.
Engine 902 with no loads, 163 mtys, 4411 tons, class AG
Meherrin 3:31
Abilene 3:53
Cullen 4:04
Phenix 4:14
Brookneal 4:35
Seneca 5:26–5:40—coal and water
Altavista 6:15
ARR Roanoke 8:10
Easy run, engine never really extended.

Special Train Leaving Norfolk at 5:31 A.M., Thursday, November 16, 1950, enroute to New River Division, arriving Roanoke 11:41 A.M. same date, returning leaving Roanoke 6:59 P.M., Friday, November 17, 1950, arriving Norfolk 1:24 A.M., Saturday, November 18, 1950.

SECOND SUB-DIVISION

Lv- Ronaoke	6:59 P.M.
Demuth	7:07 P.M.
Hardy	7:15 P.M.
Goodview	7:25 P.M.
Westgate	7:33 P.M.
Stone Mountain	7:39 P.M.
Huddleston	7:49 P.M.
Leesville	7:59 P.M.
Altavista	8:10 P.M.
Mansion	8:16 P.M.
Taber	8:26 P.M.
Seneca	8:38 P.M.
Keever	8:46 P.M.
Brookneal	8:56 P.M.
Aspen	9:07 P.M.
Phenix	9:15 P.M.
Cullen	9:25 P.M.
Abilene	9:36 P.M.
Briery	9:46 P.M.
Meherrin	9:55 P.M.
Nutbush	10:05 P.M.
Ar- Victoria	10:14 P.M.

FIRST SUB-DIVISION

Lv Victoria	10:24 P.M.
Kenbridge	10:34 P.M.
Dundas	10:44 P.M.
Alberta	10:55 P.M.
Dolphin	11:04 P.M.
Adsit	11:11 P.M.
Purdy	11:20 P.M.
Jarratt	11:30 P.M.
Gray	11:40 P.M.
Joyner	11:47 P.M.
Sebrell	11:57 P.M.
Morgan	12:08 A.M.
Burdette	12:16 A.M.
Boaz	12:26 A.M.
Kenyon	12:35 A.M.
Suffolk	12:41 A.M.
Algren	12:53 A.M.
South Branch	1:05 A.M.
Carolina	1:11 A.M.
Tidewater	1:16 A.M.
Ar- Norfolk	1:24 A.M.

Virginian No. 737, 2-8-8-2 type, US-E class

Tractive Force	114,154 lbs.
Drivers Diameter	57 in.
Weight on Drivers	491,000 lbs.
Total Weight	547,700 lbs.
Steam Pressure	270 lbs.
Tender Capacity	16,000 gals.
	23 tons

This engine was one of the N&W Y-3a's sold to the Sante Fe, their #1797, where they served their mileage on Raton Pass as Santa Fe's 1790 class through the war. They were then sold back to the Virginian where they rendered more good service.

1950
December 8th
Virginian

Dickinson—Sewalls Point
Train—Time Freight #72, Symbol Z, 42 loads, 34 mtys, 2918 tons
Engine 724 2-8-8-2 type, class USB

LV { Dickinson NYC	5:10 a.m.
{ DB Tower	5:55–6:02 a.m.
Cut in pusher engine	714 2-8-8-2 type, class USA
Page	6:27–7:10—coal and water and set off 18 mtys
Hamilton	7:19
Oak Hill Jct.	7:42
Pax	8:01
Harper	8:27
Surveyor	8:38
Slab Fork	8:57
Maben	9:12
Gulf Jct.	9:38
ARR Elmore	9:50

Opposite page:

Virginian No. 506, 2-8-4 type, BA class

Tractive Force	69,350 lbs.
Drivers Diameter	69 in.
Weight on Drivers	295,600 lbs.
Total Weight	460,400 lbs.
Steam Pressure	245 lbs.
Tender Capacity	25,000 gals.
	21 tons

This engine is almost a duplicate of the C&O class K 4.
First Sub Div. Norfolk Div.
Photo was taken at Algren, Va. in 1947 by H. Reid.

LV Elmore	12:10 P.M.—Engine 127 (electric), class EL2B with 47 loads 0 myts 2609 tons
Herndon	12:41
Clarks Gap	—with 89 loads 0 mtys 6,431 tons
Matoaka	1:42–1:52—Met train No. 71
Princeton	2:32
Rich Creek	3:12
Pembroke	3:44
Whitethorne	4:12
Merrimac	4:32
Ellett	4:45
ARR Roanoke	5:35
LV Roanoke	8:15 P.M.—Engine 505 2-8-4 type, class BA with 43 loads, 3 mtys, 2065 tons
Altavista	9:37–9:46—Del. 4 loads Southern Ry.
ARR Victoria	11:40 with 39 loads, 3 mtys, 1875 tons
LV Victoria	12:20 A.M.—Engine 509 2-8-4 type, class BA with 38 loads, 3 mtys, 1825 tons
Alberta	12:50–1:45—Del. 11 loads SAL pick up 2 loads
Jarratt	2:15–2:56—Del. 6 loads, 1 mty ACL. Set off 3 loads
Suffolk	
Carolina	4:53
Tidewater	4:56–5:16—Set off 5 loads to Fords
ARR Sewalls Pt.	5:35 A.M. with 15 loads, 2 mtys, 784 tons

Virginian No. 128, 2B—B+B—B, EL-2B class

Tractive Force starting	260,000 lbs.
Tractive Effort continuous at 15.75 mph	162,000 lbs.
Drivers Diameter	42
Weight in Working Order total two units	1,033,832 lbs.
Capacity-Continuous at	15.75 mph 6,800 hp at rail
Maximum Speed	50 mph
Trolley Voltage	11,000

Eastward at Covel. West Virginia with 81 cars and 6,000 tons. The Grade is 2.7. 3rd Sub Div. New River Div.

1950
December 10th
Virginian

Roanoke—Sewalls Point
Train Extra 903 East, 145 loads, 13,511 tons
Engine 903 2-6-6-6 type, class AG
LV Roanoke 5:30 A.M.
Altavista 7:33–8:10
Seneca 8:37–9:12—coal and water
Brookneal 9:41
Phenix 10:11
Cullen 10:28
Abilene 10:40
Meherrin 11:14
ARR Victoria 11:14
LV Victoria 2:27 P.M. Engine 906,
145 loads, 14,574 tons, class AG
Kenbridge 2:48
Dundas 2:03
Alberta 3:19
Adsit 3:44
Purdy 3:57
Jarratt 4:09
Joyner 4:31
Sebrell 4:43
Sedley 5:32
Suffolk 6:51
Carolina 7:42
Tidewater 7:48
ARR Sewalls Pt. 8:25

VIRGINIAN'S COAL MOVE

A Day's Report to President and Chairman

GORN Norfolk, Va Nov. 17,
George D. Brooke, Chairman of Board
Frank D. Beale, President, on Special Q

Dumped 113 cars, 10 large, 6049. Total 205690. Expect to dump 25000. N&W dumped nothing. Total 116 946. C&O 132 cars, 7777. Total 258236. Coal on hand 2618 cars, 536 large, 157700. N&W 751 cars, 44927, C&O 3140 cars, 157000. Grand total, on hand 6509 cars, 359967. Ordered 1295 cars, actually loaded 1115, billed 1064 cars including 35 Old Ben, 1029 others, Sewalls 365 including 51 large, East 188, N&W 199, C&O 143, NYC 124, Co 10. No bills 160 increased 60. Ordering 967 cars, 95 large, 773 hoppers, will be ok on cars. Delivered NYC 61 coal, 25 others, received 2 inland coal, 65 others. Delivered C&O Deepwater 3 coal, 13 others, received 19 others. Delivered C&O Gilbert 93, N&W 119. 11 Tide, 4 inland, NF&G 1 Sou, no SAL, 16 ACL. Everything in good shape. Weather 62 and cloudy.

WDB 910am

Virginian #903, 2-6-6-6 type, class AG with coal train passing South Norfolk, Va. first Sub Div. Norfolk Div.

Photo taken by H. Reid on December 23rd, 1951.

Section Two

WESTERN MARYLAND RAILWAY COMPANY

Report of Dynamometer Car Tests
with
Resulting Tonnage Ratings
on the

H9a 2-8-0 type J1 4-8-4 type 12 2-10-0 type
and
M2 4-6-6-4 type with Graphs, Charts and Nine Photographs

Connellsville Sub-Division
West Sub-Division
Lurgan Sub-Division
May 26, 1947 to July 15, 1957

Office of Superintendent Motive Power,
Hagerstown, Md.,
August 1, 1947.

Foreword

The primary object of these tests was to obtain authentic information concerning the characteristics of the H9-a, I2, M2 and J1 class locomotives, particularly from the standpoint of operating efficiency and obtain any other information of practical or technical importance.

Test Personnel

S.M.Roth	Supervisor Locomotive Performance, W.M.Ry.Co. - In charge of tests
H.J.Koch,Jr.	Assistant Mechanical Engineer, W.M.Ry.Co.
L.N.Schoppert	Mechanical Draftsman, W.M.Ry.Co.
G.B.Ecker	Hulson Company Service Engineer - Draft instruments
G.W.Padgett	Baltimore & Ohio Dynamometer Car Operator
C.E.Heilig	Baldwin Locomotive Works Mechanical Engineer
H.L.Odgers	Baldwin Locomotive Works Mechanical Engineer

Selection of Territory for the Tests

The physical characteristics of the road from Bowest Junction to Deal on the Connellsville Sub-Division present the most favorable conditions for the development of locomotive efficiency. For this reason the principal tests were conducted between the points above referred to, the results of which are shown in Table Nos. 1 to 8 inclusive and Chart Nos. 1 and 2. On Page No. 6 chief results of the tests are summarized.

Tests were conducted between Hagerstown and Cumberland when going to and coming from the Elkins Division. Due to the irregularities encountered on the Hagerstown Division, test data obtained could not be consistently used for comparison in general, however, desirable information was obtained, particularly between Hancock and Big Pool where permissible speeds could be attained to develop higher drawbar horsepower, especially on the J1 and M2 class locomotives, which require higher speeds to develop the maximum drawbar horsepower. Chart No. 2 shows the maximum drawbar horsepower developed.

A special test was conducted from Cumberland to Rutherford, Pa., using Engine 1410 to get authentic information on the operating characteristics of the J1 class locomotives operating in through service on coal trains between the above mentioned points. Table No. 11 shows the results of this test and Table No. 12 shows the results of test from Rutherford, Pa. to Hagerstown.

Duration of Tests

Tests were started May 26, 1947 and completed July 15, 1947. They were conducted on the Elkins Division between Cumberland and Bowest or Dickerson Run, Pa., and Hagerstown Division between Hagerstown and Cumberland, including one test from Cumberland to Rutherford, Pa., and return to Hagerstown.

Condition of the Locomotives

The four classes of locomotives tested were given classified repairs (except the J1 class, new locomotive) and were in good condition in every respect.

Comparison of Test Data between Locomotives Classes

The test data accepted for comparison between locomotive classes was in close agreement in every respect.

Method of Conducting Tests

The method used with respect to obtaining and calculating test data is in accordance with A.S.M.E. recommended practice. The coal used for tests between Bowest Junction and Deal was supplied from Consolidation Coal Company and of the same quality and weighed on the tender by scale measurement in pounds.

The amount of water used from tender was determined by one inch scale measurements of depth of tank, calibrated in gallons. The same procedure was followed with respect to coal and water measurement during all tests. The quality of the coal, however, was irregular, except as previously stated, between Bowest Junction and Deal.

Due to variable conditions on Connellsville Sub-Division during westward trips, test data could not be consistently used for comparison, however, information of practical importance was obtained, particularly drawbar pull when starting maximum tonnage trains and operating at slow speeds on the heavy grade from G.C. Junction to Colmar.

General Test Analysis

Table Nos. 1 to 4 inclusive show the results that can be expected on the four classes of locomotives when they are operated at or near maximum capacity for periods of long duration. It is of course understood that where the road profile is undulating, the firing and water evaporation rates are reduced and evaporation per pound of coal is increased, which favorably affects the economy of locomotive operation. The difference in efficiency of locomotive operation between the four classes of locomotives tested from Bowest Junction to Deal, as shown in Table Nos. 1 to 4 inclusive, is reflected under operating conditions more favorable for economic locomotive operation.

The actual overall results during the tests from Bowest or Dickerson Run to Cumberland are shown in Table Nos. 5 to 8 inclusive. It is interesting to note that the difference of percentages of coal used and pounds coal per thousand gross ton miles between the class locomotives on which comparisons were made are in most every instance in close agreement with that shown during the efficiency test period from Bowest Junction to Deal.

Referring to Item 7 of Table Nos. 9 and 10, it will be observed that the average back pressure of the J1 class is slightly higher than on the other classes tested, during the test period, between Bowest Junction and Deal. It will be noted in Items 4 and 9 of Table Nos. 9 and 10 that the average speed is considerably higher, and the average steam pressure drop from boiler to steam chest is decidedly lower on the J1 class locomotive. With an average pressure drop from boiler to steam chest of only eight pounds, a relatively higher average sustained steam chest pressure at cylinders is attained on the J1 over the H9-a, I2 and M2 class locomotives. The high average steam chest pressure of 247 pounds, along with higher average speed on the J1 class over the other classes of locomotives tested accounts for the slight increase in back pressure. The tests revealed that the Class J1 locomotive, under all operating conditions, working from minimum to maximum cut-off at speeds up to

50 M.P.H., developed back pressures ranging from 4 pounds to 19 pounds respectively. With this locomotive working at maximum capacity at 50 M.P.H., the back pressure was 10 pounds.

Based on the rated tractive effort of the four classes of locomotives tested, Chart No. 1 shows that when the train speed is more than 5 to 7 M.P.H., the J1 class is superior with respect to drawbar pull in relation to speed, which is largely due to the high steam chest pressure attained in relation to boiler pressure on the J1 class locomotive under all operating conditions.

Operating Characteristics

Connellsville Sub-Division

J1 versus H9-a Class Locomotives

It will be observed from Table Nos. 1 and 2 where the operating conditions were comparable during the tests, Bowest Junction to Deal, that the J1 class shows definite and notable superiority over the H9-a class locomotive in every respect, except drawbar pull at speeds below 5 M.P.H., as shown on Chart No. 1. The rated tractive effort of the H9-a class is 900 pounds more than the J1 class, and the difference in the actual calculated tractive effort of the two locomotives was 1488 pounds in favor of the H9-a class during the tests, due to the latter having undersize driving tires.

The tests definitely show that both locomotives have the same hauling capacity up to 5 M.P.H., after which the J1 class shows improvement in drawbar pull and drawbar horsepower, and this feature progressively increases with the increase of train speed. Due to the possibility of stopping heavy tonnage trains on ruling grades, the maximum tonnage rating for ruling grades for the J1 class should not exceed the tonnage rating for the H9-a class locomotives on the Connellsville Sub-Division.

I2 versus M2 Class Locomotives

Referring to Table Nos. 3 and 4, it will be noted that the operating efficiency of the two locomotives for the most part is in close agreement, but favorable in some respects to the M2 class locomotive, particularly with respect to drawbar pull and drawbar horsepower above 20 M.P.H. There is 800 pounds difference in the rated tractive effort favorable to the I2 class, but the difference of actual calculated tractive effort between the two locomotives during the tests was inconsequential, as shown on Table No. 10.

The tests show that the drawbar pull is slightly greater up to 20 M.P.H. on the I2 class locomotive. At train speeds more than 20 M.P.H. the drawbar pull and drawbar horsepower is greater on the M2 class locomotive, and this feature progressively increases with the increase of train speed.

The tests developed that the present tonnage rating for Classes I2, M2 and H9-a is correct for economical operation on the Connellsville Sub-Division, and that the tonnage rating for the J1 class should be the same as the H9-a class locomotives. On heavy grade territory the cost of operation is ordinarily less when operating the larger locomotives having the greater tractive effort. However, the tests show in Table Nos. 5 to 8 inclusive on the Connellsville Sub-Division that the J1 class is comparable to the I2 and M2 class locomotives from the standpoint of cost per thousand gross ton miles, and of course, less maintenance and more availability.

Between Hagerstown and Cumberland

J1 versus H9-a Class Locomotives

The tests show that the present maximum tonnage rating for H9-a is approximately correct for the J1 class, except from Hagerstown to Cumberland the tonnage rating can be consistently increased over the H9-a class, which is due to the road profile westward and the operating characteristics of the J1 class locomotive.

I2 versus M2 class Locomotives

The operating characteristics of the I2 and M2 class locomotives between Hagerstown and Cumberland are comparable to the Connellsville Sub-Division.

The difference between the four classes tested from the standpoint of economical operation can be based proportionately on the results obtained, as shown in Table Nos. 1 to 8 inclusive, regardless of the territory over which they are operated.

Cumberland to Rutherford

J1 Class Locomotive

As previously stated, one test was conducted from Cumberland to Rutherford, Pa., to obtain detailed information concerning the performance of this class locomotive operating in through service with heavy tonnage coal trains between the above mentioned points. The results of this test are disclosed in Table No. 11, and as a matter of pertinent information Table No. 12 shows the results of the eastward trip, Rutherford to Hagerstown.

Significance of Charts

Chart No. 1 shows the drawbar pull in relation to train speeds up to 50 M.P.H. on J1 and M2 class, and up to 40 M.P.H. on H9-a and I2 class locomotives.

Chart No. 2 shows the drawbar horsepower in relation to train speeds up to 50 M.P.H. on J1 and M2 class, and up to 40 M.P.H. on H9-a and I2 class locomotives.

The information shown on Chart Nos. 1 and 2 is the result of Dynamometer car tests for the duration of the tests under all operating conditions.

Referring to Chart No. 1, it is interesting to note the points where the drawbar pull curve of the J1 class crosses the curves of the H9-a and I2 classes, i.e., at 5 and 28 M.P.H. respectively, also the point where the curves intersect on the I2 and M2 class locomotives.

It will be observed on Chart No. 2 the drawbar horsepower in relation to speed corresponds with the drawbar pull at the various speeds shown on Chart No. 1, and the curves intersect at the same points.

The improvements of the J1 and M2 class locomotives over class H9-a and I2 with respect to drawbar pull and drawbar horsepower, as shown in Table Nos. 1 and 2, is a matter of no small importance and should not be overlooked.

The information revealed by Chart Nos. 1 and 2 is substantiated by Table Nos. 1 to 4 inclusive, particularly Items 7 which show an increase in average speed of 21.9% to 40.0% on J1 class over H9-a class, and 13.1% to 16.6% on M2 class over I2 class locomotives. The four classes of locomotives were operated at or near maximum capacity for the duration of the test period from Bowest Junction to Deal under comparable operating conditions.

Summary of Tests

Improvements in favor of J1 Class versus H9-a Class Locomotives

This data is the result of tests from Bowest Junction to Deal, coal trains and fast freight trains, with locomotives working at or near maximum capacity under comparable operating conditions, except Items 13 and 14, which are the results of entire test or trip.

1. Actual running time reduced 17.8 to 28.6%
2. Average speed increased 21.9 to 28.6%
3. Average drawbar pull increased 7.4 to 16.1%
4. Average drawbar horsepower increased 27.9 to 30.0%
5. Maximum drawbar horsepower increased 33.6 to 44.1%
6. Water used from tender decreased 3.1 to 7.0%
7. Water per drawbar horsepower hour from tender, 25.5 to 27.3% less
8. Coal saving 18.0 to 23.6%
9. Coal used per square foot grate area per hour, 24.8 to 29.8% less
10. Coal per drawbar horsepower hour - lbs. decrease 35.8 to 41.3%
11. Coal per M.G.T.M., decrease 19.2 to 23.7%
12. Evaporation per pound of coal, increase 13.45 to 26.75%
13. Coal saving including terminal use 18.2 to 19.8%
14. Cost per M.G.T.M. - duration of trip - decrease 13.0 to 13.4%

I2 Class versus M2 Class Locomotives

This data is the result of tests from Bowest Junction to Deal, coal trains and fast freight trains, with locomotives working at or near maximum capacity under comparable operating conditions, except Items 13 and 14, which are the results of entire test or trip.

1. Actual running time, decrease in favor of M2 class 11.5 to 14.3%
2. Average speed, increase in favor of M2 class 13.1 to 16.6%
3. Average drawbar pull, increase in favor of M2 class 1.5 to 5.0%
4. Average drawbar horsepower, increase in favor of M2 class 15.1 to 16.1%
5. Maximum drawbar horsepower, increase in favor of M2 class 10.8 to 16.1%
6. Water used from tender, decrease in favor of I2 class on coal trains 6.4%
   Water used from tender, decrease in favor of M2 class on fast freight trains .3%

7. Water per drawbar horsepower hour from tender - lbs. decrease in favor of M2 class 7.7 to 16.2%
8. Coal saving in favor of I2 class on coal trains 2.5%
   Coal saving in favor of M2 class on fast freight trains 7.5%
9. Coal used per square foot grate area per hour - lbs. decrease in favor of I2 on coal trains 2.0%
   Coal used per square foot grate area per hour - lbs. decrease in favor of M2 on fast freight trains 5.1%
10. Coal per drawbar horsepower hour - lbs. decrease in favor of M2 10.9 to 20.3%
11. Coal per M.G.T.M., decrease in favor of I2 class on coal trains .7%
    Coal per M.G.T.M., decrease in favor of M2 class on fast freight trains 8.3%
12. Evaporation per pound of coal, increase in favor of M2 class 3.8 to 7.9%
13. Coal saving including terminal use in favor of I2 class on coal trains 3.67%
    Coal saving including terminal use in favor of M2 class on fast freight trains 4.3%
14. Cost per M.G.T.M. - duration of trip - same on coal trains
    Cost per M.G.T.M. - duration of trip - decrease favorable to M2 class on fast freight trains 2.9%

Conclusion

The overall operating characteristics in favor of J1 class locomotive versus Classes H9-a, I2 and M2 as revealed by the tests are as follows:

1. Flexibility of locomotive account of its adaptability for all classes of service.

2. Availability for service.

3. Practicability of operating in through service without terminal attention at intermediate points. This was previously demonstrated during a test run of locomotive No. 1401 which was operated in through service from Bowest, Pa. to Rutherford, Pa. and return to Hagerstown, a distance of 333 miles, without cleaning the fire or dumping the ash pan. This locomotive could have been run on to Cumberland without cleaning fire or dumping the ashes, making a total of 412 miles.

4. Based on the rated tractive effort of the four classes of locomotives tested, ability to handle same tonnage and maintain higher sustained speeds under comparable operating conditions. More rapid acceleration with rated tonnages.

5. Operating efficiency and fuel economy.

Table No. 1

Test of J1 Class versus H9-a Class Locomotives
Coal Trains Bowest Junction to Deal - 63 Miles

	Locomotive No. 1410	Locomotive No. 847	Difference	Difference Percent
1. Test No.	3	14	---	---
2. Weather condition	Clear	Clear	---	---
3. Duration of test - hrs. mins.	2 - 48	3 - 15	27	13.8
4. Number of stops and mins.	2 - 20	1 - 15	---	---
5. Running time - hrs. mins.	2 - 28	3 - 0	32	17.8
6. Working distance - miles	63	63	---	---
7. Average speed - M.P.H.	25.6	21.0	4.6	21.9
8. Maximum speed - M.P.H.	40	37	3	8.1
9. Number of cars - loads, empties	40 - 0	40 - 0	---	---
10. Tonnage	3097	3059	38	1.2
11. Gross ton miles	195111	192717	2394	1.2
12. Average drawbar pull	48137	41457	6680	16.1
13. Average drawbar horsepower	3250	2540	710	27.9
14. Drawbar horsepower hours - equated	7995	6248	1747	28.0
15. Maximum drawbar horsepower	3900	2920	980	33.6
16. Water used from tender - gals.	17648	18981	1333	7.0
17. Water used including condensed exhaust steam - gals.	19413	20879	1466	7.0
18. Water per hour from tender - gals.	7174	6327	847	13.4
19. Water per hour from tender and condensed exhaust steam - gals.	7891	6960	931	13.4
20. Water used from tender and condensed exhaust steam - lbs.	161775	173992	12217	7.0
21. Water per drawbar horsepower hour from tender - lbs.	18.4	25.3	6.9	27.3
22. Water per drawbar horsepower hour from tender and condensed exhaust steam - lbs.	20.2	27.8	7.6	27.3
23. Water per thousand ton miles - gals.	99.5	108.3	8.8	8.1
24. Coal used - lbs.	24600	30000	5400	18.0
25. Coal used - tons	12.3	15.0	2.7	18.0
26. Coal used per hour - lbs.	10000	10000	---	---
27. Coal used per hour - tons	5.0	5.0	---	---
28. Coal used per square foot grate area per hour - lbs.	93.7	133.5	39.8	29.8
29. Coal per drawbar horsepower hour - lbs.	3.08	4.80	1.72	35.8
30. Coal per thousand gross ton miles - lbs.	126	156	30	19.2
31. Evaporation per pound of coal including condensed exhaust steam - lbs.	6.58	5.80	.78	13.45

Table No. 2

Test of J1 Class versus H9-a Class Locomotives
Fast Freight Trains Bowest Junction to Deal - 63 Miles

	Locomotive No. 1410	Locomotive No. 847	Difference	Difference Percent
1. Test No.	5	16	---	---
2. Weather condition	Clear	Rain	---	---
3. Duration of test - hrs. mins.	2 - 49	3 - 38	49	22.5
4. Number of stops and mins.	2 - 34	2 - 29	---	---
5. Running time - hrs. mins.	2 - 15	3 - 9	54	28.6
6. Working distance - miles	63	63	---	---
7. Average speed - M.P.H.	28.0	20.0	8	40.0
8. Maximum speed - M.P.H.	40	36	4	11.1
9. Number of cars - loads, empties	46 - 2	51 - 2	---	---
10. Tonnage	2887	2873	14	.5
11. Gross ton miles	181881	180999	882	.5
12. Average drawbar pull	45283	42152	3131	7.4
13. Average drawbar horsepower	3290	2530	760	30.0
14. Drawbar horsepower hours - equated	7403	5693	1710	30.0
15. Maximum drawbar horsepower	3920	2720	1200	44.1
16. Water used from tender - gals.	17989	18570	581	3.1
17. Water used including condensed exhaust steam - gals.	19788	20427	639	3.1
18. Water per hour from tender - gals.	7995	5895	2100	35.8
19. Water per hour from tender and condensed exhaust steam - gals.	8795	6485	2310	35.8
20. Water used from tender and condensed exhaust steam - lbs.	164900	170225	5325	3.1
21. Water per drawbar horsepower hour from tender - lbs.	20.25	27.18	6.93	25.5
22. Water per drawbar horsepower hour from tender and condensed exhaust steam - lbs.	22.27	29.90	7.63	25.5
23. Water per thousand ton miles - gals.	108.8	112.9	4.1	3.6
24. Coal used - lbs.	24000	31400	7400	23.6
25. Coal used - tons	12.0	15.7	3.7	23.6
26. Coal used per hour - lbs.	10666	9968	698	7.0
27. Coal used per hour - tons	5.3	5.0	.3	7.0
28. Coal used per square foot grate area per hour - lbs.	100.0	133.1	33.1	24.8
29. Coal per drawbar horsepower hour - lbs.	3.24	5.52	2.28	41.3
30. Coal per thousand gross ton miles - lbs.	132	173	41	23.7
31. Evaporation per pound of coal including condensed exhaust steam - lbs.	6.87	5.42	1.45	26.75

Table No. 3

Test of I2 Class versus M2 Class Locomotives
Coal Trains Bowest Junction to Deal - 63 Miles

	Locomotive No. 1111	Locomotive No. 1205	Difference	Difference Percent
1. Test No.	20	26	---	---
2. Weather condition	Clear	Clear	---	---
3. Duration of test - hrs. mins.	3 - 0	2 - 45	15	8.3
4. Number of stops and mins.	1 - 15	1 - 19	---	---
5. Running time - hrs. mins.	2 - 45	2 - 26	19	11.5
6. Working distance - miles	63	63	---	---
7. Average speed - M.P.H.	22.9	25.9	3.0	13.1
8. Maximum speed - M.P.H.	35	39	4	11.4
9. Number of cars - loads, empties	50 - 0	55 - 0	---	---
10. Tonnage	3997	4024	27	.7
11. Gross ton miles	251811	253512	1701	.7
12. Average drawbar pull	53143	55785	2642	5.0
13. Average drawbar horsepower	3520	4050	530	15.1
14. Drawbar horsepower hours - equated	8553	9842	1289	15.1
15. Maximum drawbar horsepower	3970	4400	430	10.8
16. Water used from tender - gals.	23775	25297	1522	6.4
17. Water used including condensed exhaust steam - gals.	26153	27827	1674	6.4
18. Water per hour from tender - gals.	8645	10410	1765	20.4
19. Water per hour from tender and condensed exhaust steam - gals.	9510	11451	1941	20.4
20. Water used from tender and condensed exhaust steam - lbs.	217938	231889	13950	6.4
21. Water per drawbar horsepower hour from tender - lbs.	23.2	21.4	1.8	7.7
22. Water per drawbar horsepower hour from tender and condensed exhaust steam - lbs.	25.5	23.6	1.9	7.5
23. Water per thousand ton miles - gals.	103.9	109.8	5.9	5.7
24. Coal used - lbs.	36000	36900	900	2.5
25. Coal used - tons	18.00	18.45	.45	2.5
26. Coal used per hour - lbs.	13091	15185	2094	16.0
27. Coal used per hour - tons	6.55	7.59	1.04	16.0
28. Coal used per square foot grate area per hour - lbs.	125.3	127.8	2.5	2.0
29. Coal per drawbar horsepower hour - lbs.	4.21	3.75	.46	10.9
30. Coal per thousand gross ton miles - lbs.	143	144	1	.7
31. Evaporation per pound of coal including condensed exhaust steam - lbs.	6.05	6.28	.23	3.8

Table No. 4

Test of I2 Class versus M2 Class Locomotives
Fast Freight Trains Bowest Junction to Deal - 63 Miles

	Locomotive No. 1111	Locomotive No. 1205	Difference	Difference Percent
1. Test No.	22	28	---	---
2. Weather condition	Rain	Clear	---	---
3. Duration of test - hrs. mins.	3 - 7	2 - 55	12	6.4
4. Number of stops and mins.	1 - 26	3 - 37	---	---
5. Running time - hrs. mins.	2 - 41	2 - 18	23	14.3
6. Working distance - miles	63	63	---	---
7. Average speed - M.P.H.	23.5	27.4	3.9	16.6
8. Maximum speed - M.P.H.	37	40	3	8.1
9. Number of cars - loads, empties	66 - 2	54 - 2	---	---
10. Tonnage	3795	3833	38	1.0
11. Gross ton miles	239085	241479	2394	1.0
12. Average drawbar pull	53164	53965	801	1.5
13. Average drawbar horsepower	3530	4100	570	16.1
14. Drawbar horsepower hours - equated	8119	9430	1311	16.1
15. Maximum drawbar horsepower	3715	4650	935	25.2
16. Water used from tender - gals.	23890	23826	64	.3
17. Water used including condensed exhaust steam - gals.	26279	26208	71	.3
18. Water per hour from tender - gals.	8914	10359	1445	16.2
19. Water per hour from tender and condensed exhaust steam - gals.	9806	11395	1589	16.2
20. Water used from tender and condensed exhaust steam - lbs.	218992	218400	592	.3
21. Water per drawbar horsepower hour from tender - lbs.	24.52	21.05	3.47	14.2
22. Water per drawbar horsepower hour from tender and condensed exhaust steam - lbs.	26.97	23.16	3.81	14.1
23. Water per thousand ton miles - gals.	109.9	108.5	1.4	1.3
24. Coal used - lbs.	37600	34800	2800	7.5
25. Coal used - tons	18.8	17.4	1.4	7.5
26. Coal used per hour - lbs.	14029	15130	1101	7.9
27. Coal used per hour - tons	7.01	7.57	.56	7.9
28. Coal used per square foot grate area per hour - lbs.	134.2	127.3	6.9	5.1
29. Coal per drawbar horsepower hour - lbs.	4.63	3.69	.94	20.3
30. Coal per thousand gross ton miles - lbs.	157	144	13	8.3
31. Evaporation per pound of coal including condensed exhaust steam - lbs.	5.82	6.28	.46	7.90

Table No. 5

Test of J1 Class versus H9-a Class Locomotives
Coal Trains Bowest to Cumberland (Knobmount Yard) - 90 Miles

	Locomotive No. 1410	Locomotive No. 847	Difference	Difference Percent
1. Test No.	3	14	---	---
2. Duration of trip - hrs. mins.	4 - 42	5 - 24	42	12.9
3. Total delays (including terminals) - hrs. mins.	0 - 49	1 - 2	13	21.0
4. Running time actual - hrs. mins.	3 - 53	4 - 22	29	11.0
5. Average speed - M.P.H.	23.17	20.61	2.56	12.9
6. Number of cars - loads, empties	40 - 0	40 - 0	---	---
7. Tonnage	3097	3059	38	1.2
8. Gross ton miles	278700	275300	3400	1.2
9. Water used from tender including condensed exhaust steam - gals.	21965	22696	731	3.2
10. Coal used (including terminals) - tons	14.4	17.6	3.2	18.2
11. Coal per thousand gross ton miles - lbs.	103	128	25	19.5
12. Cost per thousand gross ton miles	.267	.307	.040	13.0

Table No. 6

Test of J1 Class versus H9-a Class Locomotives
Fast Freight Trains Dickerson Run to Cumberland (Knobmount Yard) - 96 Miles

	Locomotive No. 1410	Locomotive No. 847	Difference	Difference Percent
1. Test No.	5	16	---	---
2. Duration of trip - hrs. mins.	5 - 33	5 - 33	---	---
3. Total delays (including terminals) - hrs. mins.	1 - 25	0 - 39	46	1.2
4. Running time actual - hrs. mins.	4 - 8	4 - 54	46	15.6
5. Average speed - M.P.H.	23.22	19.59	3.63	18.5
6. Number of cars - loads, empties	46 - 2	51 - 2	5	---
7. Tonnage	2887	2873	14	.5
8. Gross ton miles	282900	281600	1300	.5
9. Water used from tender including condensed exhaust steam - gals.	23505	23972	467	1.9
10. Coal used (including terminals) - tons	14.6	18.2	3.6	19.8
11. Coal per thousand gross ton miles - lbs.	103	129	26	20.1
12. Cost per thousand gross ton miles	.258	.298	.040	13.4

Table No. 7

Test of I2 Class versus M2 Class Locomotives
Coal Trains Bowest to Cumberland (Knobmount Yard) - 90 Miles

	Locomotive No. 1111	Locomotive No. 1205	Difference	Difference Percent
1. Test No.	20	26	---	---
2. Duration of trip - hrs. mins.	5 - 15	4 - 32	43	13.5
3. Total delays (including terminals)- hrs. mins.	1 - 5	0 - 44	21	32.30
4. Running time actual - hrs. mins.	4 - 10	3 - 48	22	8.8
5. Average speed - M.P.H.	21.60	23.64	2.04	9.4
6. Number of cars - loads, empties	50 - 0	55 - 0	5	---
7. Tonnage	3997	4024	27	.67
8. Gross ton miles	359700	362200	2500	.69
9. Water used from tender including condensed exhaust steam - gals.	28268	30716	2442	8.6
10. Coal used (including terminals) - tons	21.8	21.0	.8	3.67
11. Coal per thousand gross ton miles - lbs.	121	116	5	4.21
12. Cost per thousand gross ton miles	.267	.267	---	---

Table No. 8

Test of I2 Class versus M2 Class Locomotives
Fast Freight Trains Dickerson Run to Cumberland (Knobmount Yard) - 96 Miles

	Locomotive No. 1111	Locomotive No. 1205	Difference	Difference Percent
1. Test No.	22	28	---	---
2. Duration of trip - hrs. mins.	5 - 10	5 - 7	3	.97
3. Total delays (including terminals) - hrs. mins.	0 - 45	1 - 8	23	51.0
4. Running time actual - hrs. mins.	4 - 25	3 - 59	26	9.8
5. Average speed - M.P.H.	21.75	24.50	2.75	12.6
6. Number of cars - loads, empties	66 - 2	54 - 2	12	---
7. Tonnage	3795	3833	38	1.00
8. Gross ton miles	371900	375600	3700	.99
9. Water used from tender including condensed exhaust steam - gals.	30374	31197	823	2.7
10. Coal used (including terminals) - tons	23.0	22.0	1.0	4.3
11. Coal per thousand gross ton miles - lbs.	124	117	7	5.6
12. Cost per thousand gross ton miles	.268	.260	.008	2.9

Table No. 9

Test of J1 Class versus H9-a Class Locomotives
Data Obtained Bowest Jct. to Deal on Fast Freight Trains - 63 Miles

	Average			
	Locomotive No. 1410	Locomotive No. 847	Difference	Difference Percent
1. Test No.	5	16	---	---
2. Throttle position	F	F	---	---
3. Cut-off percent	57.5	55.0	2.5	4.5
4. Speed - M.P.H.	28.0	20.0	8.0	40.0
5. Boiler pressure - lbs.	255.0	220.0	35.0	15.9
6. Steam chest pressure - lbs.	247.0	204.6	42.4	21.2
7. Exhaust or back pressure - lbs.	18.0	17.3	.7	4.0
8. Pressure drop through superheater - lbs.	6.3	7.4	1.1	14.8
9. Pressure drop, boiler to steam chest - lbs.	8.0	15.4	7.4	48.0
10. Superheat temperature - degrees F.	721	705	16	2.3
11. Water delivery temperature to boiler - degrees F.	241	237	4	1.7
12. Front end draft arrester drum	15.8	15.6	.2	1.3
13. Front end draft back of arrester drum	11.3	11.6	.3	2.6
14. Firebox draft	1.88	2.05	.17	8.3
15. Ash pan draft	.22	.19	.03	---
16. Smoke reading No.	Clear	2	---	---
17. Nozzle opening actual - square inches	40.38	34.02	6.3	18.5
18. Boiler H.P.	5260	3450	1810	52.4
19. Rated tractive effort - lbs.	70600	71500	900	1.2
20. Actual tractive effort - lbs.	70600	72088	1488	2.0
21. Boiler working pressure - lbs.	255	220	---	---
22. Cylinders - dia. x stroke	26½x32	27x32	---	---
23. Drivers - dia. - inches	69	60½	---	---

Table No. 10

Test of I2 Class versus M2 Class Locomotives
Data Obtained Bowest Jct. to Deal on Fast Freight Trains - 63 Miles

	Average				
	Locomotive No. 1111	Locomotive No. 1205		Difference	Difference Percent
		No. 1 E	No. 2 E		
1. Test No.	22	28		---	---
2. Throttle position	F	F		---	---
3. Cut-off percent	66	60		6	9.0
4. Speed - M.P.H.	23.5	27.4		3.9	16.5
5. Boiler pressure - lbs.	240	250		10	4.1
6. Steam chest pressure - lbs.	222.4	216.0	219.0	3.4	1.5
7. Exhaust or back pressure - lbs.	16.2	15.3	16.8	.6	3.7
8. Pressure drop through superheater - lbs.	9.9	27.8		18.0	1.8
9. Pressure drop, boiler to steam chest - lbs.	17.6	34.0	31.0	13.4	76.0
10. Superheat temperature - degrees F.	690	645		45	6.5
11. Water delivery temperature to boiler - degrees F.	235	235		---	---
12. Front end draft - arrester drum	14.2	18.0		3.8	26.8
13. Front end draft - back of drum	8.7	12.9		4.2	48.2
14. Firebox draft	1.84	2.14		.30	16.3
15. Ash pan draft	.188	.081		.107	56.9
16. Smoke reading No.	2	1		---	---
17. Nozzle opening actual - square inches	45.72	29.40	29.40	16.32	35.6
18. Boiler H.P.	4680	6156		1476	31.5
19. Rated tractive effort - lbs.	96300	95500		800	.8
20. Actual tractive effort - lbs.	96711	96542		169	.2
21. Boiler working pressure - lbs.	240	250		---	---
22. Cylinders - dia. x stroke	30x32	22-1/8x32		---	---
23. Drivers - dia. - inches	60-3/4	69		---	---

Table No. 11

Test of J1 Class Locomotive with Coal Train
from Cumberland, Md. to Rutherford, Pa. - 160 Miles

	Locomotive No. 1410
Cumberland to Hagerstown	
1. Test No.	8
2. Weather condition	Clear
3. On duty - hrs. mins.	5 - 14
4. Road delays - hrs. mins.	0 - 54
5. Terminal time Cumberland - hrs. mins.	0 - 28
*6. Terminal time Hagerstown - hrs. mins.	0 - 48
7. Running time - hrs. mins.	3 - 4
8. Average speed - M.P.H.	25.1
9. Number of cars - loads, empties	102 - 0
10. Tonnage	7975
11. Water used from tender - gals.	16499
12. Coal used on test - tons (excluding terminals)	10.95
13. Kind of coal	Slack Gas
14. Gross ton miles	631700
15. Coal per thousand gross ton miles - lbs.	60
16. Cost per thousand gross ton miles	.163
* Changing crews, taking water and air test	
Hagerstown to Rutherford	
1. On duty - hrs. mins.	4 - 6
2. Road delays - hrs. mins.	0 - 5
3. Terminal time Rutherford - hrs. mins.	1 - 11
4. Running time NC Tower to Lurgan - hrs. mins.	1 - 12
5. Average speed - M.P.H.	27.5
6. Running time NC Tower to Rutherford - hrs. mins.	2 - 45
7. Average speed - M.P.H.	29.8
8. Number of cars - loads, empties	100 - 0
9. Tonnage	7825
10. Water used from tender - gals.	11371
11. Coal used Hagerstown to Lurgan - tons	4.35
12. Coal used Lurgan to Leesburg - tons	1.0
13. Coal used Hagerstown to Rutherford (excluding terminals) - tons	7.8
14. Kind of coal	Good quality gas
15. Gross ton miles	643400
16. Coal per thousand gross ton miles - lbs.	61
17. Cost per thousand gross ton miles	.165
Cumberland to Rutherford	
1. On duty - hrs. mins.	9 - 20
2. Road delays - hrs. mins.	0 - 59
3. Terminal time - hrs. mins.	2 - 27
4. Running time - hrs. mins.	5 - 54
5. Average speed - M.P.H.	27.1
6. Train in transit - hrs. mins.	7 - 41
7. Water used from tender - gals.	28400
8. Coal used (including terminals) - tons	21.2
9. Gross ton miles	1275100
10. Coal per thousand gross ton miles - lbs.	61
11. Cost per thousand gross ton miles	.164
Two helpers used Williamsport to Hagerstown	
One H9 class helper used Hagerstown to Leesburg	

Table No. 12

Test of J1 Class Locomotive
from Rutherford, Pa. to Hagerstown, Md. - 82 Miles

	Locomotive No. 1410
1. Test No.	9
2. Weather condition	Clear
3. On duty - hrs. mins.	5 - 15
4. Road delays - hrs. mins.	0 - 45
5. Terminal time Rutherford - hrs. mins.	1 - 5
6. Terminal time Hagerstown - hrs. mins.	0 - 23
7. Running time - hrs. mins.	3 - 2
8. Average speed - M.P.H.	27.03
9. Number of cars - loads, empties	42 - 6
10. Tonnage	2222
11. Water used from tender - gals.	13153
12. Coal used on test - tons (excluding terminals)	8.8
13. Coal used - tons (including terminals)	11.0
14. Kind of coal	R. M. Gas Inferior quality
15. Gross ton miles	183900
16. Coal per thousand gross ton miles - lbs.	120
17. Cost per thousand gross ton miles	.336

Cumberland, Md. to Rutherford, Pa.
and return to Hagerstown, Md. - 242 Miles

	Locomotive No. 1410
1. Total gross ton miles	1459000
2. Total coal used - tons	32.2
3. Total pounds of coal per thousand gross ton miles	68
4. Total cost per thousand gross ton miles	.186

Tonnage Ratings of Classes H9, H9-a, J1, I2 and M2 Locomotives
Based on Dynamometer Car Tests

Lurgan Sub-Division

Westward		Eastward	
Class Engine	Lurgan to Hagerstown	Hagerstown to Lurgan	
		Drag	Fast Frt.
J1	2250	3800 * 8000	3600

West Sub-Division

Westward		Eastward			
Class Engine	Hagerstown to Cumberland	Cumb. to Williamsport			Williamsport to Hagerstown
		Drag	Fast Frt.	WM-4	
H9,H9-a	3600	8000	3600	2200	2500
J1	4000	8000	5500	3600	2500
I2	4800	10500	7500	5000	3400
M2	4800	10500	7500	5000	3400

Connellsville Sub-Division

Westward		Eastward	
Class Engine	Cumberland to Deal	Bowest to Deal	
		Drag	Fast Frt.
H9,H9-a	1100	3100	2500
J1	1100	3100	2800
I2	1600	4000	3700
M2	1600	4000	3700

* H9 or J1 Class Helper

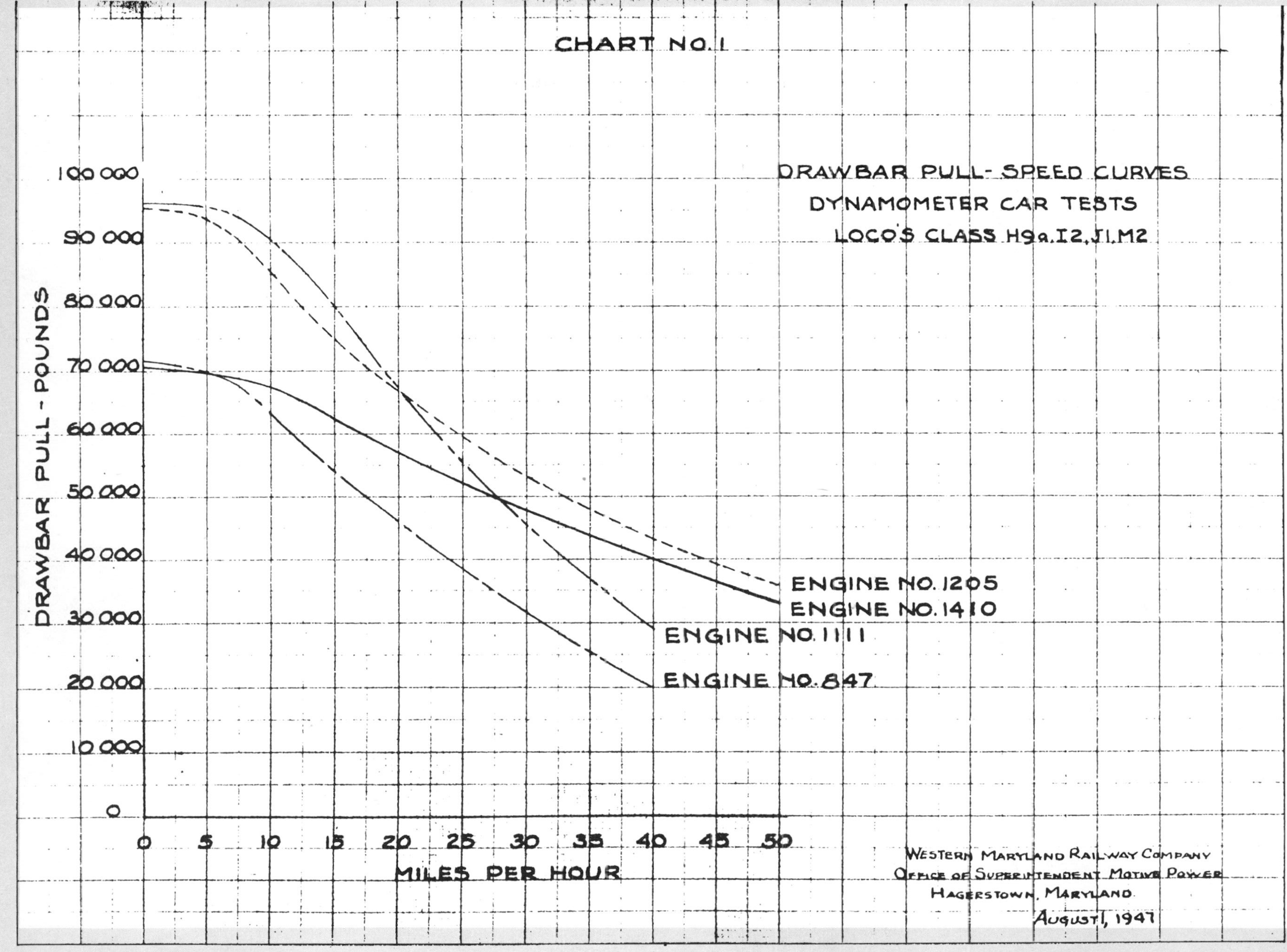
CHART NO. 1
DRAWBAR PULL-SPEED CURVES
DYNAMOMETER CAR TESTS
LOCO'S CLASS H9a. I2. J1. M2
DRAWBAR PULL - POUNDS
100 000
90 000
80 000
70 000
60 000
50 000
40 000
30 000
20 000
10 000
0
0
5
10
15
20
25
30
35
40
45
50
MILES PER HOUR
ENGINE NO. 1205
ENGINE NO. 1410
ENGINE NO. 1111
ENGINE NO. 847
WESTERN MARYLAND RAILWAY COMPANY
OFFICE OF SUPERINTENDENT MOTIVE POWER
HAGERSTOWN, MARYLAND
AUGUST 1, 1947

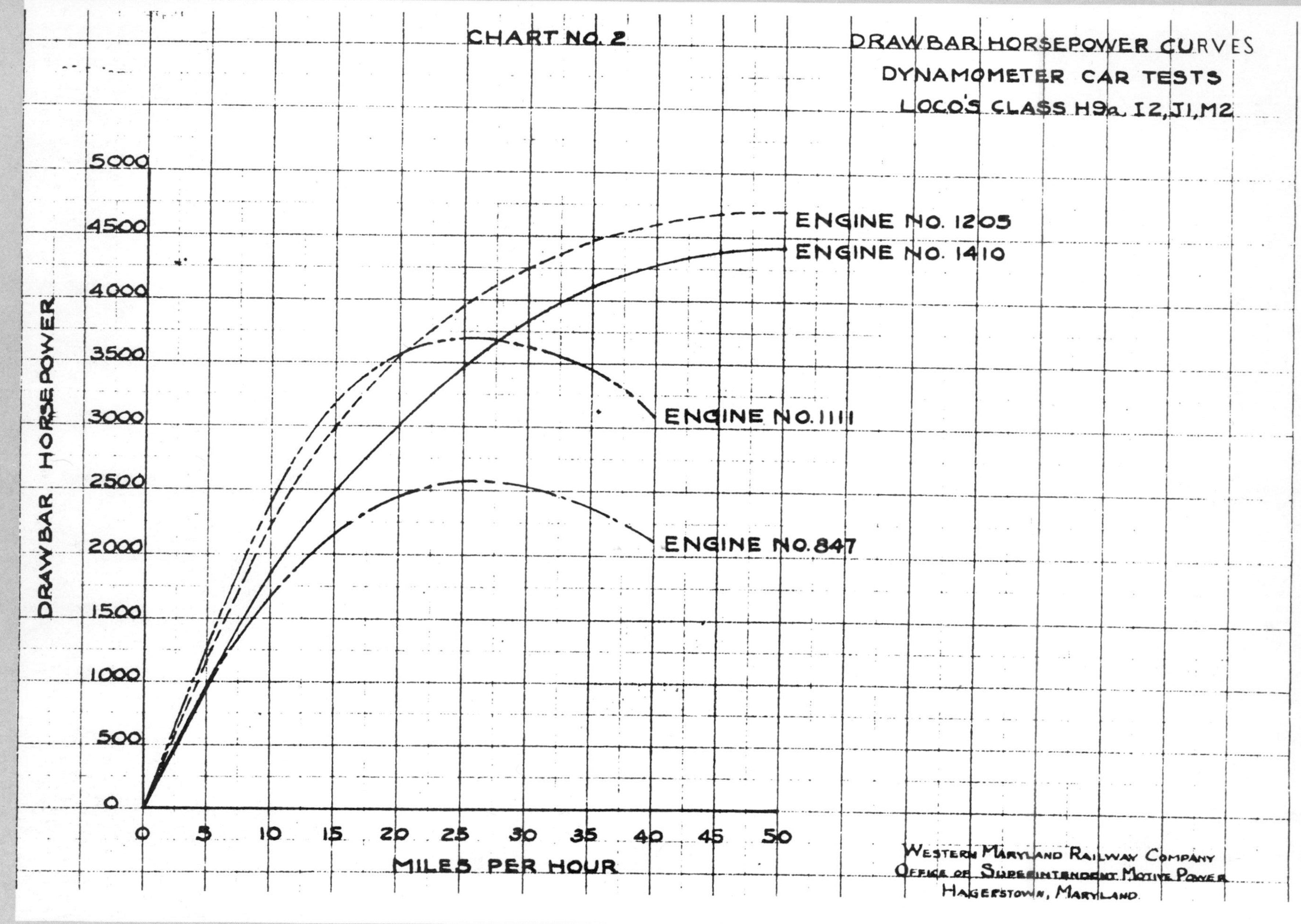
CHART NO. 2
DRAWBAR HORSEPOWER CURVES
DYNAMOMETER CAR TESTS
LOCO'S CLASS H9a I2, J1, M2
DRAWBAR HORSEPOWER
5000
4500
4000
3500
3000
2500
2000
1500
1000
500
0
0
5
10
15
20
25
30
35
40
45
50
MILES PER HOUR
ENGINE NO. 1205
ENGINE NO. 1410
ENGINE NO. 1111
ENGINE NO. 847
WESTERN MARYLAND RAILWAY COMPANY
OFFICE OF SUPERINTENDENT MOTIVE POWER
HAGERSTOWN, MARYLAND

ENGINE RATINGS
ELKINS DIVISION

(Effective August 9, 1948)

Office of Superintendent Transportation, Hagerstown, Md.

FOURTH DISTRICT - EAST Dickerson - Run Bowest to Cumberland	Class	Single	Double	Class of Helper
Fast Freight:	750	1200		
	770	1400		
	800 - 1400	2500	5000	800
			6200	1111
	1111 - 1200	3700	6200	800
			7400	1111
	900	3800		
WM-4	800 - 1400	2250		
	1111 - 1200	2250		
Drags	750	1400		
	770	1800		
	800 - 1400	3000	6000	800
			7200	1111
	1111 - 1200	4200	7200	800
			8400	1111
	900	4400		
Locals	700 - 750	1000		
	770	1300		
	800	2400		
	1111	3000		
	900	3500		
Gray	700	1050		
	750	1200	2600	750
	770	1600	3400	770
	800	2850	4050	750
			4450	770
			5700	800
	900	3750		
FOURTH DISTRICT - WEST (Cumberland to Bowest - Dickerson Run)				
Fast Freight	750	600		
	770	700		
	800 - 1400	1000	1700	750
			2000	800
			2600	1111
	1111 - 1200	1600	2600	800
			3200	1111
For 900 Helper add 1800 Tons				
Drags	700 - 750	700		
	770	800		
	800 - 1400	1100	2200	800
			2800	1111
	1111 - 1200	1700	2800	800
			3400	1111
For 900 Helper add 1900 tons				
Locals	700 - 750	500		
	770	600		
	800	750		
	1111	1400		
	900	1800		
Gray	700 - 750	700		
	770	800		
	800	1100	1800 2200	750 800
	900	1900		

FIFTH DISTRICT - EAST Elkins to Cumberland	Class	Single	Double	Class of Helper
Through	1101	850		Increase according to class for each engine up Haddix.
	750	950		
	770	1150		
	800	1350		
Local Diesel	180	950		
	750	950		
	770	950		
Thomas to Cumberland	1101	1200		
	750	1400	2800	750
			3000	770
			3700	800
	770	1600	3000	750
			3200	770
			3900	800
	800	2300	3700	750
			3900	770
			4600	800
Locals-Thomas to Cumberland	1101	1200		
	750	1400		
	770	1600		
	800	2300		
W. Va. Central Jct. - East	750	8000		
Diesel	140	3400		
Out of Fairfax	750	1300		
Durbin Branch - East	750	1150		
	770	1440		
	1101	1100		
Elk River Branch-Bergoo to Spruce	700	450		Increase for each engine up Laurel Bank.
	750	600		
	770	750		
Elk River Branch-Spruce to Elkins	700	1200		Increase for each engine from Bowden.
	750	1300		
	770	1450		
	1101	1100		
Elk River Branch-Bergoo to Byers				
	770	2000		

FIFTH DISTRICT - WEST Cumberland to Elkins		Class	Single	Double	Class of Helper
Through	Diesel	102 - 103	550		
	"	105 - 107	700		
		450	735		
		1101	1400		
		750	1600	3200	750
				3400	770
				4100	800
		770	1800	3400	750
				3600	770
				4300	800
		800	2500	4100	750
				4300	770
				5000	800
		900	2000		
Locals	Diesel	102 - 103	550		
	"	105 - 107 - 140	700		
	"	180	1600		
		1101	1400		
		750	1600		
		770	(If 770 Class Engine used on Local, use same rating as 750 Class, as this class of engine used to get power to and from shop)		
		800	2500		
Shaw Traveling Switcher		450	650		
		1101	1000		
Westernport: (Georges Creek)					
		1101	750		
Westernport - Harrison					
		1101	1000		
Thomas to Elkins		1101	750		Increase according to Class for each engine up Haddix.
		750	850		
		770	1000		
		800	1250		
Locals					
		750	850		
Durbin Branch - West		500	500		
		700	600		
		750	700		
		770	750		
		1101	650		
Huttonsville Branch					
		351	340		
Belington Branch		351	1600		
		700	2150		
		750	2250		
		770	2900		
		1101	2300		
Elkins to Spruce	Diesel	142	900		
		770	750		
Yard Engines-Thomas to Davis					
		770	800		
Spruce - L. Bank					
		770	720		
Bergoo - Webster Spring		770	1000		
W. Va. Central Jct. West		750	900		
		800	1200		

SIXTH DISTRICT - EAST Chiefton to Bowest	Class	Single	Double	Class of Helper
	700	1200	2760	1-B&O 6100
	750	1300	2860	1-B&O 6100
	770	1440	3000	1-B&O 6100
	800	1680	2540	1-B&O 4700 or 4800
			3240	1-B&O 6100 or 6200
			3640	1-B&O 7100
			3140	1-B&O 7500
	900	2900	3760	1-B&O 4700 or 4800
			4460	1-B&O 6100 or 6200
			4860	1-B&O 7100
			4360	1-B&O 7500
	B&O 2800	560		
	" 4400	1060		
	B&O 4700-4800	860		
	B&O 6100-6200	1560		
	B&O 7100	1960		
	B&O 7500	1460		
SIXTH DISTRICT - WEST **Bowest to Chiefton**	700	800		
	750	900		
	770	1000		
	800	1260	2600	800 out of Bowest
	900	1890		
Switcher				
	700	800		
	750	900		
	770	900		

August 11, 1948

RATING OF W. M. RY. ENGINES FOR EFFECT ON BRIDGES

ACTUAL RATING	CLASS	ENGINE NUMBERS	TYPE	SYMBOL	WHEEL ARRANGEMENT	WEIGHT (IN POUNDS) ON			WEIGHT OF ENGINE WITHOUT TENDER	TRACTIVE POWER	MAXIMUM CURVE	MAXIMUM CLEARANCE			
						PILOTS	DRIVERS	TRAILERS				CYLINDER	RUN. BD.	CAB	HEIGHT
		SHAY No. 4							156,500*	28800	100 Ft.		8'-6"		13'-1"
		SHAY No. 5							302,400*	52200	150 Ft.		10'-0"		14'-2¾"
220	K-2	201-209	PACIFIC	4-6-2	<ooOOOo	43,900	160500	49900	254,300	39736	22°	10'-5"	10'-5"	10'-2"	15'-3"
120	H3-c	348	CONSOL	2-8-0	<oOOOO	11,500	118100		129,600	27126	22°	9'-4½"	9'-10"		14'-0¾"
150	H3-f	351	"	2-8-0	<oOOOO	15,000	125,000		140,000	34110	22°	9'-2¼"	9'-7"		15'-4½"
160	H4-a	416	"	2-8-0	<oOOOO	17,400	141,600		159,000	37026	22°	9'-6"	9'-10"		14'-8½"
190	H4-b	451,454-458	"	2-8-0	<oOOOO	16,300	157,600		173,900	43773	22°	9'-5½"	10'-3"		14'-11"
200	H5	506, 509	"	2-8-0	<oOOOO	19200	163,500		182,700	45173	22°	9'-5½"	10'-3"	10'-2¾"	14'-5½"
210	H6	615-616	"	2-8-0	<oOOOO	18000	182,000		200,000	43305	22°	9'-8"	10'-2"	9'-11"	14'-7"
210	H6-a	626	"	2-8-0	<oOOOO	18,000	182,000		200,000	43305	22°	9'-8"	10'-2"		14'-7"
200	H5-a	513,518	"	2-8-0	<oOOOO	19200	163500		182,700	45173	22°	9'-5½"	10'-3"	10'-2¾"	14'-5½"
240	H7-a	707-736	"	2-8-0	<oOOOO	26,000	215,000		241,000	48960	22°	10'-10½"	10'-3"	10'-2"	15'-2⅞"
240	H7-b	750-764	"	2-8-0	<oOOOO	27,000	216,000		243,000	53125	22°	10'-3"	10'-3"	10'-2"	15'-3"
240	H8	770-789	"	2-8-0	<oOOOO	27,000	217500		244500	61298	22°	10'-3"	10'-3"	10'-2"	14'-11⅞"
300	H9	801-840	"	2-8-0	<oOOOO	22,000	287,910		309910	71500	22°	11'-1"	11'-0		15'-10"
300	H9-a	841-850	"	2-8-0	<oOOOO	22,000	287,910		309910	71500	22°	11'-1"	11'-0"		15'-10"
290	L1	901-904 908-910	MALLET	2-8-8-2	<oOOOO OOOOo	24,000	451800	30700	506500	C-105600 S-126700	22°	11'-4"	11'-4"	11'-4"	15'-11½"
290	L1-a	911, 913-915	"	2-8-8-2	<oOOOO OOOOo	23600	455600	23900	503100	C-105600 S-126700	22°	11'-4"	11'-4"	11'-4"	15'-11½"
290	L2	916, 917, 919-921, 923-925	"	2-8-8-2	<oOOOO OOOOo	23400	459900	21600	504900	C-105600 S-126700	22°	11'-3½"	11'-4"	11'-4"	15'-11½"
280	M1	951-952	"	0-6-6-0	˩ OOO OOO		350000		350,000	74124	22°	10'-6½"	10'-6"		15'-9½"
280	M1-a	953-959	"	0-6-6-0	˩ OOO OOO		351700		351700	74124	22°	10'-6½"	10'-5½"	10'-1"	15'-10½"
200	B2	1003, 1004	6-WHEEL SW.	0-6-0	˩ OOO		140000		140000	36309	22°	9'-6½"	10'-1"		14'-1⅛"
200	B2-a	1006, 1008	"	0-6-0	˩ OOO		142300		142300	36309	22°	9'-6½"	10'-1"		14'-1⅛"
230	B3	1009-1013	"	0-6-0	˩ OOO		164700		164700	41160	22°	10'-4¾"	10'-5½"		15'-4¾"
250	C1	1051-1052	8-WHEEL SW.	0-8-0	˩ OOOO		210700		210700	55900	22°	10'-0½"	10'-2"		15'-1½"
260	C1-a	1053	"	0-8-0	˩ OOOO		221000		221000	65200	22°	10'-0½"	10'-2"		15'-1½"
250	C2	1062, 1066-1067	"	0-8-0	˩ OOOO		200000		200,000	43305	22°	9'-8"	10'-2"		15'-1½"
210	I1	1101-1110	DECAPOD	2-10-0	<oOOOOO	23800	195200		219000	51500	16°	10'-3"	10'-3"		15'-11⅝"
360	I2	1111-1130	"	2-10-0	<oOOOOO	32480	386800		419280	96300	16°	11'-2"	11'-0"	11'-0"	16'-2"
360	M2	1201-1212	MALLET	4-6-6-4	<ooOOO OOOoo	81500	402266	117234	601000	95500	16°	10'-10"	11'-0"	11'-0"	16'-2"
250	C2-a	1073	8-WHEEL SW.	0-8-0	˩ OOOO		200000		200000	43305	22°	9'-8"	10'-2"		15'-1½"
80	DS6	75, 76	DIESEL	0-4-4-0	OO OO		88000		88000	22000				10'-1"	13'-2⅜"
160	DS1-DS2	101, 102	DIESEL	0-4-4-0	OO OO		198000		198000	59400	50 Ft.			10'-2"	14'-4⅜"
160	DS3	103-105	DIESEL	0-4-4-0	OO OO		196000		196000	58800	75 Ft.			10'-2"	14'-0"
180	DS4	125-127	DIESEL	0-4-4-0	OO OO		230000		230000	69000				10'-1"	14'-8"
180	DS5	128-132	DIESEL	0-4-4-0	OO OO		240000		240000	72090				10'-2"	14'-0"
	J-1	*1401*		*4-8-4*	*Loo oooo oo*	*117700*	*290267*	*98533*	*506500*						

* With Tender

Opposite page:

Western Maryland Engine Terminal at Hagerstown, Md. Engine No. 920 at left is 2-8-8-2 type, L-2 class.

Tractive Force	126,700 lbs.
Drivers Diameter	52 in.
Weight on Drivers	459,900 lbs.
Total Weight	504,900 lbs.
Steam Pressure	220 lbs.
Tender Capacity	15,000 gals.
	16 tons

Note B&O Engine in round house with Vanderbilts Tender.

Western Maryland No. 1205, 4-6-6-4 type, M-2 class hauling W.M. 2 out of Brush Tunnel Mile Post 172 at AU crossover. The tunnel is 914 ft. long and is 7 miles west of Cumberland on the Elkins Div. and 3 miles east of the Lap Crossover. The grade is 1.75% and the engine is on a 6 degree curve.

Western Maryland No. 850, 2-8-0 type, H-9a class duplicate of Engine 847 used in test.

Tractive Force	68,200 lbs.
Drivers Diameter	61 in.
Weight on Drivers	268,000 lbs.
Total Weight	296,000 lbs.
Steam Pressure	210 lbs.
Tender Capacity	15,000 gals.
	20½ tons

Photo from H. L. Broadbelt collection.

Western Maryland No. 1125, 2-10-0 type, I-2 class with WM-1 at Big Pool Junction, Md. where the Western Maryland connects with B&O's Cumberland Div. The train was running 40 mph with 68 cars in November 1947. This is a duplicate of Engine No. 1111 used in the test.

Photo by Bruce D. Fales.

Western Maryland No. 1404, 4-8-4 type, J-1 class being washed at the Hagerstown, Md. Engine Terminal.

N.Y.C. Dynamometer Car X8006.

Interior of Dynamometer Car belonging to N.Y.C. built in 1923 at the West Albany Shops. It weighs 62 tons, it is 52 ft. long and is 8 ft. 8 in. wide. Graphs show drawbar pull, steam indicator cards, position of reverse lever and throttle, brake cylinder and air pressure.

N.Y.C. No. 3016, 4-8-2 type, L-3a class ready to leave Harmon, N.Y. with test train. Note the test equipment for protecting test engineers on the pilot and running board of the locomotive.

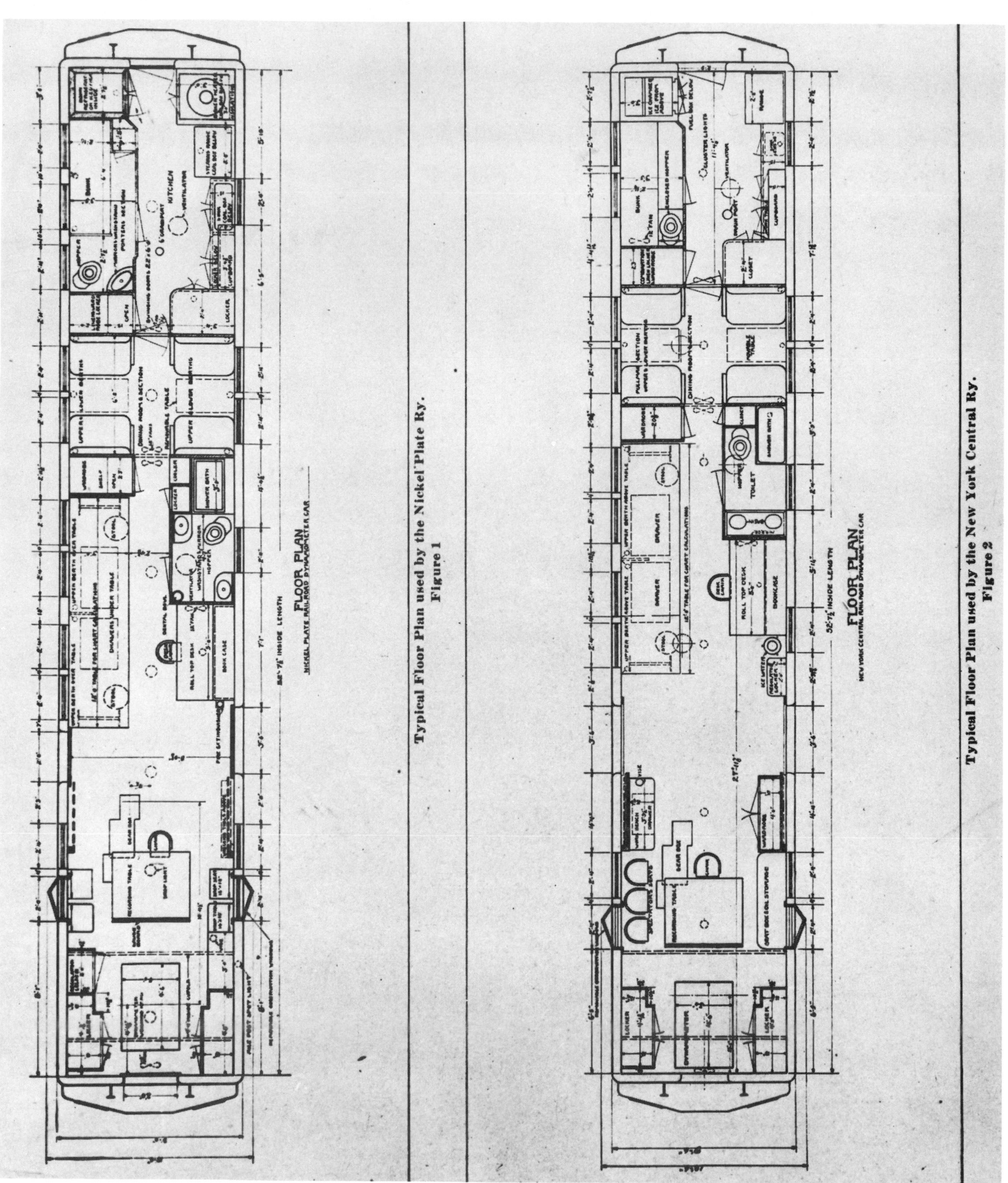

Floor plans of Nickel Plate (upper) and N.Y.C. Dynamometer Cars.

Section Three

PASSENGER TRAIN REPORT

Mileage—U. S. Railroads and Trains Ridden, with Marvelous "On Time Performance"

Second Only to the Railroads Service given the Country's Shippers with the "Ahead of" and "On Time" Performance of Todays Fast Freight Trains October 5, 1962—November 20, 1963

Grand Total of Railroad Mileage 71,055.5 (Not including Long Island Railroad from East Hampton to New York—round trips 205.2 miles)

115 Train Movements

Airlines only flown to get home on occasional Friday nights.

Only three late arrivals, one voluntary, on all roads. All connections made. Some only 20 minutes.

All tickets and Pullman reservations handled and sold through Rail Credit Card by

Frank Hrehocik, Manager of Ticket Sales & Services
Pennsylvania Railroad, New York, New York

with no double sales, no errors and 100% service at window 10, Pennsylvania Station, New York City. All first class transportation.

Grand total of railroad mileage 51,899.2 (Not including Long Island Railroad from East Hampton to New York—round trips 205.2 miles Pennsylvania Railroad—New York—Philadelphia round trips—181 miles and New York—Harrisburg round trips 389.2 Miles)

81 TRAIN MOVEMENTS

Only seven late arrivals on all roads. All connections made. All luncheon, dinner dates and business appointments kept promptly on time.

DATE	FROM	TO	R.R.	TRAIN	NO.	MILES	
1962							
Oct. 5	New York	Pittsburg	P.R.R.	Pittsburger	61	439.	O.T.
6	Pittsburg	Youngstown	P & L E	———	269	64.2	O.T.
7	Youngstown	Pittsburg	P & L E	———	264	64.2	O.T.
7	Pittsburg	Brownsville, Pa.	P & L E	Hy Rail Insp. Car	Extra	54.9	——
7	Connelsville, Pa.	Pittsburg	P & L E	Hy Rail Insp. Car	Extra	54.9	——
7	Pittsburg	New York	P.R.R.	Pittsburger	60	439.3	O.T.
14	New York	Chicago	P.R.R.	Broadway Ltd.	29	907.7	O.T.
14	Chicago	New York	N.Y.C.	20th Century	26	960.7	O.T.
24	New York	Chicago	P.R.R.	Broadway Ltd.	29	907.7	O.T.
24	Chicago	Pampa, Tex.	Santa Fe	San Francisco Chief	1	968.50	O.T.
25	Amarillo	Kansas City	Santa Fe	San Francisco Chief	2	558.3	O.T.
26	Topeka	Chicago	Santa Fe	Chief	20	515.2	O.T.
27	Chicago	New York	P.R.R.	Broadway Ltd.	28	907.7	O.T.
Nov. 6	New York	Washington	P.R.R.	Congressional Ltd.	153	226.6	O.T.
7	Washington	Huntington, W.Va.	C & O	FFV	3	436.9	O.T.
7	Huntington	New York	C & O	FFV	6		
			P.R.R.		148	663.5	O.T.
15	New York	Chicago	P.R.R.	Broadway Ltd.	29	907.7	O.T.
15	Chicago	Topeka	Santa Fe	San Francisco Chief	1	515.2	O.T.
16	Topeka	Chicago	Santa Fe	Chief	20	515.2	O.T.
17	Chicago	Hoboken, N. J.	Erie-Lackawanna	Erie Ltd.	2	975.3	O.T.
Dec. 5	New York	Chicago	P.R.R.	Broadway Ltd.	29	907.7	O.T.
5	Chicago	LaJunta	Santa Fe	Super Chief	17	990.1	O.T.
6	LaJunta	Chicago	Santa Fe	Super Chief	18	990.1	O.T.
6	Chicago	New York	N.Y.C.	20th Cent.	26	960.7	O.T.
1963							
Jan. 5	New York	Washington	P.R.R.	Federal Express	173	226.6	O.T.
5	Baltimore	Washington	P.R.R.	Colonial	171	40.1	O.T.
6	Washington	New York	P.R.R.	Congressional	152	226.6	O.T.
11	New York	Cleveland	N.Y.C.	Cleveland Ltd.	57	620.5	O.T.
12	Cleveland	New York	N.K.P.	E.L. New Yorker	8	615.9	O.T.
17	New York	Cleveland	P.R.R.	Gen.-Clevelander	49-39	574.2	O.T.
18	Cleveland	New York	N.Y.C.	5th Avenue Spec.	6	620.5	O.T.

DATE	FROM	TO	R.R.	TRAIN	NO.	MILES	
Feb. 25	New York	Chicago	P.R.R.	Broadway Ltd.	29	907.7	60 Min late
25	Chicago	St. Paul	C.B.Q.	Black Hawk	47	427.	O.T.
26	St. Paul	Chicago	C.B.Q.	Black Hawk	48	427.	O.T.
Mar. 11	New York	Chicago	P.R.R.	Broadway Ltd.	29	907.7	O.T.
12	Chicago	St. Paul	C.B.Q.	Black Hawk	47	427.	O.T.
13	St. Paul	Fargo	G.N.	Western Star	27	244.	O.T.
13	Fargo	Grand Forks	G.N.	Hy Rail Insp. Car	Extra	79.	——
13	Grand Forks	St. Paul	G.N.	Winnipeg Ltd.	8	323.	O.T.
13	St. Paul	Duluth	G.N.	Badger	24	163.	O.T.
13	Duluth	St. Paul	G.N.	Gopher	19	163.	O.T.
13	St. Paul	Chicago	C.B.Q.	Black Hawk	48	427.	O.T.
16	New York	Chicago	P.R.R.	Broadway Ltd.	29	907.7	O.T.
17	Chicago	St. Louis	Wabash	Bluebird	121	285.7	O.T.
18	St. Louis	New York	P.R.R.	St. Louisan	32	1050.6	O.T.
23	New York	Chicago	P.R.R.	Broadway Ltd.	29	907.7	O.T.
24	Chicago	St. Louis	G.M.O.	Midnight Spec.	7	283.9	O.T.
25	St. Louis	New York	P.R.R.	Spirit of St. Louis	30	1050.6	O.T.
Apr. 22	New York	Chicago	P.R.R.	Broadway Ltd.	29	907.7	O.T.
23	Chicago	Winslow	Santa Fe	Super Chief	17	1623.0	O.T.
25	Winslow	Los Angeles	Santa Fe	Super Chief	17	599.2	O.T.
27	Los Angeles	Williams Jtc.	Santa Fe	Chief	20	510.4	O.T.
28	Williams Jct.	Phoenix	Santa Fe	Passenger	47	209.2	O.T.
28	Phoenix	Williams Jct.	Santa Fe	Passenger	42	209.2	O.T.
28	Williams Jct.	Chicago	Santa Fe	Chief	20	1711.8	O.T.
30	Chicago	New York	P.R.R.	Broadway Ltd.	28	907.7	O.T.
May 13	New York	Chicago	P.R.R.	Broadway Ltd.	29	907.7	O.T.
14	Chicago	Denver	C.B.Q.	Denver Zephyr	1	1034.	O.T.
17	Denver	Salt Lake City	D.R.G.	Calif. Zephyr	17	745.1	O.T.
17	Salt Lake City	Oakland	W.P.	Calif. Zephyr	17	917.	O.T.
21	Oakland	Portland	S.P.	Cascade	12	712.	O.T.
22	Portland	Seattle	U.P.	Domeliner	457	183.4	O.T.
22	Seattle	St. Paul	G.N.	Empire Builder	32	1783.	O.T.
24	St. Paul	Chicago	C.B.Q.	Afternoon Zephyr	24	427.	O.T.
		American Air Lines - Chicago to Idlewild, N.Y.					
June 10	New York	Chicago	P.R.R.	Broadway Ltd.	29	907.7	O.T.
10	Chicago	Topeka	Santa Fe	San Francisco Chief	1	515.2	O.T.

DATE	FROM	TO	R.R.	TRAIN	NO.	MILES	
12	Kansas City	St. Louis	M.P.	Missouri River Eagle	16	279.	O.T.
13	St. Louis	New York	P.R.R.	Spirit of St. Louis	30	1050.6	O.T.
17	New York	Chicago	P.R.R.	Broadway Ltd.	29	907.7	O.T.
18	Chicago	St. Paul	C.B.Q.	Black Hawk	47	427.	O.T.
19	St. Paul	Dickinson, N.D.	N.P.	North Coast Ltd.	25	552.	O.T.
20	Dickincon	Livingston	N.P.	Mainstreeter	1	447.	O.T.
22	Livingston	Seattle	N.P.	Mainstreeter	1	893.	O.T.
24	Seattle	St. Paul	N.P.	North Coast Ltd.	26	1892.	O.T.
26	St. Paul	Chicago	C.B.Q.	Afternoon Zephyr	24	427.	O.T.
	American Airlines - Chicago to Idlewild, N. Y.						
July 8	New York	Chicago	P.R.R.	Broadway Ltd.	29	907.7	O.T.
9	Chicago	Omaha	C.M.St. P.-U.P.	City of Portland	105	488.	O.T.
10	Omaha	Denver	U.P.	City of Portland	105	560.	O.T.
11	Denver	St. Louis	D.R.G.-M.P.	Colorado Eagle	12	1020.4	O.T.
12	St. Louis	Terre Haute	P.R.R.	Spirit of St. Louis	30	168.	O.T.
13	Indianopolis	St. Louis	P.R.R.	Penn Texas	3	240.	O.T.
16	St. Louis	Atlanta	L.N.	Hummingbird-Georgian	53-93	609.	15 min. late
17	Atlanta	Washington	So.R.R.	Southerner	48	633.3	O.T.
18	Washington	New York	P.R.R.		148	226.6	O.T.
22	New York	Chicago	P.R.R.	Broadway Ltd.	29	907.7	O.T.
23	Chicago	North Platte	C.M. St. P.-U.P.	City of Los Angeles	103	769.	O.T.
24	North Platte	Cheyenne	U.P.	Fast Mail	7	226.	O.T.
24	Cheyenne	Los Angeles	U.P.	Passenger	5	1304.	O.T.
27	Los Angeles	Houston	S.P.	Sunset Ltd.	2	1635.	O.T.
Aug. 1	Houston	Cleburne	Santa Fe	Texas Chief	16	287.2	O.T.
1	Dallas	St. Louis	M.P.	Texas Eagle	22-2	710.	O.T.
	T. W. A. St. Louis to Idlewild, N. Y.						
19	New York	Chicago	P.R.R.	Broadway Ltd.	29	907.7	O.T.
20	Chicago	St. Louis	Wabash	Blue Bird	121	285.7	O.T.
21	St. Louis	Springfield	Frisco	Meteor	9	239.3	O.T.
22	Springfield	Kansas City	Frisco	Sunnyland	108	201.3	O.T.
22	Kansas City	Belen, N.M.	Santa Fe	San Francisco Chief	1	917.7	O.T.

DATE	FROM	TO	R.R.	TRAIN	NO.	MILES	
24	Albuquerque	Los Angeles	Santa Fe	Chief	19	886.7	O.T.
25	Los Angeles	San Francisco	S.P.	Coast Daylight	99	470.	O.T.
27	Oakland	Portland	S.P.	Cascade	12	712.	O.T.
28	Portland	Omaha	U.P.	City of Portland	106	1784.	90 min. late

Ran off 90 minutes.

Held at Portland three hours due to threat of railroad strike

DATE	FROM	TO	R.R.	TRAIN	NO.	MILES	
Aug. 30	Omaha	Chicago	R.I.	Rocky Mt. Rocket	8	493.	O.T.
	Chicago to Idlewild, N. Y., American Airlines						
Sept. 23	NewYork	Chicago	P.R.R.	Broadway Ltd.	29	907.7	O.T.
24	Chicago	St. Paul	C.B.Q.	Black Hawk	47	427.	O.T.
25	St. Paul	Chicago	C.B.Q.	Black Hawk	48	427.	O.T.
Oct. 1	New York	Chicago	P.R.R.	Broadway Ltd.	29	907.7	O.T.
2	Chicago	Topeka	Santa Fe	San Francisco Chief	1	515.	O.T.
4	Kansas City	Chicago	Santa Fe	Chicagoan	12	449.	O.T.
9	New York	Chicago	P.R.R.	Broadway Ltd.	29	907.7	O.T.
10	Chicago	New York	N.Y.C.	20th CenturyLtd.	26	960.7	O.T.
Nov. 19	New York	Pittsburg	P.R.R.	Pittsburger	61	439.3	O.T.
20	Pittsburg to Idlewild, N. Y., United Airlines						

1964							
Feb.							
17	New York	Chicago	P.R.R.	Broadway Ltd.	29	907.7	On Time
18	Chicago	St. Paul	C.B.Q.	Black Hawk	47	427	On Time
19	St. Paul	Chicago	C.B.Q.	Black Hawk	48	427	On Time
20	Chicago	New York	N.Y.C.	20th Century	26	960.7	On Time
Mar. 3	New York	St. Louis	P.R.R.	Spirit of St. Louis	31	1050.6	On Time
4	St. Louis	Houston	M.P.	Texas Eagle	1-41	815	On Time
7	Houston	Dallas	Rock Island F.W.D.C.	Sam Houston Zephyr	4	249	On Time
10	Texarkana	St. Louis	M.P.	Texas Eagle	2	493	On Time
11	St. Louis	New York	P.R.R.	Spirit of St. Louis	30	1050.6	90 minutes late

Hit automobile Carnegie, Pa.

DATE	FROM	TO	R.R.	TRAIN	NO.	MILES	
Mar.							
17	New York	Chicago	P.R.R.	Broadway Ltd.	29	907.7	On Time
18	Chicago	Omaha	C.B.Q.	California Zephyr	17	496.1	50 minutes late
		Elderly lady walked into diesel Wyanet, Illinois					
19	Omaha	Denver	U.P.	City of Denver	111	560	On Time
23	Denver	Chicago	C.B.Q.	Denver Zephyr	10	1050	On Time
24	Chicago	New York	N.Y.C.	20th Century Ltd.	26	960.7	On Time
Apr.							
21	New York	St. Louis	P.R.R.	Spirit of St. Louis	31	1050.6	On Time
22	St. Louis	Springfield	Frisco	Meteor	9	239.3	On Time
23	Springfield	Kansas City	Frisco	Sunnyland	108	201.3	50 minutes late
		Meeting 3 symbol fast freight trains					
23	Kansas City	Topeka	Santa Fe	San Francisco Chief	1	64	On Time
24	Topeka	Richmond	Santa Fe	San Francisco Chief	1	2022	On Time
29	Oakland	Portland	S.P.	Cascade	12	712	15 minutes late
		Meeting fast freight Coast Expediter 377 Clackamas, Oregon					
30	Portland	Spokane	S.P.S.	Empire Builder North Coast Ltd.	2	379.5	On Time
30	Spokane	Seattle	G.N.	Empire Builder	31	329.2	On Time
May							
2	Seattle	St. Paul	G.N.	Empire Builder	32	1783	On Time
5	St. Paul	Chicago	C.B.Q.	Black Hawk	48	427	On Time
6	Chicago	New York	P.R.R.	Broadway Ltd.	28	907.7	On Time
June							
10	New York	Pittsburg	P.R.R.	Pittsburger	61	469	On Time
12	Pittsburg	New York	P.R.R.	Pittsburger	60	469	On Time
16	New York	Chicago	P.R.R.	Broadway Ltd.	29	907.7	On Time
17	Chicago	Houston	Santa Fe	Texas Chief	15	1368	40 minutes late
		Mail and express Kansas City Terminal					
19	Houston	Tucson	S.P.	Sunset	1	814	On Time
22	Tucson	Los Angeles	S.P.	Golden State	1-3	546	On Time
25	Los Angeles	Salt Lake	U.P.	City of L. A.	1st 104	784	On Time

DATE	FROM	TO	R.R.	TRAIN	NO.	MILES	
June							
28	Salt Lake	Denver	D.R.G.	California Zephyr	18	570	On Time
28	Denver	Omaha	C.B.Q.	California Zephyr	18	538	On Time
29	Omaha	Chicago	R.I.	Rocky Mt. Rocket	8	493	On Time
30	Chicago	New York	P.R.R.	Broadway Ltd.	28	907.7	On Time
July							
14	New York	Chicago	P.R.R.	Broadway Ltd.	29	907.7	On Time
15	Chicago	Kansas City	Santa Fe	Kansas City Chief	9	449.4	On Time
17	Kansas City	Chicago	Santa Fe	Chief	20	449.4	On Time
18	Chicago	Hoboken	E-L	World's Fair	6	976.3	On Time
26	New York	Washington	P.R.R.	Colonial Ex.	171	226.6	On Time
26	Washington	Huntington	C. & O.	Geo. Washington	1	436.9	On Time
28	Huntington	Washington	C. & O.	Geo. Washington	2	436.9	On Time
29	Washington	New York	P.R.R.	Senator	172	226.6	On Time
Aug.							
19	New York	Chicago	P.R.R.	Broadway Ltd.	29	907.7	On Time
20	Chicago	St. Paul	C.B.Q.	Black Hawk	47	427	On Time
21	St. Paul	Spokane	G.N.	Empire Builder	31	1453	On Time
22	Spokane	Portland	S.P.S.	Empire Builder North Coast Ltd.	1	380	On Time
25	Portland	Pocatello	U.P.	City of Portland	106	725.6	On Time
26	Ogden	Omaha	U.P.	Passenger	8	989.8	On Time
Aug.							
28	Omaha	Ogden	U.P.	City of L. A.	1st103	989.8	45 minutes late
		Behind freight train break-in-two Archer, Wyoming					
29	Ogden	Oakland	S.P.	City of San Francisco	101	871.3	On Time
Sept.							
1	San Francisco	Los Angeles	S.P.	Lark	76	470	On Time
2	Los Angeles	Chicago	Santa Fe	Super Chief	18	2222.2	On Time
4		Chicago - Idlewild. N. Y. American Airlines					
27	New York	Chicago	P.R.R.	Broadway Ltd.	29	907.7	On Time
28	Chicago	St. Paul	C.B.Q.	Black Hawk	47	427	On Time
29	St. Paul	Grand Forks	G.N.	Winnipeg Ltd.	7	323	On Time
30	Grand Forks	St. Paul	G.N.	Dakotian	4	323	On Time
30	St. Paul	Chicago	Mill.	Pioneer Ltd.	4	410	On Time

DATE	FROM	TO	R.R.	TRAIN	NO.	MILES	
Oct.							
1	Chicago to New York Idlewild - American Airlines						
5	New York	Washington	P.R.R.	Midday Cong.	121	226.6	On Time
5	Washington	Cincinnati	C & O	George Washington	1	620	On Time
7	Cincinnati	Washington	C & O	George Washington	2	620	On Time
7	Washington	New York	P.R.R.	Legislator	126	226.6	On Time
Nov.							
15	New York	Washington	P.R.R.	Afternoon Keystone	149	226.6	On Time
15	Washington	Atlanta	Southern R.R.	Crescent	37	633.3	On Time
16	Atlanta	West Point	A & WP	Crescent	37	87	On Time
16	West Point	Montgomery	W. RR of Ala.	Crescent	37	88	On Time
16	Montgomery	New Orleans	L & N	Crescent	37	323	On Time
17	New Orleans	Houston	S.P.	Sunset	1	363	On Time
19	Houston	Fort Worth	Santa Fe	Texas Chief	16	316	On Time
19	Fort Worth	Kansas City	R.I.	Twin Star Rocket	18	591	On Time
20	Kansas City	Chicago	Santa Fe	Chicagoan	12	449.4	On Time
20	Chicago - Idlewild, New York - American Airlines						
1965							
Mar.							
8	New York	St. Louis	P.R.R.	Spirit of St. Louis	31	1050.6	11 minutes late
	Detouring N.Y.C. Indianapolis - Terre Haute **freight derailment, Summit, Indiana**						
9	St. Louis	Kansas City	N. & W.	City of St. Louis	209	278.1	On Time
9	Kansas City	Denver	U.P.	City of St. Louis	9	640	On Time
10	Denver	Dallas	C & S.F.W. & D.	Texas Zephyr	1	835	On Time
14	Shreaveport	Kansas City	K.C.S.	Southern Belle	2	561.4	On Time
15	Kansas Cit	Chicago	Santa Fe	Chief	20	449.4	On Time
16	Chicago	Indianapolis	N.Y.C.	Indianapolis Spec.	302	193.6	On Time
16	Cincinnati	Washington	C & O	Sportsman	4	620	On Time
17	Washington	New York	P.R.R.	Mt. Vernon	156	226.6	On Time

1962 - 1963

115 train movements - total mileage 71,055 - three late arrivals

1964 - 1965

81 train movements - total mileage 51,899.2 seven late arrivals

TWO YEAR TOTALS

Train Movements 196

Total Mileage 122,954.2

Late Arrivals 10

G.N. 1st streamlined Empire Builder passing Mt. Index on the second Sub-Div., The Cascade Div. with Diesel No. 503-2 unit E.M.D. 2,000 hp—E-7.

Chesapeake & Ohio No. 3025, 2-10-4 type, T-1 class, leaving Track 16, Russell, Kentucky, Coal Classification Yard with 160 loads and 13,500 tons, the regular makeup. 12:30 p.m., June 19, 1943.

Union Pacific No. 4002, 4-8-8-4 type with a westward Extra and 51 cars running 35 mph west of Green River, Wyoming, Wyoming Div.

Photo by Otto C. Perry.

Union Pacific No. 9082, 4-12-2 type, the Union Pacific's own, climbing the grade west of Green River, Wyoming with a 90 car westward Extra. June 26, 1948.

Photo by R. H. Kindig.

Union Pacific No. 3947, helping No. 3949, both 4-6-6-4 types on a westward Extra near Sherman, Wyoming, running 40 mph with 93 cars. (Middle of train can be seen at right.)

Photo by R. H. Kindig taken August 2, 1947.

Union Pacific Nos. 844-842 coupled, 4-8-4 type climbing Sherman Hill near Sherman, Wyoming with No. 27, San Francisco Overland, running 50 mph with 15 cars, Wyoming Div.

Photo taken September 2, 1946 by R. H. Kindig.

Union Pacific No. 822, 4-8-4 type, starting down Sherman Hill, Wyoming with No. 28, San Francisco Overland, with 16 cars, running 40 mph. Wyoming Div.

Photo taken June 1949 by R. H. Kindig.

Western Maryland No. 205, 4-6-2 type, hauling train No. 1 south of Thomas, West Virginia.

Photo taken July 1949 by R. H. Kindig.

B&O No. 4412, 2-8-2 type, Q-4 class with 64 inch wheels, Total Weight 541,400 lbs., Tractive Effort 63,200, Boiler Pressure 220 lbs. Helping No. 5093, 4-6-2 type, P-1c class, rebuilt from 2-8-2 type in 1924. Drivers 74 inches, Total Weight 299,000 lbs. Tractive Effort 44,600 lbs. Boiler Pressure 205 lbs.

They are shown coming out of the east portal Kingwood Tunnel, Tunnelton, West Virginia with train No. 30, Cumberland Div., West End.

Photo taken in October 1947 by Bruce D. Fales.

Great Northern No. 2511, 4-8-2 type, P-1 class with No. 27, The Fast Mail, leaving Belton, Montana, Kalispel Div.

Photo taken August 5, 1938 by Otto C. Perry.

N&W No. 1208, 2-6-6-4 type, with No. 91 Westward Time Freight at Blue Ridge, Va., Norfolk Div.

D.L&W. #1644 4-8-4 type Leaving Dover, N.J. with 1st #3 Lackawanna Lim. Morris and Essex Div.

Photo by Thomas T. Taber.

Section Four

SCOOPING WATER ON THE RUN

Many insulations along the right-of-way have come into the railroad picture since the days when the locomotive was young: The silent semaphore, the sentinel beside the rail; cab signals; automatic train control; color-search light signals; position light signals; dead man's brake in the cab, in case anything happened to the engineman; and now radio. These and many other devices for speeding up and yet further safeguarding roaring fast freight and passenger trains.

Time, relentless in its march, is the first enemy of the railroad. To defeat its ominous count of seconds, high speed railroads have spent vast sums and waged ceaseless war in their efforts to slow the clock. Every minute saved is a battle won. This is why track pans, or track tanks as the Pennsylvania called them, were installed by the New York Central, Pennsylvania, Baltimore & Ohio, Philadelphia and Reading, Central Railroad of New Jersey and the New York & Long Branch, a road owned and operated jointly by the Pennsylvania and Jersey Central between South Amboy and Bay Head Junction, New Jersey.

These track pans enabled the fast moving locomotives to satisfy their endless thirst without the loss of precious minutes. The locomotives took their ration of water in one prodigious gulp, only slowing to a moderate 50 mph before hitting high speed again, always with a full tank. If they didn't get it, there was something wrong with the scoop. I can remember only one or two occasions when the tank was not filled.

A track pan was merely a long trough between the rails, and the matter of taking aboard the water which filled it was childishly simple. And yet many factors were involved which required precision, careful planning and constant supervision. A track pan varied in length from 1,400 to 2,500 feet. It had, of necessity, to be located on level track; preferably on non-curving sections, though there were track pans in service on slight curves.

The pans were situated midway between the rails. They were built of rolled-steel plates, the inside cross-section dimensions being eight inches deep and nineteen inches wide, with the top of the pan one inch below the top of the rail. Markers were provided to indicate to the engine crews the exact place to drop and raise the scoops through which the water was transferred from track pan to the tank on the locomotive tender.

At each pan location there was a roadside tank of sufficient capacity to fulfill the requirements of the pan as to the volume of water used at that particular location. These tanks were kept full at all times. Water flowed from the tank to pan by gravity, passing through automatic valves, controlled by floats. When the water in the track pan fell below a certain level, the opening valve replenished the supply. In a like manner the valves closed when the water in the pan had reached a predetermined point.

In the winter months, in northern climates, it was necessary to provide heat to keep the water in the track pan from freezing. This was accomplished by means of steam furnished by adjacent stationary plants, regulated manually by the employee in charge. The steam line released live steam directly into the water contained in the pan.

The process of scooping up the water was attended by a naturally high percentage of waste, and, so far as possible, this water was caught in traps and returned to the initial supply. From the standpoint of maintaining satisfactory roadway conditions, it was extremely important to provide perfect drainage at all track-pan locations.

The equipment on the locomotive for lifting water consisted of a scoop, telescopic in construction, which had two moving parts, actuated through a cylinder by means of air pressure. Attached to the scoop was a pipe which extended up through the cistern in the tender at its approximate middle. Located laterally and longitudinally, the top of this pipe was equipped with a U bend, the outlet of which was above the water level when the tender cistern was full. This U bend was directed toward either the forward or the rear of the cistern, depending upon the necessities of the particular design.

When the scoop was lowered to take water, it was 6¼ inches below the top of the rail, 5¼ inches below the top of the track pan. Thus it was immersed into the water approximately 4½ inches. While the engine was not taking water, the scoop was 4 inches above the top of the rail. The mouth of the scoop was moved by the air-actuated cylinder through a total distance of 10¼ inches. Tests indicated that about 2½ to 2¼ gallons of water were transferred from the track pan to the tender's cistern per linear foot of scooping distance.

The engineer and fireman announced the approach to a track pan as they might call and repeat a signal. When the locomotive was opposite the "entering" marker, the engineman called again to the fireman, who immediately operated the valve which supplied air to the scoop-actuating cylinder. The scoop was left down until the tank was full, or until the "leaving" marker was reached, at which time the scoop was raised. In the meantime, the speed was reduced somewhat, perhaps to forty or fifty miles an hour. Then came again the full-throated roar as the train quickly swung back into its high-wheeling stride. The operation of slamming some 5,000 gallons of water aboard the thirsty giant took not much longer than it would for you to say Jack Robinson. A swoosh and a spatter and it was done.

The saving in time of a high-speed road like that of the New York Central or Pennsylvania between New York and Chicago was enormous. The savings in cost of starting and stopping more than offset the cost of maintaining the pans.

The Pennsylvania had 24 track tanks as well as one at Branchport, N.J. operated jointly with the Central R.R. of N.J. as already mentioned.

The location of the track tanks was as follows:

New York Division
Rahway, N.J.
Plainsboro, N.J.
Bristol, Pa.
Philadelphia Division
Radnor, Pa.
Atglen, Pa.
Landisville, Pa.
Middle Division
Bailey, Pa.
Hawstone, Pa.
Mapleton, Pa.
Bellwood, Pa.

Pittsburgh Division
Wilmore, Pa.
Saxmans, Pa.

Eastern Division
Grafton, Ohio
Millbrook, Ohio

Fort Wayne Division
Dola, Ohio
Hanna, Ind.

The above locations are from East to West.

The Pennsylvania had online coaling stations at Thorndale, Pa. Phila. Div.; Denholm, Pa. Middle Div.; Conemaugh, Pa. Pittsburgh Div.; Millbrook, Ohio Eastern Div.

Track Tanks

Maryland Division
Glenolden, Pa.
Ruthby, Del.
Edgewood, Md.
Baltimore Division
Stony Run, Md.

Belvidere Branch—N.Y. Div.
formerly Trenton Div.
Frenchtown, N.J.
Trenton Division
Delanco, N.J.
Atlantic Division—PRSL
Ancora, N.J.
South Seaville, N.J. Cape May Branch

The above are North to South.

The Royal Blue Line, as the Central Railroad of New Jersey, Reading and Baltimore and Ohio's joint service which was mighty good was called. Had the following track tanks from Jersey City to Wash. D.C.

Central Railroad of New Jersey
Central Division
Green Brook (Dunellen), N.J.
Reading
New York Division
Yardley, Pa.
(later removed to Roelofs, Pa., the next station West
and the Div name changed to Philadelphia Division)

Baltimore and Ohio
Baltimore Division–East End
Stanton, Del.
Swan Creek, Md.

These locations are from North to South.

The New York Central's track pans (as they call them) were as follows: from East to West.

Hudson Division	Clinton Point	Tracks 1–2–3–4
	Tivoli	" 1–2
Mohawk Division	Schenectady	" 1–2
	Yost's	" 1–2
	Rome	" 1–2–3–4
Syracuse Division	Seneca River	" 1–2
	East Palmyra	" 1–2
Buffalo Division	Churchville	" 1–2
	Wenda	" 1–2
Erie Division	Silver Creek, N.Y.	" 1–2–3–4
	Westfield, N.Y.	" 1–2–3–4
	Springfield, Pa.	" 1–2–3–4
	Painesville, Ohio	" 1–2–3–4
Cleveland	Huron, Ohio	" 1–2
Toledo Division	Stryker	" 1–2–3
	Corunna, Indiana	" 1–2
	Grismore, "	" 1–2
Western Division	Lydick, "	" 1–2
	Chestertown,"	" 1–2

As you readers can well imagine, keeping these track pans in service during four seasons of the year was a mighty horrendous, expensive operation, one more great expenditure that was eliminated by the diesels.

INTERIOR OF SANTA FE 4-8-4 TYPE, 2900 CLASS CAB WITH ALL VALVES AND GAUGES LABELED

1. Throttle
2. Power Reverse Control
3. Automatic Brake Valve
4. Fuel-Oil Firing Valve
5. Firebox Damper Control
6. Independent Brake Valve
7. Boiler Pressure Gauge
8. Injector Operating Lever
9. Equalizing and Main Reservoir Air Pressure Gauge
10. Trainline and Brake Cylinder Air Pressure Gauge
11. Lubricator Steam Valve
12. Gauge Lamp (Right and Left)
13. Roof Vent Regulator (Right and Left)
14. Water Glass—Engineer's Side
15. Water Glass—Fireman's Side
16. Foam-Meter
17. Electrically Controlled Blowdown Switch
18. Flagging Equipment Box
19. Whistle Cord
20. Bell Ringing Cord
21. Trainline Steam Heat Regulating Valve
22. Blower Fountain Valve
23. Trainline Steam Cutoff Valve
24. Water Pump Cutoff Valve
25. Dynamo Operating Valve
26. Main Fountain Cutoff Valve
27. Steam Heat Regulating Valve (Cab)
28. Fountain Cutoff Valve for Power Reverse
29. Injector Fountain Shutoff Valve
30. Feed-Water Pump Valve
31. Feed-Water Pump Pressure Gauge
32. Trainline Steam Heat Gauge
33. Cab Steam Heat Gauge
34. Cab Heater Valve
35. Manifold Blower Valve
36. Oil Atomizer Control Valve
37. Direct Fuel Tank Heater Valve
38. Fuel Tank Steam Heat Valve
39. Flue Sanding Hole and Fire Peephole
40. Speed Indicator and Recorder

Cab interior of Union Pacific Engine No. 822, 4-8-4 type, $\frac{\text{FEF-80-25/32-}}{\text{270-BK}}$ class.

Posed American Locomotive Company picture of right side of Union Pacific's Engine No. 4010, 4-8-8-4 type, $\frac{\text{23¾-23¾}}{\text{1-68-32-540-MB}}$ class. Note the drifting throttle and the fire box door open with no fire.

Interior of cab of N.Y.C. No. 3006, 4-8-2 type, L-3a class.

Interior of cab of N.Y.C. 4-6-4 type streamlined, J-3 class.

Interior of cab of N.Y.C. 4-8-4 type, S-1 class.

Interior of cab of Santa Fe No. 3757, 4-8-4 type, 3751 class with Duplex Stoker. The No. 3757-60 had Duplex Stokers and the 3751-3756 had Standard Stokers.

Photo from H. L. Broadbelt Collection.

Interior of right side of cab of Santa Fe No. 3465, 4-6-4 type, 3460 class.

Interior of left side of cab of Santa Fe No. 3465, 4-6-4 type, 3460 class.

Interior of cab of Santa Fe No. 5003, 2-10-4 type, 5001 class, coal burner Standard Stoker.

Front end of Norfolk & Western 2-6-6-4 type, class A.

Front end of Chesapeake & Ohio 4-8-4 type, J-3 class.

Chesapeake & Ohio Engine No. 305, 4-6-4 type, L-2 class.

Front end of Southern Pacific 4-8-8-2 type, AC-11

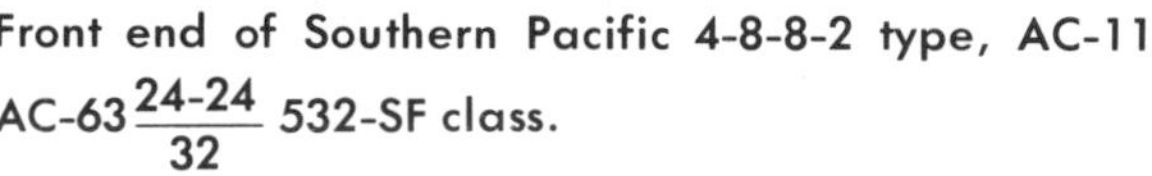
AC-63 $\frac{24\text{-}24}{32}$ 532-SF class.

Front end of Southern Pacific 2-8-8-4 type, AC-9 AC-63 $\frac{24\text{-}24}{32}$ 531-SF class.

Front end of Pennsylvania Railroad 2-C+C2 type, GG-1 class.

Front end of New York Central No. 3107, 4-8-2 type, L-4a class at Beacon Park before her first trip with side sheets. Photo by: H. W. Pontin, Railroad Photographic Club.

Front end of Southern Ry. 4-6-2 type, PS4 class.

Front end of Richmond, Fredericksburg & Potomac 4-6-2 type, 301 class.

Front end of Baltimore & Ohio 2-8-8-4 type, EM-1 class.

Front end of Santa Fe 4-8-4 type, 2900 class.

Photo from H. L. Broadbelt Collection.

Front end of Richmond, Fredericksburg & Potomac 4-8-4 type, General T. J. Jackson, 551 class.

Front end of Santa Fe 5012, 2-10-4 type, 5011 class.

Photo from H. L. Broadbelt Collection.

Front end of St. Louis & San Francisco 4-8-4 type, Engine 4521.

Front end of Santa Fe Oil Burner 2-10-4 type, 5004, 5001 class. Photo from Collection of H. L. Broadbelt.

Front end of Pennsylvania Railroad 4-4-4-4 type, T-1 class.

Front end of Sante Fe 4-8-4 type, 3765, class. Photo from H. L. Broadbelt Collection.

Front end of New Haven Engine 1400, 4-6-4 types, 1-5 class.

Front end of Santa Fe 4-6-4 type, 3460 class.

Front end of Chesapeake & Ohio 2-6-6-6 type, H-7 class.

Rear end of New York Central Engine No. 3037, 4-8-2 type, L-3a's class tender. Transients were not only in danger of being scalded by steam and hot water as the danger sign indicates but also ran the risk of being frozen after water was scooped during the winter months. On the Southern Pacific some were fatally asphyxiated riding the monkey decks on the rear end of the cab ahead AC classes, in tunnels.

Front end of Northern Pacific 4-8-4 type, A-5 class.

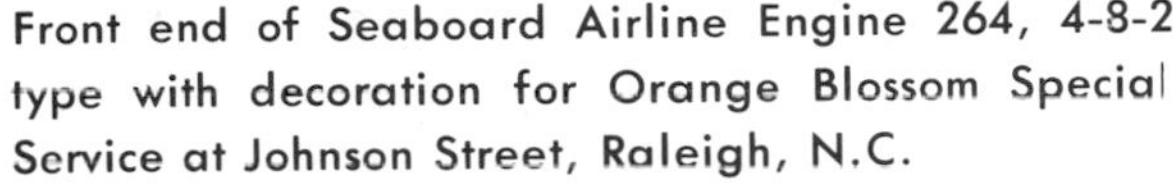

Front end of Seaboard Airline Engine 264, 4-8-2 type with decoration for Orange Blossom Special Service at Johnson Street, Raleigh, N.C.

Front end of Florida East Coast Engine 704 oil burning 2-8-2 type, 700 class shown at Long Key, Fla. prior to the 1935 hurricane which washed out the railroad, station, and the old Long Key Fishing Camp.

Front end of Florida East Coast Engine 430 oil burning 4-8-2 type at Key West, Fla.

P.R. No. 2101, 4-8-4 type, class T1. Renumbered No. 1 for Freedom Train to be used on N.E. railroads. Rebuilt in Reading, Pa. shops from 2-8-0 type 110SA in 1945-1947 by the railroad.

Tractive Effort	68,000 lbs.
Drivers Diameter	70 in.
Weight on Drivers	278,200 lbs.
Total Weight	441,300 lbs.
Steam Pressure	240 lbs.
Tender Capacity	19,000 gals.
	26 tons

ACKNOWLEDGMENTS

Going back over a period of 60 years, I have had the privilege of knowing and being friends with some of the greatest, all-around railroaders America has ever produced. These are the men who gave me permission to be on their properties so that after writing my first fishing book, I was given the invitation to write one on modern operating practices of the U.S. railroads.

Eight more followed, one being on the very important World War II operations and another, *Railroading Around The World*.

These great railroaders, some of whom are no longer with us and others who have retired, are the only ones to be named here.

The many presidents whose friendship, guidance and advice I shall never forget were:

W. N. Deramus	Kansas City Southern
W. S. Hackworth	Nashville, Chattanooga & St. Louis
Clark Hungerford	St. Louis & San Francisco
Norman Call	Richmond, Fredericksburg & Potomac
R. H. Smith	Norfolk & Western
Fred E. Williamson	New York Central
H. H. Scandrett	Milwaukee
J. D. Farrington (no relation)	Rock Island
Walter Tuohy	Chesapeake & Ohio
Paul J. Neff	Missouri Pacific
Robert A. Emerson	Canadian Pacific
A. T. Mercier	Southern Pacific
Edward T. Reidy	Chicago Great Western
F. D. Beale	Virginian
William White	Lackawanna
Harry Murphy	Burlington
Robert J. Bowman	Chesapeake & Ohio
Lynn L. White	Nickel Plate
John Davin	Nickel Plate
E. J. Engel	Santa Fe
Walter Douglas	El Paso & Southwestern and also Southern Pacific of Mexico
Hale Holden	Southern Pacific
Daniel Upthegrove	St. Louis & Southwestern
Ernest S. Marsh	Santa Fe
Eugene M. Williams	Western Maryland

and going back even before the above were:

Paul Shoup	Southern Pacific
Carl R. Gray	Union Pacific
W. W. Atterbury	Pennsylvania Railroad
W. H. Truesdale	Lackawanna
L. W. Baldwin	Missouri Pacific
W. B. Storey	Santa Fe
S. T. Bledsoe	Santa Fe
F. E. Underwood	Erie
W. J. Jenks	Norfolk & Western
Henry Swan	Chairman of the Finance Committee of the Denver, Rio Grande & Western
and	
T. M. Schumacher	Chairman of the Board, D.R.G. & W. Chairman of the Executive Committee W.P.

Retired Presidents are:

Perry M. Shoemaker	Lackawanna
D. J. Russell	Southern Pacific
H. H. Pevler	Norfolk & Western
John Barriger	Pittsburgh & Lake Erie
N. R. Crump	Canadian Pacific
William N. Brosnan	Southern Railway
Gregory Devine	Chesapeake & Ohio
George D. Brooke	Nickel Plate
W. Arthur Grotz	Western Maryland
Harry DeButts	Southern Railway
R. Russell Coulter	Toledo, Peoria & Western
John Budd	Great Northern

Operating Vice Presidents, no longer with us, who were great friends and shall always be cherished by the author:

George H. Minchin	Santa Fe
C. O. Jenks	Great Northern
C. W. Van Horn	Baltimore & Ohio
J. J. Gillick	Milwaukee
F. G. Gurley	Santa Fe
E. J. Connors	Union Pacific
R. C. White	Missouri Pacific
Thomas Jerrow	Great Northern
Clarence R. Tucker	Santa Fe
F. W. Green	St. Louis & Southwestern
G. W. Harworth	Western Maryland
W. K. Etter	Santa Fe
E. M. Rine	Lackawanna
and	
Joe H. Dyer	Southern Pacific

who, when he was Train Master at Sparks, Nevada in 1913 used to take me out on the road with him in engines and cabooses all over the Sacramento Division.

Retired Operating Vice Presidents are:

J. J. Corbett	Southern Pacific
Carl H. Burges	Northern Pacific
Ernest Potarf	Burlington
Ed West	Rio Grande
Perry Lynch	Union Pacific
William G. White	Lackwanna
Raymond D. Shelton	Santa Fe

Other Vice Presidents deceased were:

George Le Boutillier	Pennsylvania Railroad
W. S. Jenney	Lackawanna
Thomas H. Balmer	Great Northern
J. A. Appleton	Pennsylvania Railroad
W. S. McDonald	Louisville & Nashville
H.W. Schotter	Pennsylvania Railroad
F. S. McGinnes	Southern Pacific
L. O. Frith	Kansas City Southern

General Managers deceased:

R. Halowell	Southern Pacific
O. L. Grey	Santa Fe
E. B. Moffatt	Lackawanna
E. E. McCarty	Santa Fe
G. H. Jefferies	Santa Fe
H. B. Lautz	Santa Fe

General Managers retired:

L. M. Olson	Santa Fe
M. A. McIntyre	Southern Pacific
G. R. Buchanan	Santa Fe
J. N. Landreth	Santa Fe
L. H. Phetteplace	Clinchfield
I. E. Manion	Great Northern
O. H. Osborn	Santa Fe
F. N. Stuppi	Santa Fe

Chief Engineers deceased:

R. H. Brown	Burlington
G. W. Harris	Santa Fe
Tom Blair	Santa Fe
George Ray	Lackawanna

Chief Engineers retired:

Walter Bjorkholm	Ft. Worth & Denver
George V. Guerin	Great Northern
R. H. Beeder	Santa Fe
W. M. Jaekle	Southern Pacific, who is now a Vice President
H. M. Williamson	Southern Pacific

Superintendents of Motive Power Mechanical Department Heads deceased:

Paul W. Kiefer	New York Central
J. M. Nicholson	Santa Fe
John Purcell	Santa Fe
George McCormack	Southern Pacific
Frank E. Russell, Sr.	Southern Pacific
John P. Morris	Santa Fe

Superintendents of Motive Power and Mechanical Department Heads retired:

Frank E. Russell, Jr.	Southern Pacific
Jess Cannon	Northern Pacific
J. E. Bjorkholm	Milwaukee
A. R. Genin	Northern Pacific Superintendent of Livingston Montana Shops

Public Relations Officers deceased:

F. H. Johnson	Milwaukee
R. M. Van Sant	Baltimore & Ohio
Lee Lyles	Santa Fe
R. R. Hornor	Norfolk & Western
W. Rachsels	Seaboard
Clarence Dugan	New York Central

Public Relations Officers retired:

C. W. Moore	Great Northern
K. C. Ingram	Southern Pacific
George Dodge	Rio Grande

Had it not been for the men listed above, this book would not have been possible. To those whose names have been inadvertently omitted, my sincere apologies. S.K.F.

AFTERWORD
FREEDOM TRAIN

This book would not be complete without my mentioning THE AMERICAN FREEDOM TRAIN. The American Freedom Train is a steam-powered, 24 car train which will carry this nation's most treasured documents and artifacts to people in all 48 continental states during the Bi-Centennial years of 1975 and 1976, beginning the month of April 1975.

The train will exhibit in 10 specially-designed display cars a priceless collection of historical documents and memorabilia gathered from important museums and historical societies across the country. The display items will reflect American achievements in nearly every aspect of life, including art, sports, science, architecture and government. Among the hundreds of historical documents and objects expected to travel on the Freedom Train are: the first Bible printed in the United States, Benjamin Franklin's draft of the Articles of Confederation, Pennsylvania's Ratification of the Constitution, Delaware's Ratification of the Bill of Rights, Credentials of the Pennsylvania Delegates of the Continental Congress—Benjamin Franklin's credentials or those signed by Franklin, George Washington's copy of the Constitution-Committee on Detail, a lunar rover and a moon rock.

Moving walkways will carry an estimated 8,000,000 vistors through the exhibit cars during the train's 21-month journey at a rate of 1,250 people per hour.

In addition, the train has two "bubble cars." One carries the "Children's Gift Bell," a 6-foot, 2-inch high, 17,073-pound double-size replica of the original Liberty Bell—without the crack. The bell, cast in The Netherlands, was made possible by donations from the American Legion. The other "bubble car" displays several vehicles depicting American transportation.

The locomotive is the former Southern Pacific GS-4 class, 4-8-4 type #4449 which was donated to the City of Portland by that Railroad when it was taken out of service. Portland, Oregon has been so generous as to present it for use hauling the Freedom Train over all railroads which have excellent track facilities and curvature to allow its operation.

The Burlington Northern R.R. generously allowed the use of their shops in Portland to put this great locomotive back in running order.

This tremendous job was accomplished by a group of mechanical experts who volunteered their services under the leadership of Doyle McCormack. Many of them came from all over the United States and stayed with the locomotive until the work was completed.

The #4449 has a Tractive Effort of 64,800 lbs.

Drivers Diameter 80 in.

Weight on Drivers 275,700 lbs.

Total Weight 475,000 lbs.

Steam Pressure 300 lbs.

Tender Capacity 23,300 gals. water, 5,880 gals. oil.

On some of the Northeastern roads where this locomotive is too big to haul the train, a smaller 4-8-4 type Class T1 Philadelphia and Reading Railroad engine #2101 was donated by the Striggel Equipment Co. of Baltimore, Md. who had purchased it for scrap. The locomotive was put back in shape by 200 volunteers at the Chesapeake & Ohio, Baltimore & Ohio's Mt. Clare historic shop in Baltimore. The engine was re-numbered #1 for service on the Freedom Train. The locomotive was purchased by Ross Rowland and presented to the Freedom Train.

It was rebuilt in the Reading, Pa. shops from 2-8-0 type I10sa in 1945–1947 by the Railroad.

Engine 2101 has a Tractive Effort of 68,000 lbs.

Drivers Diameter 70 in.

Weight on Drivers 278,200 lbs.

Total Weight 441,300 lbs.

Steam Pressure 240 lbs.

Tender Capacity 19,000 gals., 26 tons.

Donald Kendall, Chairman of the Board of Pepsi Co. Inc., spearheaded the four public spirited corporations that donated one million dollars each for the Freedom Train. Besides Pepsi Cola they were General Motors Corp., Prudential Insurance Co. of America, and Kraft Foods.

Richard C. Gerstenberg, retired Chairman of the Board of General Motors, headed up that wonderful Corporation's enthusiasm for the project and he was ably assisted by Oscar A. Lundin, retired Vice Chairman of General Motors. J. J. MacDonald, General Assistant Treasurer, who is extremely well versed in railroad operations as well as all of General Motor's officials are, as their Electro-Motive Division at La Grange, Illinois has turned out the world's finest and most efficient diesel locomotives that have been in service in the United States since the 1930's.

The representatives of these four great companies on the National Advisory Board were as follows: the General Motors designate being Vincent C. Burke, Chairman of Riggs National Bank, Washington, D.C.; Pepsi Co. Inc.'s designate was Jack Cornelius, retired publisher of American Heritage Magazine; Kraft Foods' designate was Gordon Edwards, retired Chairman of Kraft's Board; Prudential's designate was Richard Congleton, retired General Counsel (deceased) of Prudential. Donald Kendall's enthusiasm and all round business acumen made him quick to realize what a great thing this would be for the United States and her citizens in the Centennial years.

Tentative Route of The American Freedom Train
1975-1976

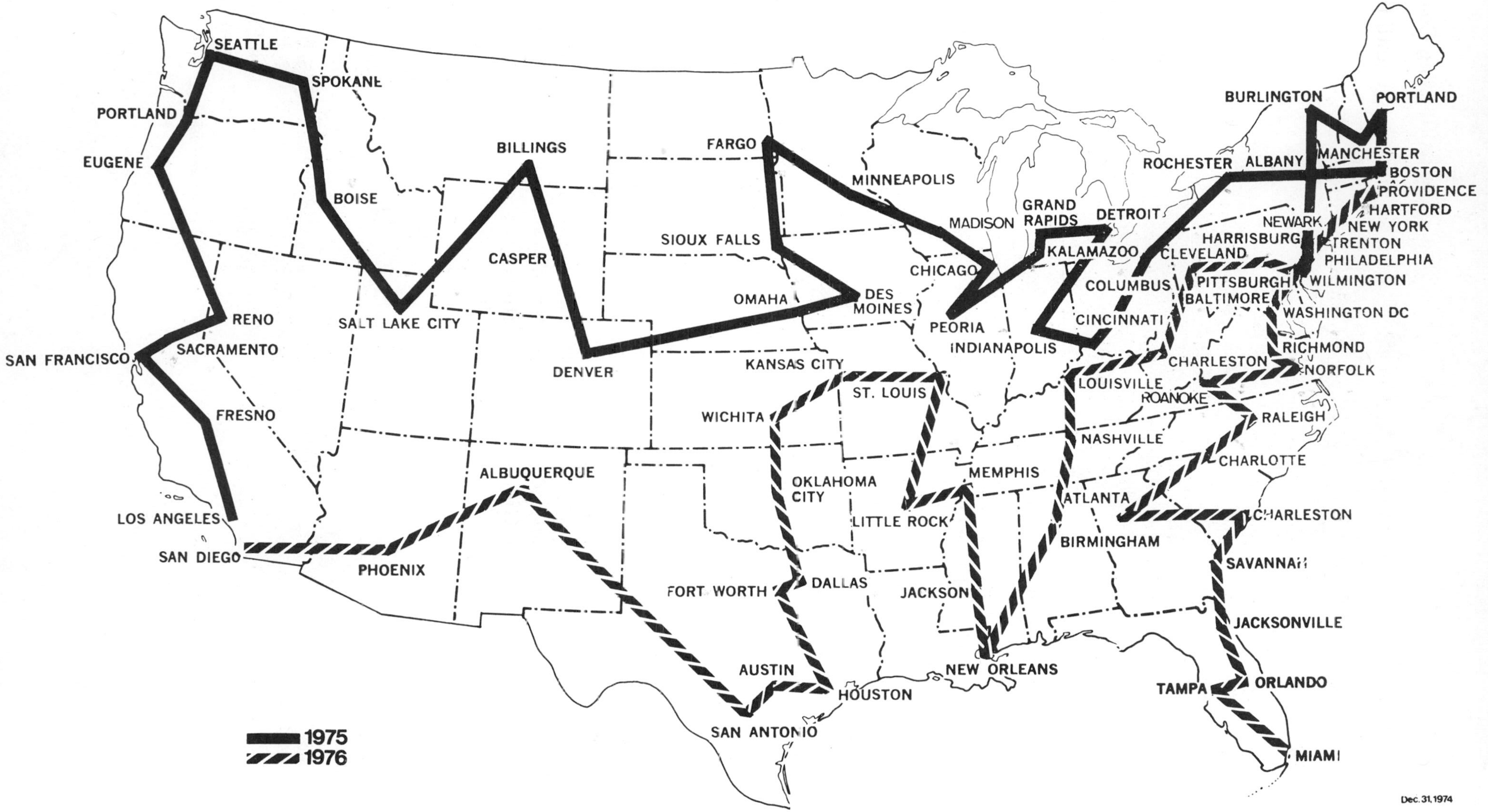

Dec. 31, 1974

GLOSSARY

OT	On Time
Dead Time	Wasting time when you are ahead of time on slow schedule.
Waiting On	For meet opposing train or being overtaken.
Slipped	Slipping—Driving Wheels slipping.
Met	Same as meet. Meeting opposing train on single track.
Being Scooped	Being run around by train of same direction.
Helper	Helping engine on head end.
Pusher	Pusher engine on rear end.
Hooking Mail	Picking up mail at speed from track side Mail Cranes.
Scooping or Scooped	Picking up water from track tanks or pans when running.
G.F.X.	Santa Fe Green Fruit Express.
C.T.X.	Santa Fe California Texas Fast Freight.
Potomac Merchandise	Richmond, Fredricksburg & Potomac Fast Freight.
Merchant's Dispatch	Richmond, Fredricksburg & Potomac Fast Green Fruit.
Symbol Train	Fast and Expedited Freight.
Time Freight	Fast and Expedited Freight.
Gold Ball	Fast and Expedited Freight.
Red Ball	Fast and Expedited Freight.
Forwarder	Fast and Expedited Freight.
Manifest Fast Freight	Fast and Expedited Freight.
Main Train	Troop or any other military move with solid train.
Tank	Engine Tender
R.P.O.	Railway Post Office Car
E.X.	Express Car
R.F.	Refrigerator Car (Reefer)
Storage	Car used for storing bagged mail, parcel post or newspapers.
Horse Car	Car used for transporting race horses, polo ponies, etc.
Combine	Baggage and coach.
P.L.B.	Pullman Club Baggage Car
P.L.	Pullman Parlor Car
S.L.	Pullman Sleeping Car
O.B.S.	Pullman Observation Sleeping Car
Tourist	Pullman Tourist Sleeping Car
Chair Car	Deluxe Coach
Dormitory Car	To provide sleeping accommodations for dining car crews.
D-70	Pennsylvania R.R. 70 Foot Steel Dining Car
P-70	Pennsylvania R.R. 70 Foot Steel Coach
PB-70	Pennsylvania R.R. 70 Foot Steel Combine Coach and Baggage Car
M-70	Pennsylvania R.R. 70 Foot Steel Postal Car
B-60	Pennsylvania R.R. 60 Foot Steel Baggage or Express Car
BS-60	Pennsylvania R.R. 60 Foot Steel Mail Storage Car

Index